The Human Experience

The Human Experience

Insights from Sociology

John Curra

Eastern Kentucky University

Boston   New York   San Francisco
Mexico City   Montreal   Toronto   London   Madrid   Munich   Paris
Hong Kong   Singapore   Tokyo   Cape Town   Sydney

Editor in Chief: *Karen Hanson*
Series Editor: *Jeff Lasser*
Series Editorial Assistant: *Andrea Christie*
Marketing Manager: *Jude Hall*
Editorial-Production Administrator: *Beth Houston*
Composition and Prepress Buyer: *Linda Cox*
Editorial-Production Service: *Walsh & Associates,Inc.*
Electronic Composition: *Peggy Cabot, Cabot Computer Services*
Manufacturing Buyer: *Andrew Turso*
Cover Administrator: *Kristina Mose-Libon*

For related titles and support materials, visit our online catalog at
www.ablongman.com.

Between the time Website information is gathered and then published, it is not
unusual for some sites to have closed. Also, the transcription of URLs can result
in typographical errors. The publisher would appreciate notification where
these errors occur so that they may be corrected in subsequent editions.

Library of Congress Cataloging-in-Publication Data

Curra, John.
    The human experience : insights from sociology / John Curra.
        p. cm.
Includes bibliographical references and index.
    ISBN 0-205-33530-6
        1. Social interaction. 2. Social psychology. 3. Human behavior.
I. Title.
    HM1111 .C87 2002
    302—dc21   2002071719

Printed in the United States of America

10 9 8 7 6 5 4 3 2 1   08 07 06 05 04 03 02

Contents

Preface

My sophomore year of college was practically over, and I had put off declaring a major as long as I could. The time had come to pick a field of study. Unfortunately, I didn't have a clue about what I wanted to be or what major I should select. What I needed was professional help. I made my way to the college's counseling center and was hooked up with a career counselor. He scheduled me for a bunch of interest tests, all guaranteed to be able to put me on the right track to fame and fortune and to help me find a perfect major. A week after I took the tests, I returned to learn the results. The counselor told me that his analysis of the data showed that I would be happy as a gym director, a car salesperson, or a sociologist. My oh my. He might just as well have told me I would make a good shepherd. None of them sounded like something I wanted to do with my life, but tests don't lie. At the time I was enrolled in a sociology class, so I decided to forego a career selling cars and directing gyms and declared sociology as a major. As I learned more about the field—and earned some degrees—I was eventually given the opportunity to teach about societies, groups, and social relationships and show students how important these are in their lives.

This book is a result of that decision long ago to major in sociology and especially of my long career teaching about societies, groups, and social relationships. It draws on sociology—and other social sciences (like anthropology)—to show just how relational and interactive we humans really are. Nothing that we are or will become can be isolated from our lifelong relationships with others. We humans are unique for many reasons, but one of our most distinctive features is that relationships are crucial for us in all that we are and all that we will become. No understanding of anything human is possible without a thorough understanding of social relationships, groups, and societies.

Organization of the Book

The book has seven chapters. Each one begins with an outline of the chapter. Concepts, theories, descriptions, and examples are included to show the many ways that societies, groups, and social relationships are responsible for making us what we are. Key terms are defined in a chapter glossary. As the book moves from chapter to chapter, it will become clear that in one way or another, our life experiences, both public and private, are social experiences. A reciprocal relationship exists between individual and society, and one cannot be understood—or even considered—apart from the other. The relationship between the wider society and personal experience must be kept at the forefront of our explanations of what it means to be human.

- **Chapter One** explores human connections, as well as the ways that we humans construct the reality within which we live. It concludes by examining social dilemmas that can occur when group members fail to honor the social contract.

- **Chapter Two** examines classic thoughts about our relational nature. No book about society and social relationships should ever fail to give prominence to the works of sociologists like Comte, Marx, Durkheim, Mead, Weber, and Goffman. They told us so much about society, and they are responsible for understandings about social relationships that can serve as an inspiration to us all.

- **Chapter Three** deals with our unique nature. Children raised in social isolation show how important relationships are—good ones—in making us the distinctive creatures that we are. This chapter explores human evolution and the human revolution based upon it. No one can understand what it means to be human without paying close attention to our symbolic and cognitive abilities.

- **Chapter Four** focuses on socialization and how humans become societies in miniature. Social forces start to have an impact on us the day we are born and then continue throughout life. We must understand how society gets in us and what this means for us as members of a society.

- **Chapter Five** looks at our more public relationships in the wider society. We live in a stratified society in a stratified world, and it is impossible to understand ourselves without understanding things about the hierarchical arrangement of society and what this means for us. A stratified society is a fertile ground for the creation of social deviance, an important subject for anyone who wants to understand what it means to be human.

- **Chapter Six** explores the private realm. We perceive, think, feel, and remember not simply as individuals or human beings, but as members of social environments. The inner experience of each of us is a reflection of relationships and interpersonal experiences.

- **Chapter Seven** deals with changing relationships. What we are individually is a direct reflection of how we have organized ourselves collectively in our societies. Changes have been particularly impressive in the United States where sociocultural changes in our institutions have transformed the views we have of ourselves and of others.

Acknowledgments

Much thanks to the folks at Allyn and Bacon, especially Jeff Lasser and Andrea Christie, his assistant. Jeff was always supportive of my efforts and very willing to let me go in whatever direction I thought best. He shared my enthusiasm over what the book could become and where it would fit. Comments and suggestions of reviewers—Dan Phillips of the University of Kentucky and Mark Edwards of Oregon State University—were of great help. Not only did they offer concrete suggestions that improved the work, their comments served as a source of encouragement and inspiration.

Much thanks to members of my family. The support and encouragement from my wife, Carolyn, my two daughters, Christy and Jennifer, and my granddaughter, Alexa, are greatly appreciated. I am particularly thankful for their patience as I spent so many hours away from them, working to put my thoughts into words. The help and support I received from my mother, Nancy, and my sister, Susan, also deserve an extra special thanks. This project would have been impossible without them.

The Human Experience

Social Interaction
The Coin of the Realm

Once upon a time, Robert Fulghum (1988:83–5), the author of *All I Really Need to Know I Learned in Kindergarten,* was given the job of entertaining about eighty children in the social hall of a church while their parents were busy elsewhere. He gathered the children together and started them playing a game that allowed them to run around, have fun, and make lots of noise. After the children had been at it for a while, Fulghum yelled to them that they had to decide *right then* whether they were GIANTS, WIZARDS, or DWARFS. He waited while the children picked the category that fit them the best. Suddenly he felt a tug at his pants leg. He looked down, and standing there was a small girl. She asked him where the mermaids were supposed to stand. Fulghum took it upon himself to straighten this child out right then and there. "There are no such things as mermaids," he told her, but the child refused to be convinced. She knew she was a mermaid, and a mermaid was what she intended to be, not a giant, a wizard, or a dwarf. What to do? Instead of trying to change her mind again, Fulghum found a place for her. He invited her to stand right next to him. In fact, he even appointed himself to the position of King of the Sea.

The coin of the human realm is **social interaction,** and social interaction is what we must understand in order to know about others and also to know about ourselves. Humans take account of one another all the time, and they let that accounting direct the course of their future activities and ongoing relationships. Asking someone out to dinner, giving someone a gift, or even honking a car horn at someone who cuts you off in traffic all involve taking account of another individual and establishing a relationship, no matter how slight. Practically everything that we humans are and do reflects our lifelong relationships with others. "Where do the mermaids stand?" is a question that can only be answered in light of how mermaids are viewed—if they are viewed at all—and treated in a particular society at a specific point in time.

To talk about humans and to understand things about them—why they conform and why they do not, why they feel and think as they do, or even how and what they remember—we need to understand the nature of human relationships and how these relationships change over time. Humans are social to a remarkable degree, and they take account of others all the time as they fit their lines of behavior together into some coordinated whole. It is no accident that humans live with, around, or near one another; we wouldn't be fully human without these connections. No creature is quite so receptive to the influence of others as we are.

The **sociological imagination** (Mills 1959:6–7) requires those who possess it to maintain a clear awareness of the reciprocal relationship between the wider society and personal experience. Changes in a society always intersect with changes in the members of that society (Mills 1959:6). The promise and the power of the sociological imagination is that it allows us to shift our gaze from impersonal and remote changes in the very public world to the very private and personal features of human character and personality and then move back again (Mills 1959:7). The sociological imagination allows us to make sense of a multitude of happenings that would otherwise remain unintelligible and to uncover the hidden meanings of social life (Portes 2000:11).

Contextualizing Humanity

The Instinct Doctrine and Human Nature

Charles Darwin's (1952/1859; 1952/1871) views of **natural selection** (certain traits fit an environment better than other traits and get transmitted from generation to generation)—even though they were developed by him as he observed nonhuman animals and plants—were ultimately applied to the explanation of human behavior. He assumed that most human behavior was determined by instincts (thus not a product of free thought and deliberation), an approach known as the **instinct doctrine.** In other words, basic human nature exists, and it is caused principally by innate or genetic factors. Are humans aggressive? If so, it must be because of an instinct for aggression. Are they compassionate? Yes? Then that must be due to an instinct, too. It was an easy leap to the view that innate differences in human nature are responsible for the arrangements of a society. Simply, genes make humans and humans make society, so, ultimately, it is genes that make society. However, this cannot really be true (Lewontin 1991:14). Whatever value instincts have in explaining the behavior of nonhuman animals, the instinct doctrine was woefully inadequate to explain humans and their social arrangements.

A fair amount of opposition existed in U.S. sociology to the attempt to use instincts to explain human behavior, especially human *social* behavior. The principal reason for the resistance was that explanations in terms of instincts left too little room for the impact of social learning and purpose on humans and their relationships. Bernard's critique of the application of the instinct doctrine to human social behavior was simple and direct: Too many instincts were being blamed for just too many things. After examining the work of 1,700 writers, Bernard was able to identify 15,789 separate instincts that these writers used to explain behavior, divisible into 6,131 different types (Hinkle and Hinkle 1954:29). What seemed to be happening was that anytime something needed explaining, an instinct was called into service to do it. Had supporters of the instinct doctrine only used instinct to explain a few types of behavior among a limited number of species, they might have been more successful in spreading their views. As it was, they killed the goose that laid the golden eggs by asking for, and expecting too much from, the instinct doctrine. The instinct doctrine just left far too little room for the role of learning and deliberation in human affairs.

Humans are neither mindless robots whose actions are determined by genes nor clean slates upon which society writes whatever it wants and thereby determines every detail of their lives (Steen 1996:21). It is beyond dispute that some of what a human does—some of the social differentiation between individuals and groups of individuals—has something to do with chromosomes, genes, body chemicals, and brain structures. Evolution exists in some form or another, and humans have evolved in some way or another from lower life forms (Udry 1995:1269). However, what is most true is that a **dialectical relationship** exists between individuals and society, each being a condition of the other's existence and progression (Berger and Luckmann 1966:61; Lewontin, Rose, and Kamin 1984:257). Simply, societies could not exist without persons, and persons could not exist—or even be persons— without social relationships. While humans cannot be cut adrift from their biological heritage, they are not enchained by it either (Lewontin, Rose, and Kamin 1984:10).

At the start of the twenty-first century, natural scientists claimed victory in the search for the human genome, the sum of the genetic material that is found in nearly every cell of the human body (Ridley 1999). Francis Collins, director of the National Human Genome Research Institute, expressed his views of the **human genome project** at a press conference in the White House East Room, Monday, June 26, 2000: "We have caught the first glimpse of our own instruction book, previously known only to God." Perhaps he is right. However, to treat this large-scale project to map the human genome as similar to the quest for the Holy Grail, a comparison that was actually drawn (Lewontin 2000:136–8), was stretching things a bit too far and a bit too soon.

Some experts believe that terrible public disillusionment will be the principal outcome of the human genome project when it is discovered that this elaborate and expensive human genetic sequencing project accomplished very little. People will still be dying of cancer, heart disease, and strokes; they will still be mentally ill, addicted to drugs, committing crimes, and killing themselves (Lewontin 1991:52). Knowledge of the human genome is far too one-sided to advance our understanding very far of how life works and what it means to be human (Lewontin 2000:149). What genes determine, if they determine anything at all, is the *range* of variation of a particular organism in response to a constantly changing environment (Lewontin 2000:68).

Dynamic Relationships and Human Development

Human bodies are historically and socially constructed in so many ways that it is impossible to separate socially constructed traits, qualities, and temperaments from those that might actually be universal and natural (Petersen 1998:67–8). Our thoughts, actions, and feelings are a product of a complex interplay between happenings in our brains and bodies and happenings in our societies and the groups to which we belong. Our personal identity is a reflection of membership in social groups, traits we show, others' interpretations of our traits, our interpretation of the traits of others, and our assessment of our own individual traits. Humans occupy **statuses** (positions defined in terms of group membership) like son or daughter, Supreme Court judge or dentist, teacher or student, and then **play the roles** (or **role play**) that are attached to those statuses. Being a son requires acting (and perhaps thinking and feeling) like one, just as being a dentist involves rights and duties that fall to any occupant of that status. Becoming a person is a dynamic and ongoing process that cannot be separated from the people, historical events, and social circumstances that surround us all (Kimmel 2000:95). What we do (or do not do) and the experiences that we have (or do not have) transform what we are as well as they transform our understandings of what we are (van den Wijngaard 1997:115). All human events are social and biological, just as they are chemical and physical (Lewontin, Rose, and Kamin 1984:282).

Groups Are Us

Because humans are so greatly influenced by social relationships, sociologists have identified the **group** as the one thing that must be thoroughly understood by anyone who wishes to understand what it means to be human. A group exists when two or more people are regularly in interaction with each other. These interactants may also define themselves as members of a group and be defined as members by others, giving that group an identity and a boundary (Merton 1968:339–40). Members of groups create symbols and rituals to establish a sense of purpose, to increase their group's persistence over time, and to reinforce their sense of collective identity (Smith-Lovin 1999:8). When this group structure is coupled with the possibility of a succession of members in and out of the group over time, it is easy to see how a group—or any collectivity—is more than the sum of its members (Rothman 1998). It can have an identity and a persistence over time even though members may come and go. A family is a group and so are fraternities and sororities, athletic teams, and bridge clubs. In fact, the term **society,** one of the central ideas in the social sciences, describes a special type of grouping, one that is large and enduring.

Members of a society share a **culture,** which is a blueprint or a system of designs for living that each generation passes on to the next. In other words, culture is shared knowledge about social life that humans use as they act together. Bodybuilders who have figured out ways to make their muscles bigger may share this information with others, or gamblers may show close friends how to win money at cards and dice. While it is certainly true that our shared knowledge about how to act, think, and feel does guide our relationships, it is equally true that behavior can and does guide the development of shared knowledge and personal thoughts (Harris 1999:22). Culture is only a partial explanation for why we behave, think, and feel the way we do (Kuper 1999). Each group in a society will have its own **subculture,** designs for living that channel and direct the relationships of the group's members in distinctive ways. A college class is a subculture, and so is one's family. While a great deal of overlap may exist between a culture and the many subcultures it contains, each subculture is unique.

While cultures and subcultures contain many forms of shared knowledge, two of the most important types are called values and norms. **Values** are shared understandings about desirable and undesirable things in social life. Some people value material success while other people value harmony with nature. **Norms** are cultural rules or shared understandings about acceptable and unacceptable ways of acting, thinking, or feeling that members of a group are expected to follow. The command to "brush and floss after every meal" is a statement of a norm, as is the "Golden Rule" that encourages us to treat others as we would want to be treated by them. Refusal to obey norms may lead to **sanctions,** which are positive or negative consequences that encourage people to obey the rules. A high grade on an exam is a positive sanction, just as a low grade is a negative one. Negative sanctions may range from mild to severe and can take the form of ridicule, dismissal, ostracism, corporal punishment, or even a killing of the rule breaker. Positive sanctions may range from moderate to excessive and take the form of things like hugs, encouragements, valuables (like money), awards, prizes, or promotions. Norms are powerful forces for stabilizing and reproducing human relationships in groups, organizations, and institutions like families and schools (Bendor and Swistak 2001; March, Schulz, and Chou 2000).

Not all norms are alike, and many different types have been identified (Sumner 1906). Some norms are called **folkways.** These are shared understandings about acceptable and unacceptable ways of acting, thinking, or feeling, that, when violated, produce only a mild reaction or sanction. In other words, these are cultural rules in regard to what members of a culture *should* or *should not* do, think, or feel. They are rules to be followed, to be sure, but they are rules that are viewed as of minor importance for the life of a group. The shared understanding that you will put a napkin on your lap during dinner and not under your chin is a folkway. Other norms are called **mores.** These are shared understandings about acceptable and unacceptable ways of acting, thinking, or feeling, that, when violated, produce a severe reaction or sanction. In other words, these are cultural rules in regard to what members of a society *must* or *must not* do, think, or feel. Mores are serious matters to be taken seriously, and failure to obey them can bring forth severe penalties. The responsibility of parents to care for their children and to protect them from harm is a *mos* (the singular of mores). Still other norms are called **laws.** Laws are formal norms. This means that the content of the law will be written down, the penalties or sanctions for the breaking of the law will be written down, and the penalties or sanctions for breaking the law will be administered by a specific agency or group like the police.

Laws often regulate behavior that is crucial for the well-being of a society and its members. Laws to protect life and property are violated by acts like murder, rape, and robbery, and specific punishments exist for these crimes. Laws, however, can also regulate more trivial matters. In Lexington, Kentucky, it is against the law to carry ice cream cones in your pocket (Seuling 1976:64).

In Boston, Massachusetts, it is against the law to hold a frog-jumping contest in a night club (Seuling 1976:31). In Idaho it is against the law to fish for trout from the back of a giraffe (Seuling 1976:42). In Washington, DC, it is against the law to punch a bull in the nose (Seuling 1976:52). In Baltimore, Maryland, it is against the law to mistreat an oyster (Seuling 1976:48). With these laws, the original reason for their creation so long ago is no longer with us—but the laws are. However, they do not get the kind of enforcement—if they get any at all—as laws created to protect life and property. They don't have to. We no longer have a reason to violate these laws because our folkways and mores—and other conditions of life—keep us on the straight and narrow. Even if it were *not* against the law, how many of us would be willing to punch a bull in the nose or to fish from the back of a giraffe?

Norms overlap, and some action may violate more than one type of rule. You may not only do something that annoys other members of your family or community, you may also do something for which you can be arrested by police. Not only is shoplifting a crime, taking things that do not belong to you may provoke negative sanctions from friends and family. In fact, reactions from people who are in a position to directly and immediately sanction you may be far more effective in getting you to follow the rules than any legal sanctions you might receive. This is one of the reasons that some laws, like those in regard to shoplifting or speeding, are not any more effective than they are. They do not receive complete support from the folkways and mores. Some people may find it very appealing to be able to get something for nothing or to be able to get where they want to be as quickly as possible even if these actions violate the law.

Norms also vary, and what is appropriate in one situation may be distinctly inappropriate in some other situation. The folkways, mores, or laws of one group or situation may be very different from the folkways, mores, or laws of some other group or situation. Laughing at a performance at the local comedy club is perfectly proper; failure to do so might seem odd. You are supposed to stay loose and have a good time. However, if you laugh, stay loose, and have a good time at a funeral, this would be most inappropriate. In pre-Christian Scandinavia, suicide was a good and noble way to die; it guaranteed that you would reach Valhalla, the Viking paradise (Colt 1991:134–5). Nowadays things are different, at least in parts of the United States, and suicide is condemned for many reasons. Standards for acting, thinking, and feeling change as we move from place or time to some other place or time.

Groups are not all alike, and they vary along a number of dimensions. Some are **primary groups,** characterized by face-to-face interaction, cohesion, and intimacy; others, like a college class, are **secondary groups** (task-oriented and less personal). Some of our more important primary and secondary groups are the ones to which we belong, called **membership groups.** However, others that we use all the time are groups to which we do not belong but to which we compare ourselves and from which we learn standards for behavior. These latter groups—called **reference groups**—may also be membership groups but they don't have to be, because reference groups and membership groups may not coincide (Merton 1968:335–51). A female college student who aspires to be an actress is a member of a collectivity (student body) that is different from the one she uses as a reference point (entertainers). What you think of yourself and the standards you use to conduct your daily affairs are directly related to the kinds of people you use for comparison and the kinds of groups to which you belong (Borkman 1999; Mark 1998:317; Smith-Lovin 1999:13).

So Sad and So Strange, the Days That Are No More

The ways that groups influence the flow of human relationships can be seen by considering a periodic gathering that elicits a range of feelings and thoughts in those who attend it: the high school reunion. A reunion offers a unique opportunity for reflections on past successes and failures, as well as opportunities to succeed or fail at the reunion itself. Reunions give us an opportunity to make sense of our lives and to reflect on our current situation, while we reminisce with others who once were like us (and against whom we certainly compared ourselves). While it may be fun to hark back to earlier times with former classmates, reunions present a potential threat to self-concept as well. We may learn that what we thought of ourselves in high school was not shared by our classmates (Ikeda 1998). Some of us are reminded of things that we had either forgotten or intentionally suppressed from those early days: the unsuccessful pick-up line, the botched date, the stupid answer in class, the fight we lost, the challenge to our honor that we refused to take, the unrequited love, and so on. Even under the best of circumstances, people you want to see and impress will fail to attend, teachers who were important in your life are not at the reunion, and memories of what things were like in high school are probably different from how they really were.

Although people attend their reunions for many reasons, a basic interest among many returnees is to make the past and present fit together in some sensible way (Vinitzky-Seroussi 1998:158). Reunions have the potential to demonstrate graphically the contrast between what one was in high school and what one has become. Most individuals who attend a reunion try in one way or another to appear successful. Some of them may even prepare for the gathering by exercising, losing (or gaining) weight, buying (or renting) a new car, and purchasing new clothes. They may even create new autobiographies to cover their post-high school days (for example, telling their former classmates that they invented post-its). Their labors may be worth the effort. Vinitsky-Seroussi's (1998) analysis suggests that at high school reunions the prevailing assumption is one of continuity in self-development with the past being filtered through the present in the construction of some kind of "true" self. The class nerd who becomes a famous entertainer is described as someone who always had it in him or her; the star athlete in high school who becomes unsuccessful and unpopular in adulthood is described as someone who was always insecure and shallow. Adult roles and adult successes or failures seem to be what matter most in the assessment of an individual at high school reunions. Some of the individuals who attend a high school reunion, however, will fall back on the same role that they played in high school. The class clown will still be a clown, the outsiders will still be outsiders, and members of the in-crowd will still stay pretty much to themselves. Some of the things that we were in high school we still are years later: the good, the bad, and the ugly.

Families, Marriages, and Social Relationships

One of the most important relationships in every society is the marital relationship, and one of the most important groups is the family (Hareven 2000). **Families** are found in every human society, and this institution, wherever it is found, helps to fulfill certain recurring social needs like socializing the young, regulating sexual expression, and bringing new members of the human race into existence. The ways that families meet these needs, however, vary widely (Newman 2002:203). Some societies follow the custom of **polygyny** (one husband and many wives), and a few even accept **polyandry** (one wife and many husbands). However, cross-cultural studies of the family show that **monogamy** (being married to only one person at a time) is now the prevailing family form (Melotti 1981). Why is monogamy so common?

One view, the **male compromise theory of monogamy,** is that polygynous males—the ones with all the wives—were also the ones with the most power and resources. Because of their prosperity (and greed), they faced a potential threat from those males who were powerless as separate individuals but who would be very powerful if they were to join together and protest against the accumulation of multiple wives by a few wealthy men. What to do? The polygynous males saw that it was in their economic and political interest to release their tight hold over women, abandon the custom of having multiple mates, and get the political and social support of men lower in rank who were now much happier because they too could have wives (Ridley 1993). As men of lower standing became a political threat, polygynous men found it in their best interest to compromise; women were then more accessible to men who formerly would have had to do without (Kanazawa and Still 1999:28).

A problem with the male compromise theory—a very *big* problem—is that it credits men with too much power and influence in the determination of marriage customs. The relational nature of this most basic human arrangement reminds us that we must look at the negotiations that are made among a large number of people in any society (Kanazawa and Still 1999:33). Females do have power, oftentimes a great deal of it, to control with whom they marry and reproduce and under what conditions. While both women and men experience a number of societal pushes and pulls as they contemplate marriage, the final outcome is still strongly influenced by what *both* women and men want and need in a relationship (Small 1995:152). Monogamy became more popular and predominant because (1) men became more equal to one another *and* (2) women became more powerful.

> As men have become more equal in their wealth and status over time, more women have chosen to marry monogamously because it was more beneficial for them to do so. The separate and independent decisions of a large number of women to marry monogamously rather than polygynously have brought about the institutional change from polygyny to monogamy (Kanazawa and Still 1999:33).

Polygyny is best for women when a lot of inequality exists among prospective husbands. Finding a husband with abundant resources is more important than having him all to yourself, especially if you're without much power yourself. However, when men become more alike in what they can offer to a wife, everything changes. Being the first and only wife is far more attractive and beneficial, and monogamy becomes the best choice for women and their children.

Groups and Human Evolution

Groups are important to humans for all kinds of reasons, and they are inextricably tied up with the evolution of our species (Alexander 1979:64). The first human groupings were probably loose-knit and fluid, and the first humans were probably more independent than we are today (Maryanski and Turner 1992:165). Eventually, cultural processes like language and stronger social bonds were layered over the loose social networks, which altered somewhat the existing human tendencies toward individualism and self-interest (Maryanski and Turner 1992:165). Even ancient hunters and food gatherers had extensive relationships, and they almost always hunted and gathered with a clear sense of group purpose and shared what they caught or found with others (Cox, Sluckin, and Steele 1999:369; Wood and Hill 2000:124–5). Groups and relationships are so important for human development and so much a part of all that we are that it seems unlikely that we were ever without them. In fact, we were social long before we were human.

The Social Construction of Reality

The world is different to a salamander than it is to an eagle; this is true even if they both are together at the same time and place. Organisms do not simply respond to environments. They create them out of the bits and pieces of the natural world through their activities (Lewontin 1991:109; Piliavin and Lepore 1995:21). Each and every physical fact of nature has an effect that is a direct consequence of the nature of the organism itself and the relationship between that organism and its environment (Lewontin, Rose, and Kamin 1984:276). Even the operation of gravity depends on characteristics of an organism and its relationship to the outer world. A bacterium in a liquid environment is so small that it does not feel gravity, so its size is what determines whether gravity exists and has an influence (Lewontin 1991:117). This is also true for small insects called water striders. They are so light that they can walk across water without sinking. Humans are in a unique position, however, because they have so many opportunities to participate in a **social construction of reality.** They are able to form relationships and work together to construct the world in which they live, including ideas and theories about what they are and why. In the dialectical relationship between humans and their environment, both are changed in the process (Berger and Luckmann 1966:61).

Even something that seems as natural as the passage of time really is not. The sociotemporal order—the temporal order that regulates the routines of social entities like families, religious organizations, bureaucracies and organizations, or even entire societies—is actually a socially constructed artifact that rests upon many arbitrary social conventions (Zerubavel 1981:xii). These social facts of time and scheduling are no less compelling (and seem no less natural) just because they are socially constructed. Just like natural facts, social facts can impose themselves ruthlessly on individuals and influence and determine all that they do.

While it is unlikely that anyone would mistake a day for a night or a hot summer day for a cold winter day, it is not at all unusual for groups of individuals to vary in how they handle sociotemporal elements. The seven-day week is not universal. Different societies have had—or at least tried—three-day, four-day, five-day, six-day, eight-day, nine-day, ten-day, twelve-day, thirteen-day, nineteen-day, and twenty-day weeks. The French adopted a ten-day schedule in order to get rid of the seven-day week that was so closely associated with Christianity. New names for the days and months were created and placed on the calendar to make it necessary for people to abandon the old regime and its traditions and symbols and to embrace the new way of doing things (Nisbet 1966:39–40). The Russians once tried, first, a five-day and then a six-day week (Zerubavel 1981:73). These various "temporal tinkerings" never attained enough popularity to supplant the seven-day cycle, but this is not because the seven-day week is necessarily the best or most natural. It was simply that the force of tradition and the power of the Christian Church made it difficult to challenge the supremacy of the seven-day week (Zerubavel 1985:44).

Curiously enough, time can go faster or slower depending on social relationships and individual needs. Our sense of the passage of time is directly influenced by our movement from one social situation or phase of social experience to another (Flaherty 1999). I was once told that a watched coffee pot never boils. That's silly. Of course a watched coffee pot boils, and a physicist could tell us exactly how long it will take and why it boils when it does; furthermore, if it does not boil, a physicist could tell us why that happened, too. However, you don't have to be a physicist to see that a different reality exists for someone who really REALLY wants a cup of coffee and someone who does not. That coffee pot takes longer to boil—or seems to—when you're waiting anxiously for it to get hot. A child waiting for the arrival of a special day like Christmas or a birthday finds that the minutes pass oh so slowly, while the child's parents (who must make all the holiday preparations) find that they pass oh so quickly.

If we track time in some biological or evolutionary sense, major features of an organism's development do follow one another in an invariant order: The one-celled organism precedes the two-celled, the two-celled precedes the four-celled, and so on (Lewontin 2000:125). However, what is most important is that humans constantly make and remake features of the natural world and so make them meaningful in their lives (Eder 1996). "Where do the years go?" individuals in the twilight of their years ask. As soon as one birthday passes, another one arrives. However, a young person may think that life will go on forever. Something that seems as natural as "middle age" or "midlife" really is not. While middle age certainly is correlated with physical changes that, say, childhood is not, middle age (like other transitions in life) also carries many cultural meanings that help to make it what it is. The aging process is not viewed in the same way in all places and times (Shweder 1998:x–xi), and bodily changes are impacted by cultural understandings (Gullette 1998:4).

It is very possible for people in some places and times to get *older* much *younger* than people at other places and times (Gullette 1998:17). The Japanese are as anxious over the aging process and physical decline as are some Westerners. However, in Japan, it is more likely that one cultural compensation for advancing age is the belief that it brings unique insight and wisdom to the individuals who have achieved it (Lock 1998:68). In the United States, the Amish reserve an important role for their elders; they do not want them to become obsolete just because they are no longer as sprightly as they once were (Kephart 1976). In India, middle age is not a question of age but of family dynamics: Middle age starts when the first son is married. With his marriage comes a new reproductive sequence, and the parents can then transfer many of their family responsibilities to the next generation (Kakar 1998:85). If anything universal does characterize the arrival of middle age in the many cultures of the world, it is that middle age is a social and relational event, not simply an evolutionary or biological one (Weisner and Bernheimer 1998:216).

The Social World

Once social routines are created, implemented, and legitimated, they are likely to persist over time. They are cast into a pattern, and they can then be repeated with an economy of time and effort. Who would want to continue to reinvent the wheel, especially if it is unnecessary? When customs are passed on to others, their arbitrary and conventional nature is likely to be forgotten. They take on a thickness and a firmness that they once lacked, maybe that they never were intended to have, and probably that they will never be rid of again (Berger and Luckmann 1966:58–9). These social constructions have lost their transparency, and they are now serious matters to be taken seriously. At this point it is correct to speak of a social world that is as real and as embracing as any natural world.

Some social constructions make a great deal of sense, and it is not hard to understand why they exist. Social constructions allow us to know that we should be very careful around poisonous snakes, look both ways before crossing the street, and eat the right foods. If a social construction were to be too outlandish and out of synch with our biological properties and physical laws, then it would soon disappear. Think what would happen if someone tried to make eating iron ore or skydiving without a parachute customary for us all. Few of us—and none of us for long—would follow these customs; even fewer of us would teach them to our young. They certainly would not get thicker and firmer as the days passed.

Some social constructions made good sense a long time ago when they were created, but they have persisted way beyond their shelf life. Men's shirts have buttons on the right while women's shirts have buttons on the left. Why are buttons gendered? The buttons were originally placed on the right of men's shirts because it is easier for right-handed people to push *right* buttons through *left* holes. Most men are right-handed so their buttons were placed in the position to make it easiest for them to get dressed. Very sensible. Most women, however, are also right-handed, so what gives? Why aren't their buttons also on the right? When buttons came into being, they were a mark of privilege, and only the wealthy could afford them. Wealthy women were almost always dressed by maids, who faced the women they were dressing. Dressmakers sewed buttons on women's garments in a position that made it easiest for *maids* to do their jobs, which put the buttons on the left side of the women who were being dressed. That's where they've been ever since (Smith 1991:6). We in the United States often shake hands to show friendship. Why? The custom started long ago when men traveled heavily armed. When two men met, each one had to show the other man that he came in peace and could be trusted. The right hand was extended forward to show that it contained no weapon. The proffered hand was then grabbed and held tightly so that it could not be used to grab a weapon at the last moment. The vigorous hand shaking may have been intended to dislodge any weapons that might have been hidden in a sleeve (Smith 1991:12). We continue to follow these customs even though the reasons that they were created in the first place no longer exist.

Sometimes social constructions are a result of chance, ignorance, or prejudice. Men's trousers have cuffs on the bottom. Why? In the late 1880s, a nobleman from England was making his way to a high-society wedding in New York. It was raining heavily, and water was standing in the streets. Before leaving his carriage, he rolled up the bottom of his pants to keep them dry. He forgot to unroll them before he entered the church. Men noticed the cuffs, thought it was the newest style from England, and started telling their tailors that they wanted pants with cuffs, too (Smith 1991:36). A wedding ring is customarily worn on the third finger of the left hand. Why? It used to be believed—incorrectly—that a vein of blood ran directly from the third finger of the left hand to the heart. It seemed appropriate that this special finger should be the one to wear the ring (Smith 1991:62). Baby boys in the United States are regularly dressed in blue, and baby girls are regularly dressed in pink. Why? At one time it was believed that evil spirits lurked in nurseries waiting for a chance to enter the bodies of young children. The color blue was thought to have the power to repel these evil forces and keep children free from harm. Because boys were viewed as more valuable than girls, they were given the protective color to keep away the demons. The default color for little girls was pink, the color of a rose (Smith 1991:9). Social constructions, sensible or not, have a power and a force. We may not know why they came into being or even care, but we may still follow them without question. In fact, we may have little choice in the matter.

Berger and Luckmann (1966:53–67) identified and discussed three **moments** in the social construction **of reality.** The first is **externalization.** This is the process in which some bit or piece of knowledge (or behavior based on it) moves from the private or personal experience of an individual or a small group of individuals to be shared by a wider audience. Somebody (or some-bod*ies*) had to decide that blue was a better color for boys than for girls. The second moment is **objectivation.** This is achieved when those human products that have been externalized no longer are viewed as being human products; they are now separate and autonomous from the individuals who created them. We may have forgotten who told us spinach was healthy, but we continue to eat it for its nutritional value. The last moment is **internalization.** This exists when the externalized and objectivated social facts become part of the consciousness of new "recruits" as they learn the way of life of a group. When we wear our clothing with the gendered buttons, we are responding to the internalization of a social construction. Social order is a human product and an ongoing human production (Berger and Luckmann 1966:52). The curious thing is that a social order, once constructed, resists efforts to change it any further (Soeffner 1997).

Even though much of our world is socially constructed, it does not mean that social construction is the only way for something to exist in our world. The processes of nature, both inside our bodies and external to us in the physical world, can and do impact social constructions and social relationships. Physical laws and biological factors work together to impose limits on what people think, feel, and do (Hacking 1999). Some facts are **brute facts.** They exist separate from any human institution or understanding (although the relationship between even brute facts and humans is a dialectical one). Brute facts may require the existence of words or language to make it possible to describe them, but the facts themselves exist without words, languages, or institutions (Searle 1995:27). Other facts, however, are **institutional facts.** These facts require human institutions and human relationships for their very existence (Searle 1995:27). It is a brute fact that the earth is the third rock from the sun (as it is that rocks exist); it is an institutional fact that I am both a college professor and my parents' first-born child. The separation of brute from institutional facts makes us aware of a reality that is separate from us and beyond human ability to control or manage it entirely. Some of the brute facts of evolution and of the repetitive movement of atomic particles will have an influence in one way or another on what humans do, think, and feel no matter where they live or when.

It is our human capacity to construct intentionally plans of action and then to work together to implement them that allows us to overcome the constraining effects of both biology and physical forces. No one individual human being could fly by flapping his or her arms, nor could a group of human beings—even if it numbered in the millions—fly though all its members flapped their arms simultaneously (Lewontin 1991:121; Lewontin, Rose, and Kamin 1984:286). However, we can fly by using flying machines and the accompanying social technologies of airports, pilots, baggage handlers, and flight attendants. We may not be able to leap over buildings in a single bound, but we can build tall buildings and reach the top of them on elevators so jumping over them is unnecessary. We may not be able to control entirely the elements, but we can plan for them and build structures that will protect us from them. (If all else fails, we can blow that meteor heading toward earth out of the sky.) We may not like the kind of nose, hairline, or body shape that we inherited from our parents. Through surgery, exercise, or diet, we can alter those features of our appearance, too. The joint operation of collective intentionality and social organization makes it possible for us to be the kind of people who can do or be practically anything we want.

Cosmic Events and Social Constructions

On May 24, 1985, in a small town south of Naples, Italy, called Oliveto Citra, a group of boys between the ages of 8 and 12 reported that they had seen the Madonna. The feast of Saint Macarius the Abbot, patron of the town, was in progress. The boys were enjoying the festivities when they saw what they later said was a luminous track in the sky, heading toward a nearby castle. Their first thought was that they had seen a falling star; then they thought it might be Martians. Shortly thereafter (or so the boys claimed later) they heard the sound of a crying baby coming from inside the castle gate. They looked toward the castle and saw a beautiful woman with a baby in her arms (Apolito

1998:14–15). The boys ran through the town telling everyone what they had seen. The people who heard the boys' story accepted it as true, and the sighting of the Virgin Mary became a "real event" in the life of the community.

Town leaders, especially the parish priest, had a decisive influence in transforming the claims of the children into objective facts (Apolito 1998:9). Town leaders became the filter through which messages from the Madonna were interpreted. The boys were defined as "seers" or "visionaries," rather than as "nuts," "liars," or "dreamers." Even when adults could not agree exactly on what the boys had seen, they still agreed that the boys had seen something extraordinary. This tacit acceptance encouraged even more reporting of visions, which circled back to reinforce the leaders' beliefs and convictions about the tangible nature of the apparition in the first place (Apolito 1998:10). As time passed, fewer and fewer people wondered *if* something cosmic or supernatural had actually occurred; they tried simply to determine *what* kind of supernatural event it was.

No matter how convincing the seers were or how influential the leaders came to be, people would not have believed in the Madonna, at least not for long, unless the conditions of their lives had given them a reason to want to see and believe in her. In general, those towns that sent the greatest number of pilgrims to Oliveto Citra were places characterized by recent socioeconomic changes, increases in social inequality, community deterioration, feelings of insecurity, graft and corruption by politicians, and the expansion of organized crime into the government apparatus (Apolito 1998:31). Those people who were the most likely to see the Madonna (or to believe that something cosmic was happening) were those people who needed to see her or to believe in her the most. The subdued expression of religiosity that characterized the earlier sightings gave way to a more frenzied display of piety as people farther and farther away from the Castle of Oliveto made the pilgrimage (Apolito 1998:31). Group prayer, crying, moaning, physical gyrations, fainting spells, great emotional excitement—all of these were eventually found every night all through the town, not simply at the castle gate. Some of these emotional displays may have been faked. The rumor spread that owners of travel agencies paid people to claim that they saw the Madonna in order to boost the tourist trade (Apolito 1998:32).

The events at Oliveto are superb examples of the social construction of reality. New views of the world were created and then externalized by a group of boys. Through their efforts and, more important, through the efforts of others who were prominent in the community (or who became prominent because of their visionary abilities), the apparition of Madonna attained a life of its own, no longer connected to the people who were responsible for creating (or envisioning) it in the first place. An important event that helped to externalize and objectify the social constructions about the Madonna was the publication of a written rendition of what had happened. Initially, it was nothing more than an anonymous sheet; however, the parish priest eventually signed the document, and it was included in several additional publications. This written version provided an opportunity for the priest to reconstruct details of the visions in ways more consistent with church doctrine (Apolito 1998:12). If a seer had reported that Madonna had told the faithful to "party down," this claim would not have made its way into the official version of the event. It would not have fit the priest's judgment about what the Virgin Mary would say. While some people remained forever skeptical about the presence of the Madonna at Oliveto Citra, the claims about her became thicker and firmer with the passage of time, and the details of the visions became more widely known as they were told and retold by visitors to the town.

It's a Small World after All

The South African poet Jeremy Cronin wrote from his prison cell that a person is a person because of other people (*"Motho ke Motho ka batho babang"*). The fascinating thing about humans is how connected they are—or can be—to one another. Many of us have had the experience of meeting a complete stranger, getting into a polite conversation, and finding unexpectedly that we share a mutual acquaintance. "It's a small world!" we say. Is this mere fancy, or is there some complex underlying structure that joins us all together? Is the **small-world phenomenon** a real feature of the social world? Just how relational are we?

The Small-World Phenomenon

Stanley Milgram (1967:62) asked the question, "Given any two people in the world, person X and person Z, how many intermediate acquaintance links are needed before X and Z are connected?" This question can be answered in the abstract, but the real world is far more complicated. People and groups of people are differentiated on the basis of class, race, ethnicity, age, and several other divisions that make it very unlikely that any two individuals who are selected at random can get in touch with each other. The small-world phenomenon is unlikely—or seems that way—in any place with the following characteristics: (1) A large number of people live there; (2) we know only a small number of them; (3) our immediate circle of family, friends, and acquaintances is insulated from most other circles; and (4) no central individual is around who could be relied upon to contact everyone else for us (Watts 1999:496). As Milgram (1967:63) noted: Poor people probably are acquainted with other poor people, and the rich speak mostly to the rich.

Milgram was given $680 by the charitable folks at the Laboratory of Social Relations at Harvard University to find out what he could about the smallness of the world. He started his study by designating *two* target persons (the persons who would be contacted). One was from Cambridge, Massachusetts—

she was the wife of a divinity school student—and the other target person was a stockbroker who lived in Sharon, Massachusetts. Letters were sent to prospective starting persons in Wichita, Kansas, and in Omaha, Nebraska, asking them to participate in a study of social contact. All those who agreed to participate were sent a packet of information that contained the name and description of the target person, the directions to send a folder to the target person or to someone likely to know him or her, and instructions to keep the chain going. The participants were told that folders could only be sent to someone they knew on a first-name basis.

What Milgram found was surprising and suggested that it is a small world after all. The Kansas study met with remarkable success. Not long after the folders had been mailed, a teacher at the Episcopal Theological Seminary came up to the target person and handed her a folder. A starting person (a wheat farmer from Kansas) had given it to his own minister, who had sent it to the seminary teacher, who had given it to the target person. Only two intermediate links were required for the folder to move forward to its final destination, the shortest of all of those in Milgram's study. The lengths of chains to get from Nebraska to Massachusetts also were surprisingly short. Milgram found that they varied from two to ten intermediate acquaintances, with the median being five. This number of links is probably far less than most people would think possible to get a message from Omaha, Nebraska, to Sharon, Massachusetts. In fact, one of Milgram's intelligent friends really missed the mark. He estimated that it would take 100 intermediate links. Milgram concluded from his study that anyone in the United States could contact anyone else in a small number of steps, unless the target person is a hermit, in which case no amount of effort would be sufficient to contact him or her (Milgram 1967:67). The small-world phenomenon does seem to exist in real social networks (Watts 1999:516).

The Electronic Community

In certain respects, the world is getting smaller all the time, and long-distance relationships are becoming more and more significant in our lives (Wellman 1999). Through the Internet and other forms of electronic communication, no longer must we wait for days to receive a letter from that special someone. Messages can fly back and forth continually throughout the day. It is even possible to belong to an online community that lacks both physical territory and a sense of shared identity; entrance and exit are as close as the flick of the wrist. These relationships are very different from the more standard face-to-face relationships that are found in primary social groups (Adams 1998:161–2). These electronic relationships allow a great deal of personal freedom: You can interact no matter what you're wearing, even if you're wearing nothing at all, no matter how you look, without embarrassment. They also exert much less social control and have far fewer implications for personal identity (Adams

1998:176–7)—it is unlikely your mom will e-mail you to tell you to eat your spinach. In fact, these electronic relationships may be nothing more than pure entertainment.

Online capacities allow people outside your network of family, friends, and acquaintances to get to you, people you might just as soon avoid. The Milgram study only looked at relationships in one direction, that is, from Kansas to Cambridge or from Oklahoma to Sharon, and his experiment had a playful quality. However, in the real world, YOU could be the target person, something that is not always to your advantage. Creditors or salespeople can maintain contact with you once they have an address even when you wish they would not, and the person to whom you owe money may be relentless. It is true that these messages can be deleted with a click, but they may still be quite annoying. Increases in the transmission of computer viruses mean that your life can be made more difficult by online participation in ways that once were impossible.

Returning to the Nest

The world is getting smaller in another way. More and more adult children "return to the nest" to once again live with their parents. In fact, from 1925 to 1985, the likelihood that young adults in the United States who had left home would return and stay for at least as long as they had been gone increased from 22 percent to about 40 percent (Goldscheider, Goldscheider, St. Clair, and Hodges 1999:695). Why the near doubling? The trends in returning home reflected both changes in the leaving home process and changes in how parents and their offspring relate. Those adult children who left home to get married or to be parents themselves were less likely to return to their family home than were those who left to attend school, to cohabit, to get a job, or just to be on their own. The individuals most likely to return and stay, at least for a while, were those who had left home to serve in the military. A significant factor in the increase in returning home is the likelihood that adult children with dead or dying marriages, or those who find that they cannot go it alone, will return home. Adult children may simply find that their childhood home was much more attractive than they once thought and a nice safety net in times of need (Goldscheider, Goldscheider, St. Clair, and Hodges 1999:710–16).

The Dilemma of Social Dilemmas

Social relationships do not occur automatically, and they often require a great deal of effort and commitment from us all if they are to work. If groups break into a mass of conflicting individuals who look out only for themselves, then we have the making of a **social dilemma.** A social dilemma exists when members of a group care less about others than they do about themselves, and each individual pursues only his or her own interest. This undermines or destroys collective sentiments and the benefits that come from cooperating with others, and it creates a situation in which all members will eventually suffer (Yamagishi 1995; Yamagishi and Cook 1993:236). Social dilemmas are found everywhere: in small and large social groups as well as in formal and informal organizations (Liebrand and Messick 1996:1). If the conflicts are extensive and ongoing, eventually the collectivity will simply disappear.

The Tragedy of the Commons

Hardin (1968:1244) provides a good example of a social dilemma in his discussion of what he called the **tragedy of the commons.** In colonial towns like Williamsburg, Virginia, it was customary for residents to graze their sheep on a common ground. The tragedy occurred when some villagers decided that they would act without restraint and graze as many sheep as they could on the public land. If all villagers were to act selfishly, the commons would eventually be overgrazed and all would lose. Moderation is most likely when individuals believe that preservation of a community resource is vital for their own well-being and for the well-being of their descendants (Sell and Wilson 1999), or when they must pay directly for their overuse of a collective resource (Catton 1979). When individuals trust each other to cooperate rather than compete, then they are all more likely to work together for the good of the community (Seligman 1997:155; Yamagishi and Cook 1993:240).

The nature and amount of cooperation that exist in a group depend on the characteristics of the members, the context of the relationship, and memories of past interactions (Axelrod 1984:28; Cox, Sluckin, and Steele 1999:372). It may be difficult to get individuals to cooperate because they are actually better off—or think that they are—by not cooperating (Axelrod 1984:173). This is especially true if individuals are strangers, because the urge to take advantage of someone whom you will never see again is often too great to resist (Macy and Skvoretz 1998:650). Individuals may not always know or do what is in their best interests, and the pursuit of immediate pleasure may produce long-term disaster.

> A poor Japanese peasant, from his hilltop farm, saw the ocean rapidly withdrawing and knew that a tidal wave was in the making. His neighbors were working in low fields, too far off to hear him call out a warning. Without a moment's thought, he set fire to his own rice ricks and energetically rang the temple bell. The far-off neighbors looked up, saw the smoke, and rushed up the hill to help him, narrowly escaping death (Hunt 1990:154).

The peasant destroyed his rice crop but saved his friends from certain death, a heroic but personally costly act. However, any of his neighbors who decided it was easier to stay put and work in the low field lost his or her life. Reciprocal exchange relationships that are characterized by mutual reward will develop only if interactants are able to accept some short-term costs. Without this sacrifice, the benefits of cooperation will never be recognized and the greater good will never be achieved (Molm, Peterson, and Takahashi 1999).

Altruism and Social Relationships

One frigid afternoon in January 1982, Air Florida's Flight 90 left Washington National Airport on its way to Tampa, Florida. However, the plane never reached its final destination. Ice and snow had accumulated on the wings and tail section and dragged the plane down, and the engine had sucked up too much slush from the runway to get the plane high enough. The tail slammed into a bridge, and the plane then plunged into the freezing waters of the Potomac River where it quickly sank; only the tail remained visible above water. Most of the seventy-four passengers and crew on board died instantly or within seconds of crashing into the river; four motorists were killed when the plane hit the bridge. Six individuals survived the initial crash, and they held onto the tail section, literally for dear life. The arrival of a rescue helicopter gave them a measure of hope. A rope with a life preserver was lowered to the survivors, one man caught it, and he was taken safely to shore. Another survivor had injured her arm, so the pilot of the helicopter had to hover the craft right at the water's edge; his partner leaned out to grab the injured woman and she was taken to safety, too. On the next trip, a Ms. Tirado was taken close to shore. A man who was watching her, Lenny Skutnik, jumped into the freezing water and helped her to reach land safely (Kelly 1982). The helicopter made another trip to the downed plane. The rope was lowered to Arland Williams, Jr., a middle-aged bank examiner, and he caught it. However, rather than use it himself, he passed it to a woman in the water near him. She was saved. The helicopter returned, and the rope was lowered again. Mr. Williams caught the rope again, and again he passed it to another person, who was also taken safely to shore. Every time Arland Williams caught the rope, he passed it to someone else. When the helicopter returned the very last time to save Mr. Williams, it was too late; he had already drowned in the bitterly cold waters of the Potomac (Hunt 1990:11–12).

Mr. Williams's brave and selfless act was made even more unforgettable by the fact that he extended such remarkable charity to people whom he did not know. Altruism—true altruism—is unique behavior (Heckert 2000:33). First named by Auguste Comte in 1851 (Heckert 2000:33; Hunt 1990:26), **altruism** is behavior that benefits another at some cost to the benefactor, and it is done selflessly without the anticipation of rewards from some outside source (Hunt 1990:21). One way to explain the seemingly inexplicable is to insist that, despite all appearances, the donor actually *is* getting some reward from his or her acts of charity and that is the reason for the donation (Hunt 1990:12). In **generalized exchange,** an individual donates something to another individual in what seems to be an act of pure charity, but the donor eventually is rewarded, just not from the person to whom the donation was made (Takahashi 2000:1107). An example of generalized exchange is the donation of blood to a blood bank during a blood drive. You will not benefit right here and now from your contribution, but at some future time you very well might, especially if you are ever in an accident and need a transfusion. It is possible that what looks like altruism is simply a form of generalized exchange (Takagi 1996:313–7).

A more charitable view of human relationships is that altruism exists, and humans perform acts of charity and kindness all the time, even for strangers (Sober and Wilson 1998). Even infants show some empathic arousal, and they become unhappy when they see suffering in others (Hunt 1990:51). While most relationships probably do contain elements of either complete selfishness or mutual exchange/reciprocity, humans can and do help others, even total strangers, without calculating what it will do for them personally (Lieberman 1991:166). If Mr. Williams got anything of value from what he did, it was certainly fleeting, and it could hardly compensate him for his great sacrifice.

Bystander Intervention

If the altruism of Arland Williams, Jr., seems difficult to understand, so does what happened one spring night long ago. It was March 13, 1964, and the place was Kew Gardens in Queens, a borough of New York City. Catherine Genovese, age 28, was returning home from her job as a manager at a local bar. It was 3:30 A.M. and "Kitty," as she was known to most of the people in the community, parked her car, turned off its lights, locked its door, and headed for her apartment. She had not gone far when she noticed a man watching her. She stopped walking toward her apartment and started in a different direction, intending to call police from a nearby call box. She never made it. The man jumped her and then stabbed her. Ms. Genovese started screaming, and lights went on in an apartment building. One man from a window in the apartment building yelled at the attacker to leave the woman alone. That was enough for him to stop and walk away. Lights went out in the apartment, and everyone stopped paying attention to the stabbed woman. The attacker returned and stabbed Ms. Genovese again. Again she screamed for help. Windows again were opened and lights were turned on in some of the apartments; however, this time nobody even bothered to shout at the attacker. Still, he got into a car and left the crime scene again. It was now 3:35 A.M., and Catherine Genovese regained her footing and tried to reach safety. The attacker returned one last time. He found her lying at the back of a building at the foot of some stairs. He approached her, stabbed her again, and then left. The police received their first call about the attack at 3:50 A.M., twenty minutes after it had started; within minutes they were at the crime scene.

They found that Catherine had died from her wounds. At 4:25 A.M., an ambulance carted off her mortal remains. It was then that people came out of hiding (Adler, Mueller, and Laufer 2001:268). Police eventually arrested Catherine's killer, a 29-year-old man named Winston Moseley, and he was tried, convicted, and imprisoned for the crime (Hunt 1990:128–9).

Many people—thirty-eight according to the *New York Times*—had seen the attack and heard Ms. Genovese's screams, but they had done nothing, not even phoned police, until the attack was over and it was too late. How on earth can we make sense of this incredible callousness and failure to help another human being when it would have cost so little and meant so much for Catherine Genovese? It is difficult, of course, to understand the behavior of the killer: Why would someone stab and kill someone else without rhyme or reason? It is as difficult—maybe more so—to understand why thirty-eight people would refuse to come to the aid of another human. The simple answers that described the spectators as monstrous, apathetic, or alienated were too simple. It was the nature of human relationships and characteristics of the situation that explained much of the passivity of the witnesses to the crime and not their distressingly high levels of sadism, apathy, or alienation (Hunt 1990:126–7).

When many people witness an emergency situation, it is unlikely that any one of them will come to the aid of an individual in trouble; if only *one* individual witnesses an emergency, he or she is likely to help (Darley and Latane 1968; Latane and Darley 1968). This tendency for lone observers to help others even while crowds of individuals will not is known as the **bystander effect,** and it helps to explain human reactions to emergency situations that would otherwise be inexplicable. Bystanders will not help unless they are encouraged or forced to help by elements of the situation; the first response of bystanders to an emergency situation is *no* response.

Why does the bystander effect occur? One factor that explains it is called **diffusion of responsibility.** Each bystander may believe that someone else will help so no one does, a classic example of pluralistic ignorance (Darley and Latane 1968:378). The belief that some other individual will intervene means that one's own sense of urgency and obligation to help evaporates. When a diffusion of responsibility is operating, everyone believes that everyone else will act so no one does. The presence of others can also be inhibiting if it contributes to the ambiguity or uncertainty of a situation. Before a bystander is likely to help others, he or she must decide that an emergency does exist and then decide that his or her involvement will do some good (Latane and Darley 1968). An individual who witnesses inactivity on the part of other bystanders may conclude that the situation is not too serious and the emergency is not a real one (Latane and Darley 1968:217–9). One other inhibiting factor may be that individuals refuse to intervene because they do not want to embarrass themselves in front of other people by responding to something that is better left alone (Latane and Darley 1968:216).

The United States is not organized structurally or culturally to encourage high levels of social support or altruism (Cullen 1994:531). The mobility, heterogeneity, and anonymity of U.S. social life make it difficult for altruism, mutual help, and trust to flourish. Even though we live in groups, we may still find them to be lonely places (Riesman 1961:21–2). This is unfortunate. Everyone benefits from living in a well-connected society, even an individual who is a poorly connected member of it (Putnam 2000:20). Paxton's (1999) analysis of the nature of social integration (or what she calls **social capital**) from 1975 to 1994 in the United States found a strong and consistent decline in trust in individuals. However, she found no huge decline in the general trust in institutions, although some specific institutions were temporarily damaged by scandals. While we should not credit social support and social capital with more than they can deliver—conflict is ubiquitous and often instrumental in the creation of new and sturdier forms of social capital and social support—it is likely that the deterioration of social bonds has produced real social costs for us all (Putnam 2000:402–14).

Conclusions

This chapter explored the relational nature of being human. Groups and social relationships are an important part of human experience, and they are an important part of understanding that human experience. We belong to different kinds of groups, ranging from those primary groups, characterized by face-to-face interaction and cohesion, to those secondary groups, which are more task-oriented and impersonal. Some of our groups are reference groups—they provide standards for us to live by—and others are membership groups, the ones to which we belong. When humans interact, one of the more important things that they do is to construct the reality within which they live and then incorporate bits and pieces of this constructed reality into their cultures and subcultures. Individuals externalize some belief about the world, objectivate it, and then make it available for other people to internalize and use. The creation of values and norms are important parts of culture that channel human relationships in a variety of ways. Humans create and change social relationships as they act together, and humans themselves are then re-created in the process.

Humans are always social but they are not always sociable. They can and do act selfishly without concern for the common good. When groups contain members who are selfish and egocentric, the group has a social dilemma. Eventually, every member of the group suffers because the group itself may simply disappear. While self-interest and greed are parts of human relationships—the bystander effect is a common occurrence where observers to some emergency situation do not render aid to others—humans are capable of great altruism and charity. Some individuals have given their lives to help others, even total strangers.

Chapter One at a Glance

- The sociological imagination is the state of mind that allows us to understand the intersections between social conditions and individual experiences.
- We must understand social interaction in order to understand what it means to be human.
- The evolution of the human species is tied up with the evolution of groups, and our ancestors of long ago were probably social even before they were human.
- Humans construct the world within which they live in fundamental ways, and they are themselves reconstructed in the process.
- Social capital and feelings of group solidarity are threatened as group members pursue individual self-interest and fail to work together to achieve collective goals or to assist one another in times of need.

Glossary

altruism behavior that benefits another at some cost to the benefactor; done selflessly without the anticipation of rewards

brute facts these exist independently from any human institution or social relationship

bystander effect the tendency for a lone observer to render aid at the scene of an emergency situation even while crowds of individuals will not

culture knowledge or designs for living that people share and transmit to other members of the group; the system of values, norms, symbols, technologies, and material objects that humans create and use as they act together

dialectical relationship individuals construct social relationships and are themselves reconstructed in the process; or social relationships transform individuals who then reconstruct their relationships

diffusion of responsibility individuals who are part of a crowd are unlikely to render aid to others in an emergency situation because they all think that someone else will help

externalization a piece of knowledge or an idea about the world is created by an individual or individuals

family two or more people related by blood, marriage, or adoption who form a social and emotional unit and who often live together

folkways norms that tell members of the society what they should or should not do, think, or feel

generalized exchange an individual gives something to another and is eventually rewarded for it, but not from the person to whom the donation was made

group two or more people in interaction with one another; members of a group may define themselves as members of a group and be defined that way by others

human genome project   the undertaking to map out the elements of the human genome, the sum of the genetic material found in practically every cell in the human body

instinct doctrine   an instinct is behavior that is hereditary and unlearned, making it predetermined and preorganized in the life of a creature

institutional facts   these are created in and through social relationships and only exist because of them

internalization   a piece of shared knowledge is learned and used by humans as they act together

laws   formal norms that are written down and enforced by a specific agency such as the police

male compromise theory of monogamy   prosperous males gave up their possession of multiple wives in order to defuse the political threat from men who were angry because they had no wives

membership group   the group to which an individual belongs

moments of reality construction   the social construction of reality proceeds along three phases or moments: externalization, objectivation, and internalization

monogamy   a marriage that unites two partners into a family

mores   norms that tell members of the society what they must or must not do, think, or feel

natural selection   certain traits work better in some environments than in others; these are what survive and get transmitted from generation to generation

norm   cultural rule or shared understanding about acceptable and unacceptable ways of acting, thinking, and feeling that, if violated, produces a negative reaction

objectivation   a piece of shared knowledge has existed long enough that its origin is unknown and it seems objective and unbiased

play the roles (or **role play**)   acting out the rights and duties attached to a status, for example, students take tests and teachers prepare them

polyandry   a marriage that unites one female with two or more males

polygyny   a marriage that unites one male with two or more females

primary group   a group characterized by cohesion, intimacy, and face-to-face interaction

reference group   the group with which an individual identifies and uses as a point of comparison and evaluation

sanctions   positive responses to the following of norms (called positive sanctions) or negative responses to the breaking of norms (called negative sanctions); both positive and negative sanctions are intended to encourage individuals to obey norms

secondary group   a group characterized by large size and high levels of impersonality; the principal objective is to accomplish a specific task

small-world phenomenon   a structure of relationships exists that joins us all together in many direct and indirect ways

social construction of reality   the dynamic process through which humans work together to form and transform the world in which they live

social capital   the level of social support or integration that exists in a society

social dilemma   each member of a group works only for himself or herself, a situation that will undermine and perhaps destroy any cooperative or collective sense that group members might have

social interaction   two or more people take account of one another and fit their lines of action together in some meaningful way

society   the largest and most encompassing social group; members of a society share a culture and system of action, occupy a territory, and transmit their shared knowledge and social arrangements to others over time

sociological imagination   a clear awareness of the ways in which happenings in the social world and happenings in our private lives are interconnected

status a social position defined in terms of group membership that can be occupied by an individual (e.g., daughter, aunt, college student, athlete)

subculture a distinctive system of shared knowledge and a blueprint for living that is separable and separate from the dominant culture; a subculture is a culture within a culture

tragedy of the commons the damage done by the overuse of a collective or public resource (e.g., common grazing lands or joint fishing waters)

values shared understandings about desirable and undesirable things in social life, for example, success is a value in some societies as is democracy

References

Adams, Rebecca. 1998. "The Demise of Territorial Determinism: Online Friendships." Pp. 153–82 in *Placing Friendship in Context*, edited by R. Adams and G. Allan. Cambridge, UK: Cambridge University Press.

Adler, Freda, Gerhard O. W. Mueller, and William Laufer. 2001. *Criminology*, 4th ed., Boston: McGraw-Hill.

Alexander, Richard. 1979. *Darwinism and Human Affairs*. Seattle: University of Washington Press.

Apolito, Paolo. 1998. *Apparitions of the Madonna at Oliveto Citra: Local Visions and Cosmic Drama*, translated by William Christian, Jr. University Park: Pennsylvania State University Press.

Axelrod, Robert. 1984. *The Evolution of Cooperation*. New York: Basic Books.

Bendor, Jonathan and Piotr Swistak. 2001. "The Evolution of Norms." *American Journal of Sociology* 106: 1493–545.

Berger, Peter and Thomas Luckmann. 1966. *The Social Construction of Reality*. Garden City, NY: Doubleday.

Borkman, Thomasina Jo. 1999. *Understanding Self-Help/Mutual Aid: Experiential Learning in the Commons*. New Brunswick, NJ: Rutgers University Press.

Catton Jr., William. 1979. "Depending on Ghosts." Pp. 355–66 in *Sociology Readings for a New Day*, 2nd ed., edited by T. F. Hoult. New York: Random House.

Colt, George. 1991. *The Enigma of Suicide*. New York: Summit.

Cox, S. J., T. J. Sluckin, and J. Steele. 1999. "Group Size, Memory, and Interaction Rate in the Evolution of Cooperation." *Current Anthropology* 40:369–77.

Cullen, Francis. 1994. "Social Support as an Organizing Concept for Criminology: Presidential Address to the Academy of Criminal Justice Sciences." *Justice Quarterly* 11:527–59.

Darley, John and Bibb Latane. 1968. "Bystander Intervention in Emergencies: Diffusion of Responsibility." *Journal of Personality and Social Psychology* 8:377–83.

Darwin, Charles. 1952/1859. *The Origin of Species by Means of Natural Selection*. William Benton, Publisher. Chicago, IL: Encyclopaedia Britannica.

———. 1952/1871. *The Descent of Man and Selection in Relation to Sex*. William Benton, Publisher. Chicago, IL: Encyclopaedia Britannica.

Eder, Klaus. 1996. *The Social Construction of Nature: A Sociology of Ecological Enlightenment*. Thousand Oaks, CA: Sage.

Flaherty, Michael. 1999. *A Watched Pot: How We Experience Time*. New York: New York University Press.

Fulghum, Robert. 1988. *All I Really Need to Know I Learned in Kindergarten: Uncommon Thoughts on Common Things*. New York: Villard Books.

Goldscheider, Frances, Calvin Goldscheider, Patricia St. Clair, and James Hodges. 1999. "Changes in Returning Home in the United States, 1925–1985." *Social Forces* 78:695–720.

Gullette, Margaret Morganroth. 1998. "Midlife Discourses in the Twentieth-Century United States: An Essay on the Sexuality, Ideology, and Politics of 'Middle-Ageism.'" Pp. 3–44 in *Welcome to Middle Age! (And Other Cultural Fictions)*, edited by Richard Shweder. Chicago, IL: University of Chicago Press.

Hacking, Ian. 1999. *The Social Construction of What?* Cambridge, MA: Harvard University Press.

Hardin, Garrett. 1968. "The Tragedy of the Commons." *Science* 162:1243–48.

Hareven, Tamara. 2000. *Families, History, and Social Change: Life Course and Cross-Cultural Perspectives*. Boulder, CO: Westview Press.

Harris, Marvin. 1999. *Theories of Culture in Postmodern Times*. Walnut Creek, CA: AltaMira Press.

Heckert, Druann Maria. 2000. "Positive Deviance." Pp. 29–41 in *Constructions of Deviance: Social Power, Context, and Interaction*, 3rd edition, edited by P. Adler and P. Adler. Belmont, CA: Wadsworth.

Hinkle, Jr., Roscoe, and Gisela Hinkle. 1954. *The Development of Modern Sociology: Its Nature and Growth in the United States*. New York: Random House.

Hunt, Morton. 1990. *The Compassionate Beast: What Science Is Discovering about the Humane Side of Humankind*. New York: William Morrow and Company.

Ikeda, Keiko. 1998. *A Room Full of Mirrors: High School Reunions in Middle America*. Stanford, CA: Stanford University Press.

Kakar, Sudhir. 1998. "The Search for Middle Age in India." Pp. 75–98 in *Welcome to Middle Age! (And Other Cultural Fictions)*, edited by Richard Shweder. Chicago, IL: University of Chicago Press.

Kanazawa, Satoshi and Mary Still. 1999. "Why Monogamy?" *Social Forces* 78:25–50.

Kelly, James. "We're Not Going to Make It." *Time* (January 25, 1982):16–7.

Kephart, William. 1976. *Extraordinary Groups: The Sociology of Unconventional Life-Styles*. New York: St. Martin's Press.

Kimmel, Michael. 2000. *The Gendered Society*. New York: Oxford University Press.

Kuper, Adam. 1999. *Culture: The Anthropologists' Account*. Cambridge, MA: Harvard University Press.

Latane, Bibb and John Darley. 1968. "Group Inhibition of Bystander Intervention in Emergencies." *Journal of Personality and Social Psychology* 10:215–21.

Lewontin, Richard. 1991. *Biology as Ideology: The Doctrine of DNA*. New York: HarperPerennial.

———. 2000. *It Ain't Necessarily So: The Dream of the Human Genome and Other Illusions*. New York: New York Review of Books.

Lewontin, Richard, Steven Rose, and Leon Kamin. 1984. *Not in Our Genes: Biology, Ideology, and Human Nature*. New York: Pantheon.

Lieberman, Philip. 1991. *Uniquely Human: The Evolution of Speech, Thought, and Selfless Behavior*. Cambridge, MA: Harvard University Press.

Liebrand, Wim B. G. and David Messick. 1996. "Social Dilemmas: Individual, Collective, and Dynamic Perspectives." Pp. 1–9 in *Frontiers in Social Dilemmas Research*, edited by Wim Liebrand and David Messick. Berlin, Germany: Springer-Verlag.

Lock, Margaret. 1998. "Deconstructing the Change: Female Maturation in Japan and North America." Pp. 45–74 in *Welcome to Middle Age! (And Other Cultural Fictions)*, edited by Richard Shweder. Chicago, IL: University of Chicago Press.

Macy, Michael and John Skvoretz. 1998. "The Evolution of Trust and Co-operation between Strangers: A Computational Model." *American Sociological Review* 63:638–60.

March, James, Martin Schulz, and Xueguang Chou. 2000. *The Dynamics of Rules: Change in Written Organizational Codes*. Stanford, CA: Stanford University Press.

Mark, Noah. 1998. "Beyond Individual Differences: Social Differentiation from First Principles." *American Sociological Review* 63:309–30.

Maryanski, Alexandra and Jonathan Turner. 1992. *The Social Cage: Human Nature and the Evolution of Society.* Stanford, CA: Stanford University Press.

Melotti, Umberto. 1981. "Towards a New Theory of the Origin of the Family." *Current Anthropology* 22:625–38.

Merton, Robert K. 1968. *Social Theory and Social Structure,* enlarged edition. New York: Free Press.

Milgram, Stanley. 1967. "The Small-World Problem." *Psychology Today* 1:60–7.

Mills, C. Wright. 1959. *The Sociological Imagination.* New York: Oxford University Press.

Molm, Linda, Gretchen Peterson, and Nobuyuki Takahashi. 1999. "Power in Negotiated and Reciprocal Exchange." *American Sociological Review* 64:876–90.

Newman, David. 2002. *Sociology: Exploring the Architecture of Everyday Life,* 4th edition. Thousand Oaks, CA: Pine Forge Press.

Nisbet, Robert. 1966. *The Sociological Tradition.* New York: Basic Books.

Paxton, Pamela. 1999. "Is Social Capital Declining in the United States? A Multiple Indicator Assessment." *American Journal of Sociology* 105:88–127.

Petersen, Alan. 1998. *Unmasking the Masculine: "Men" and "Identity" in a Sceptical Age.* London: Sage.

Piliavin, Jane Allyn and Paul Lepore. 1995. "Biology and Social Psychology: Beyond Nature versus Nurture." Pp. 9–40 in *Sociological Perspectives on Social Psychology,* edited by Karen Cook, Gary Alan Fine, and James House. Boston: Allyn and Bacon.

Portes, Alejandro. 2000. "The Hidden Abode: Sociology as Analysis of the Unexpected." 1999 Presidential Address. *American Sociological Review* 65:1–18.

Putnam, Robert. 2000. *Bowling Alone: The Collapse and Revival of American Community.* New York: Simon & Schuster.

Ridley, Matt. 1993. *The Red Queen: Sex and the Evolution of Human Nature.* New York: Penguin.

———. 1999. *Genome: The Autobiography of a Species in 23 Chapters.* New York: HarperCollins.

Riesman, David, with Nathan Glazer and Reuel Denney. 1961. *The Lonely Crowd.* New Haven, CT: Yale University Press.

Rothman, Barbara Katz. 1998. *Genetic Maps and Human Imaginations: The Limits of Science in Understanding Who We Are.* New York: W. W. Norton.

Searle, John. 1995. *The Construction of Social Reality.* New York: Free Press.

Seligman, Adam. 1997. *The Problem of Trust.* Princeton, NJ: Princeton University Press.

Sell, Jane and Rick Wilson. 1999. "The Maintenance of Cooperation: Expectations of Future Interaction and the Trigger of Group Punishment." *Social Forces* 77:1551–70.

Seuling, Barbara. 1976. *You Can't Eat Peanuts in Church and Other Little-Known Laws.* Garden City, NY: Dolphin.

Shweder, Richard. 1998. "Welcome to Middle Age!" Pp. ix–xvii in *Welcome to Middle Age! (And Other Cultural Fictions),* edited by Richard Shweder. Chicago, IL: University of Chicago Press.

Small, Meredith. 1995. *What's Love Got to Do with It: The Evolution of Human Mating.* New York: Anchor.

Smith, Douglas. 1991. *Ever Wonder Why?* New York: Ballantine.

Smith-Lovin, Lynn. 1999. "Core Concepts and Common Ground: The Relational Basis of Our Discipline," presidential address given April 9, 1999, at the Southern Sociological Society Meetings in Nashville, Tennessee. *Social Forces* 78:1–23.

Sober, Elliott and David Sloan Wilson. 1998. *Unto Others: The Evolution and Psychology of Unselfish Behavior.* Cambridge, MA: Harvard University Press.

Soeffner, Hans-Georg. 1997. *The Order of Rituals: The Interpretation of Everyday Life,* translated by Mara Luckmann. New Brunswick, NJ: Transaction Publishers.

Steen, R. Grant. 1996. *DNA and Human Destiny: Nature and Nurture in Human Behavior.* New York: Plenum.

Sumner, William Graham. 1906. *Folkways: A Study of the Sociological Importance of Usages, Manners, Customs, Mores, and Morals.* Boston: Ginn.

Takagi, Eiji. 1996. "The Generalized Exchange Perspective on the Evolution of Altruism." Pp. 311–36 in *Frontiers in Social Dilemmas Research*, edited by Wim B.G. Liebrand and David Messick. Berlin, Germany: Springer-Verlag.

Takahashi, Nobuyuki. 2000. "The Emergence of Generalized Exchange." *American Journal of Sociology* 105: 1105–34.

Udry, J. Richard. 1995. "Sociology and Biology: What Biology Do Sociologists Need to Know?" *Social Forces* 73: 1267–78.

van den Wijngaard, Marianne. 1997. *Reinventing the Sexes: The Biomedical Construction of Femininity and Masculinity.* Bloomington: Indiana University Press.

Vinitzky-Seroussi, Vered. 1998. *After Pomp and Circumstance: High School Reunion as an Autobiographical Occasion.* Chicago, IL: University of Chicago Press.

Watts, Duncan J. 1999. "Networks, Dynamics, and the Small-World Phenomenon." *American Journal of Sociology* 105:493–527.

Weisner, Thomas and Lucinda Bernheimer.

——. 1998. "Children of the 1960s at Midlife: Generational Identity and the Family Adaptive Project." Pp. 211–57 in *Welcome to Middle Age! (And Other Cultural Fictions)*, edited by Richard Shweder. Chicago, IL: University of Chicago Press.

Wellman, Barry. 1999. *Networks in the Global Village: Life in Contemporary Communities.* Boulder, CO: Westview Press.

Wood, Brian and Kim Hill. "A Test of the 'Showing-Off' Hypothesis with Ache Hunters." *Current Anthropology* 41: 124–5.

Yamagishi, Toshio. 1995. "Social Dilemmas." Pp. 311–35 in *Sociological Perspectives on Social Psychology*, edited by Karen Cook, Gary Alan Fine, and James House. Boston: Allyn and Bacon.

Yamagishi, Toshio and Karen Cook. 1993. "Generalized Exchange and Social Dilemmas." *Social Psychology Quarterly* 56:235–48.

Zerubavel, Eviatar. 1981. *Hidden Rhythms: Schedules and Calendars in Social Life.* Chicago, IL: University of Chicago Press.

——. 1985. *The Seven Day Circle: The History and Meaning of the Week.* New York: Free Press.

Sages and Superstars
Classic Thoughts about
Our Relational Nature

People have always thought about, or so it would seem, societies and social relationships. Some individuals, however, have done it more thoroughly and formally, and they have written down their ideas for the rest of us to use. Classical theorists were convinced that **supernatural explanations** of social behavior would have to be supplanted by **scientific explanations** (Martindale 1960:29). This would make it possible for social relationships to be objectively examined and rationally explained. The growth of the **social sciences** made it possible to use methods of science and scientific observation to explain (and help to predict) relationships and regularities in human behavior. Early sociologists believed that they could identify laws of social order and social change by using scientific procedures (Eisenstadt 1976:16). Just as the natural world was governed by forces like the law of gravity, so was the social world governed by its own laws that could be discovered through the use of science.

The views of European sociologists were influenced by two sweeping social changes: the Industrial Revolution and the French Revolutions. These revolutions transformed and altered customary ways of doing things, while they called into question the very notion of tradition itself (Nisbet 1966:22). The **Industrial Revolution** was a series of changes—economic, cultural, social—that transformed those societies in which it occurred from a social order based on farming and agriculture to a social order based on industry and manufacturing. The Industrial Revolution encouraged growth of cities (with attendant problems), rise of large-scale organizations and bureaucracies, growth in the number and size of institutions, and changes in population size and characteristics. Social mobility—both upward and downward—occurred more often. The **French Revolutions of 1789 and 1848** reinforced the importance of equality, freedom, and popular control of government (Nisbet 1966:39). They called into question the prevailing social order and, more important, the ways in which property was distributed and owned (Aron 1968:303–33). These social revolutions changed people's relationships to each other and to society. As a result, social theorists were forced to rethink their views of both social and human nature.

If European sociology was a response to industrialization and political unrest, U.S. sociology was a response to industrialization and the growth of factories and to urbanization and the growth of cities (Hinkle and Hinkle 1954:2). Early U.S. sociologists shared a rural and small-town background, which encouraged them to view a social problem as anything that was *not* small-town and rural (Mills 1943). This meant, for all practical purposes, that they worried about the correlates of both urbanization and industrialization, and they were anxious about the abrupt changes that they saw happening all around them (Eisenstadt 1976:40). They believed that sociology was a system of knowledge to explain human relationships and predict the course that they were likely to take. Once the laws of human interaction were discovered, they believed, it would be possible to tinker with society and change it for the betterment of humankind. Even though U.S. sociologists were influenced by European social theorists (Morgan 1997), U.S. sociology was still distinctly American (Hinkle and Hinkle 1954:7).

Some U.S. sociologists experienced both personal and professional setbacks because of their politically incorrect views of U.S. society and their dislike of the direction it seemed to be heading. Edward A. Ross, for example, was dismissed from his teaching position at Stanford University because his views were considered too radical (Eisenstadt 1976:40). He worried that the forces of social control in U.S. society would be harnessed and used by selfish individuals to get what they wanted from others (Hinkle and Hinkle 1954:13–14). Edwin Sutherland, a prominent U.S. criminologist/sociologist (he received his Ph.D. in sociology and political economy from the University of Chicago in 1913), was pressured to behave (or at least write) in more politically correct ways. His study of white-collar crime showed him that some major U.S. corporations were responsible for perpetuating harmful acts against an unsuspecting public. His plan to publish the names of the offending companies and brand them as persistent criminals made administrators at the university where he worked quite nervous. They feared that donations to the university from these businesses might stop if Sutherland scorned them (Geis and Goff 1983). Sutherland yielded to the pressure and removed the names of the offending companies from his published work (Sutherland 1949). It was not until decades later that an uncut version was published and the names of the offending companies finally appeared in print (Sutherland 1983). These are not isolated cases. The entire discipline of sociology was attacked by powerful adversaries in the United States who seemed to think that anyone who was not flagrantly supportive of the status quo was a traitor.

Many prominent sociologists came under the surveillance of the Federal Bureau of Investigation when J. Edgar Hoover was its director for what he defined as radical or un-American activities (Keen 1999:6–8). While loss of jobs did not usually occur—most of the targeted individuals had enough clout and prominence to survive an FBI investigation—the investigations still had a damaging effect. They created embarrassment, anxiety, worry, and fear among some of the brightest and the best that sociology has had to offer. Prominent African American sociologists (e.g., W. E. B. Du Bois and E. Franklin Frazier), especially when they were outspoken in their condemnation of the racist policies and discriminatory practices of the United States, were viewed as communist sympathizers and conspirators. They were the target of intrusive background checks, defined as security risks, and disallowed from leaving the country (e.g., passports would not be issued). Other prominent sociologists were defined as threats to national security and investigated and harassed. Sometimes rumor and innuendo were all that was required for a sociologist to be singled out for attention by the FBI. At other times, the spark that got an investigation going was nothing more than an expressed interest in Russia, in Cuba, or simply an affiliation, no matter how slight, with an organization that was viewed as a communist front by the FBI. Even the ability to speak Russian or the wish to travel abroad was suspect.

Hoover was aware of the potential of sociology for social criticism, and he was suspicious of sociologists and any of their ideas that might challenge the status quo (Keen 1999:47). In fact, in a handwritten note, he scribbled the following: "The sociologists at at [sic] it again!" (Keen 1999:7). It is unclear what exactly he thought "The sociologists" were up to, but Hoover certainly thought it was no good. The sociological imagination was "stalked" by the FBI for doing what it was supposed to do—unmask the pretensions and propaganda people use to order their lives (Berger 1963:38)—and some prominent sociologists were branded as subversive and un-American. The activities of FBI agents stifled dissent, subverted the principles of a democratic society, and nudged mainstream sociology—at least temporarily—more in the direction of uncritical support of the status quo (Keen 1999:207). The discipline, however, was able to fulfill its potential for social critique and criticism. It reached the point where it did offer a scientific way to understand social relationships and to describe both social integration and social change.

Because humans are capable of such a wide range of behaviors, from those that are totally self-conscious and deliberate to those that are totally irrational and mysterious, some of the happenings in the social world will never be fully understood. These uncertainties do not mean that theoretical sketches in sociology are irrelevant. Far from it. Familiarity with *who* said *what* and exactly what was said can be both valuable and inspiring. In the remainder of this chapter, a major idea of a handful of influential social theorists will be presented as a "dictum," that is, a formal statement that summarizes a theorist's view. It is true, of course, that condensing these classic theoretical sketches into one statement does a great disservice to the theorists who devoted their lives to understanding the intricacies of social life. They said a great deal more about social relationships than a construction of a single dictum could ever suggest.

Auguste Comte (1798–1857)

> Comte's dictum: Social units can be understood by a scientific analysis of their patterns of integration and change.

A Biographic Sketch

Auguste Comte was born January 19, 1798, in Montpellier, France. As he grew to adulthood, he developed a knack for scholarly activities. He had a photographic memory, and he could recite backwards any page of text after reading it only once. When he sat down to write, he did everything from memory and never used supplementary materials during the writing process. All his lectures were given without reference to notes (Ritzer 2000:16–17). He was plagued by problems and anxieties throughout his life (Coser 1971:14). In 1827, he tried unsuccessfully to drown himself in the Seine. As he reached his forties, he became disillusioned with his life's work of understanding society. He practiced "cerebral hygiene," where he refused to read or to consider anyone's scientific ideas other than his own. He spent his reading time on poetry and works of fiction. This insulation from other scientists gave his work a lack of vitality and currency. He was fired from jobs, and his wife eventually left him. In 1844, he got a new, but temporary, lease on life. He met and fell in love with Clothilde de Vaux. The relationship only lasted about a year—she died of tuberculosis—but it was to have enduring effects on Comte's outlook on life. He came to believe that emotion was more powerful than intellect; that feeling was more powerful than mind; and that altruism was more important and valuable than egoism and selfishness (Coser 1971:18–9). The man died September 5, 1857.

Social Statics and Social Dynamics

Auguste Comte is considered to be the father of sociology, primarily because he named the discipline. His first choice was "social physics"; however, he abandoned that term because he believed that it had been used already by Adolphe Quetelet, a Belgian statistician (Coser 1971:3). Comte decided upon the term **sociology** to describe the scientific study of societies, groups, and social relationships. His objective was to construct a science of social unity. Human history and human relationships are all elements of a greater and grander whole, he believed, and it is the whole that must be understood *as* a whole. Whenever living things are the object of interest, it is their organic unity that is the most important; the parts must be placed in their proper relationship to each other and to the whole of which they are a part.

Comte employed what we would now call a **biological metaphor.** The society or group is compared and contrasted with a biological organism in order to understand the society or group better. Just as a human body has different parts, so does a society; just as different parts of a human body work together, so do different parts of a society work together; just as a human body changes or evolves gradually—or returns to the equilibrium that is best for it—so does a society; and just as parts of a human body really cannot be understood in isolation from each other or from the whole, so it is true with a society. Societies have a unity that must be understood and explained scientifically.

Comte realized that a society was different from an organism. While a living creature (or even a cell of that creature) is discrete and encased in a physical or material membrane like a skin, a society is not. This does not mean that social groups lack boundaries, however. Members of groups separate themselves from other groups all the time and in many different ways. While members of a family may live together in a particular place like a house, apartment, or trailer, their identity as a family is not dependent on that physical structure. You can set the family loose in an amusement park, far away from its residence, and the members are no less of a family. Members may even die and still be included in the family history. So, what is the "skin" of the "body social" if it is not material or physical? The boundaries of human societies are spiritual and moral, but no less constricting than the skin of a creature that separates it from the outside world. The human capacity for **symbolic communication,** our involvement in **social institutions** like a family or a religion, our complex **division of labor** (where groups of people perform different tasks in a society), and our **social identities** are some of the important factors that create the boundaries that we use to mark ourselves off from others.

In Comte's *System of Positive Polity,* he established right from the beginning one of his most important ideas and one of his most enduring legacies. He insisted that sociology could be divided into the study of social statics and the study of social dynamics (Comte 1968/1875:1). **Social statics** is the category that contains those factors that integrate and stabilize a society; **social dynamics** is the category that contains those factors that change and transform it. Social statics covers the laws of integration, and social dynamics covers the laws of actual development and social progress. This specialization into these two categories was at the heart of Comte's positive philosophy, and it was at the heart of his understanding of society, its laws of relationships, and its laws of evolution. Statics and dynamics work together in human societies and they are "intimately connected" (Comte 1968/1875:1). Dynamic changes, Comte believed (1968/1876:8), actually increase levels of harmony and unity so that the society evolves over time to become more and more perfect. Comte, like the rest of us, was torn continually—in his work, in his life, and in his social relationships—between the forces of order and conflict, of stability and progress, of statics and dynamics (Coser 1971:41).

Karl Marx (1818–1883)

Marx's dictum: Humans construct and reconstruct social forms as they act together, and they themselves are changed in the process.

A Biographic Sketch

Karl Marx was born May 5, 1818, in Trier, Prussia. His early years were lived in a comfortable middle-class existence. His father practiced law, and his mother took care of the household. Young Marx was never particularly close to his mother, but his father exerted a strong influence upon him, especially on his love of learning. Marx had planned to study law like his father but found he was more interested in philosophy and history. In 1841, Marx received a doctorate in philosophy from the University of Jena. Two years later he married his childhood sweetheart, Jenny von Westphalen. Even though her parents were opposed to the marriage because of what they saw as Marx's total lack of social standing, it lasted almost forty years, and the couple had six children.

The couple moved to Paris so that Marx could find work to support his family. However, his passion for social criticism consumed him, and his family suffered. While there, he met Friedrich Engels, a man who became his close friend, supporter, and collaborator (Ritzer 2000:44). In 1845, he was forced to leave France, and he and his family moved to Brussels where he joined other radicals like himself. Four years later, he and his family moved to London, where they were to remain for the rest of their lives. The Marx family lived in desperate situations, during desperate times, among the underclass of London. Marx could not even get a job as a clerk because his handwriting was so bad. Three of his children died from starvation and lack of proper medical care. Marx could not even afford a coffin for one his children who had died, so he had to turn once again to the kindness of others, one of whom gave him enough money to buy the coffin.

> [Marx's] personal situation, the acute misery of isolation and marginality, in its turn fueled and refueled the sense of outrage and indignation that informs his works. His tension-ridden and conflictive private life predisposed him to see in conflict and contention the ultimate hidden motive force of all history (Coser 1971:85).

At the end of Marx's life, material conditions did improve for him. His friend Engels had prospered, and he continued to financially support Marx's intellectual activities. Marx wrote for a wider and wider audience. The death of his wife in 1881, followed by the death of his oldest daughter in 1882, was devastating to Marx and he never recovered. He passed away on March 14, 1883, alone in his study.

Historical Change and Class Conflict

"The history of all human history," Marx and Engels wrote, "past and present, has been the history of class struggles" (Marx and Engels 1963/1848:25). It is not without reason that Karl Marx is referred to as the father of conflict theory. For him, tension, struggle, conflict, domination, and exploitation are inevitable and inexorable in most social groups. In the Marxist scheme, social transformations come through joint human actions, but human actions are themselves constrained by the social relationships that are being created.

People are the masters of their own destinies only up to a point, because their society and its historical transformations are not exactly what these individuals would like or expect. We live in a world that is not entirely of our own making and choosing. In the network of social relationships, one set of relations is more important than all others: economic relationships. It is the way that humans interact with each other as they try to survive and live in a place where survival and livelihood are never guaranteed that shapes cultural, political, and social structures.

The economic component of society has two parts: the forces of production and the relations of production. The **forces of production** are the technological abilities of the people and the social relationships that evolve around the creation (or collection) of the goods and services that sustain human life. Forces include natural resources, the level of technology, and the particular way labor is used to produce goods and services. At one time, muscle power may be most important; at some other time, simple farming techniques will be most important; and at still some other time, machines will do practically everything. These forces of production influence the relations of production. The **relations of production** are the legally supported differences in the ownership of property, including the ownership of the forces of production. During feudal times the major social division was between those who owned land (nobles) and those who did not (serfs). In capitalist economies, the major division is between those who own machines and those who do not. In Marx's terms the owners of machines were called the *bourgeoisie* (or capitalist class) and the nonowners were the *proletariat* (or working class).

The structure of a society is an elaboration of its class structure, and social changes come directly from conflicts between classes. The capitalists and workers have an antagonistic relationship: They cannot advance together for very long. Capitalists can dish out some material resources to workers for a while, but what capitalists will not do is to relinquish their control of the *forces* of production. If they were to do so, it would mean that they would lose control of that which guarantees their superior position in a society. Even if wealth were redistributed, class inequality would not disappear until the forces of production were collectively owned and the fruits of workers' labors would go more directly to them. This is why Marx was adamant that the revolution must be ongoing, worldwide, and set to destroy the bureaucratic, authoritarian form of *bourgeois* society. Workers could not just assume the old forms of bureaucratic power and expect to end social inequality. They had to work together to eliminate capitalism as the dominant economic and social form.

False Consciousness, Class Consciousness, and Revolution

No guarantee exists that the instability of capitalist society will *inevitably* lead to revolution and change. The reason is that the capitalist class uses its extraordinary resources to "reproduce" the status quo. Because the ideas of every period are, in large part, the ideas that support the interests of the ruling class and because institutions serve as mechanisms for indoctrinating persons into the capitalist conceptions of reality, Marx insisted that a **false consciousness** exists. False consciousness is the acceptance of ruling class ideas and the failure to confront the *bourgeoisie* and overthrow the existing social order through revolutionary action.

Capitalist society will end when social conditions are right to set the stage for the emergence of a class-conscious working class, whose numbers are legion, armed with a set of ideas that justifies their revolutionary activities. **Class consciousness** exists when a class in itself becomes a class for itself, and members of the working class understand that they have much in common and work together to further their shared interests. This is where Marx's sociology is so apparent. Members of the capitalist class, lacking a sense of unity because each of them is selfish and competitive, will be unable to survive for long the challenge posed by a class conscious *proletariat* whose members are more altruistic and connected with each other. Marx and Engels (1963/1848:68) show as much in the concluding words of their *The Communist Manifesto:* "Proletarians have nothing to lose but their chains. They have a world to win. PROLETARIANS OF ALL LANDS, UNITE!" These authors' mission, one of them at any rate, was to show members of the working class how exploited workers were and to move them in the direction of greater class consciousness and revolutionary action. Workers could not just sit back and wait for the good life to arrive. They had to work and struggle together to create a world, and then, of course, no guarantees existed that they would get what they all wanted (Ritzer 2000:46).

Emile Durkheim (1858–1917)

Durkheim's dictum: The whole is more than the sum of its parts.

A Biographic Sketch

Emile Durkheim was born April 15, 1858, in Epinal, France. His father was a rabbi, and his mother worked in the home as an embroiderer, an early example of a two-income family. Emile's grandfather and great-grandfather had also been rabbis, and everyone expected Durkheim to follow the family tradition and become a rabbi, too. However, he decided by his early teens that a rabbi was not what he wanted to be (Ritzer 2000:80). His life's work was to be the creation of a scientific sociology that would serve as a moral platform for the direction and guidance of members of society (Coser 1971:145). Durkheim developed a strong interest in the forces of regulation and deregulation that were responsible for social order and disorder. During his formative years, wars were being fought, political regimes were coming and going, populations were changing rapidly, and economic changes were all around. He carried with him an overwhelming sense of community lost, and it is not at all surprising that he turned the full power of his intellect to understanding what happens when societies and people in them lose their moral rudder and society becomes deregulated (Jones 1999).

By age 29, Durkheim was already viewed as a rising star in the social sciences (and philosophy). In 1887, he got a teaching job at the University of Bordeaux, and that same year he married Louise Dreyfus. In the course of their marriage, they had two children, Marie and Andre. While Emile devoted his energies to his teaching, writing, and research, his wife took care of family matters and also helped him with proofreading and other secretarial duties (Coser 1971:146). These were productive years for him. Emile wrote a number of important books, developed into a masterful lecturer who captivated his students, and increased his status as a social scientist. He earned his doctorate at age 35, and in 1896 he was promoted to a full professorship in social science at Bordeaux, the first position of its kind in France (Coser 1971:147). He finished his teaching career at the Sorbonne in Paris as a professor of the science of education and sociology.

Shortly before Christmas day, 1915, he received the tragic news that his son had died from wounds received in World War I. Andre was his father's pride and joy, who expected him to establish himself as one of the leading social scientists of his day (sociolinguistics was Andre's specialty). Durkheim never recovered from the death of his son, and his interest in his work and in his life dwindled. Emile Durkheim died on November 15, 1917, at the age of 59.

The Priority of the Social

Durkheim is considered to be the father of structural-functional theory, and his views of society and social relationships certainly illustrate the fundamentals of this approach. Durkheim's inclination was to conceive of society as a whole or totality—a *sui generis*—that is above and beyond individuals, a view that he inherited from Comte. Like Comte, Durkheim viewed societies as organic wholes that could not be understood by examining—no matter how closely or scientifically—the biologies or psychologies of the individuals who were members of the group (Turner 1974:18).

> We have here, I think, the outline of what is to be one of Durkheim's central ideas throughout his career—the idea with which he defines sociology—namely, the priority of the whole over the parts, or again, the irreducibility of the social entity to the sum of its elements, the explanation of the elements by the entity and not of the entity by the elements (Aron 1970:17).

When people get together, it sets the foundation for the construction or building of social relationships. When these relationships become durable and enduring, a social level of reality forms. Durkheim believed this social level is both separate and separable from individuals, and it must be explained and understood in its own right. It has a power and a force that makes individuals what they are (Durkheim 1974:55).

Social Facts, Social Relationships, and Suicide

If collective events are not caused by individual factors, then what does cause them? Durkheim's answer is "social facts." **Social facts** are things that emerge from the association of people (Durkheim 1938:14), but they are then externalized and come to constrain the collective and individual actions of those people who created them. What impressed Durkheim about social facts was their exteriority and their power to cause other social facts in a society.

> Here, then is a category of facts [social facts] with very distinctive characteristics: it consists of ways of acting, thinking, and feeling, external to the individual, and endowed with a power of coercion, by reason of which they control him [or her] (Durkheim 1938:3).

One social fact that most of us have experienced is a crosswalk. These lines on the pavement have no physical capacity to keep a car from running over someone who is crossing a street; they are not physical barriers. Yet, they are not simply two lines on the pavement. They do constrain the activities of both the individuals who seek them out before crossing a street and the motorists who bring their vehicles to a complete stop to allow pedestrians to cross in front of them. Pedestrians waiting to cross at a corner without a crosswalk may not be treated so charitably by passing motorists.

At times, far too little regulation or integration exists to constrain individual desires enough to allow harmony and interdependence to develop. When this happens, the parts of the whole are in a state of anomy (Durkheim 1933:368). **Anomy** is a state of deregulation or normlessness where individuals become too self-centered to have a sense of shared destiny and a common moral direction. Durkheim thought that humans will be forever unhappy and eternally striving without a chance of fulfillment unless their passions or desires are held in check by a moral authority. Too little or too much integration or regulation was dysfunctional for a society and bad for individuals exposed to these perverse conditions. Self-interest and individualism can coexist with social integration and harmony *if* the **collective conscience**—the body of beliefs and sentiments that holds people together—allows a pinch of individualism without letting it get so out of hand that it destroys all cooperation and interdependence (Ritzer 2000:94–5).

In order to show that social relationships influence private and personal experiences, Durkheim turned his sociological imagination to an analysis of **suicide.** Durkheim's best friend and roommate at college, Victor Hommay, committed suicide, an event that was to have a lasting effect on Durkheim's thoughts about it. Because he knew Hommay so well, Durkheim was unwilling to blame the death on some personal defect or loss of reason. Instead of doing what is so typical today and blame suicide on factors like chemicals in the brain or psychological states like extreme depression or hopelessness, Durkheim moved to the social level. He (1951/1897) identified two societal conditions that he believed caused suicide: **social integration** and **social regulation.** Either too much or too little of either of these represented a social condition that was correlated with a particular type of suicide. Too little integration produced **egoistic suicide,** while too much integration produced **altruistic suicide.** An example of the first type is the lone, sick, and tired individual who takes his or her own life because of the absence of meaningful relationships. The second type is demonstrated by a suicide bomber who sacrifices life in order to terrorize members of some society. Too little regulation produced **anomic suicide,** while too much regulation produced **fatalistic suicide.** An example of anomic suicide would be an individual who takes his or her own life in response to an immediate and abrupt economic depression. Fatalistic suicide is shown by a teenager who cannot get out from under the ruthless of control of his or her parent and commits suicide in order to be free of the stifling control.

Despite his early infatuation with **society as a *sui generis*,** Durkheim eventually came to realize that social facts could only become effective if they were internalized by individuals. The society that we each confront as something above and beyond us eventually infiltrates our consciousness and becomes a part of each of us. Even though society is more than the sum of its members, it is still in us and we must experience it as such (Durkheim 1974:55). According to Durkheim, the individual is no mere puppet at the hands of the society puppet master. Society constrains action through moral facts or rules, but it does not determine the particulars of each and every individual act (Peristiany 1974:xxx).

George Herbert Mead (1863–1931)

> Mead's dictum: Humans become societies in miniature as they internalize the perspectives of others.

A Biographic Sketch

George Herbert Mead was born February 27, 1863, in South Hadley, Massachusetts. The young Mead was encouraged to strive for intellectual excellence, and he developed a love of both reading and learning. At the age of 7, his family moved to Ohio, where his father became a chairperson at the theological seminary at Oberlin College. Mead came of age in Ohio, and he eventually attended the college. It had been founded in 1833, principally to teach theology and morals, but it did more than that. It was one of the first U.S. colleges to admit African Americans, and, in 1841, it became the first U.S. coeducational institution to grant college degrees to women. It was also one of the points on the underground railroad that made it possible for slaves from the south to escape from their servitude on plantations. Oberlin College was also the site of the emergence of the Anti-Saloon League (Coser 1971:341). It is not hard to see that the climate at the college was a puzzling one. It combined fire and brimstone fundamentalism with a heavy dose of libertarianism, egalitarianism, and social activism. The atmosphere at Oberlin was still heavily authoritarian, and an inquisitive mind like Mead's didn't have much opportunity to grow. The obligation of a responsible and dedicated Oberlin student was to master the classics and to develop a sound moral philosophy. Although he did graduate from Oberlin, Mead rebelled against its strict and stifling climate and eventually rejected the dogmas of the church; however, he never lost his sense of decency and kindness.

In 1887, he decided to go to Harvard to study philosophy. It was there that he was to fall under the influence of William James, and in due course, Mead's ideas about human behavior matured. After his years at Harvard, Mead traveled abroad to study and learn; much of this period was spent at German universities (at Leipzig and at Berlin) where he studied both psychology and philosophy. Mead, however, never did receive any graduate degrees (Ritzer 2000:343). Upon his return to the United States, he married the sister (Helen Castle) of a close friend, and they prepared for their move to Ann Arbor, Michigan, where Mead had been hired to teach in the Department of Philosophy and Psychology at the University of Michigan. It was there that he met his intellectual soulmate, the pragmatist John Dewey, and the two became lifelong friends. The Meads' son Henry, the only child they would have, was born in 1892. A year later Mead was enticed to move to Chicago to teach philosophy at the request of Dewey, who himself had been courted by administrators at the recently created University of Chicago and convinced to move. It was at Chicago that Mead would develop his thoughts about social relationships and fine-tune his vision of philosophy and social psychology.

Mead is usually referred to as the father of symbolic interaction theory. Curiously enough, he never used the term symbolic interaction theory and would probably be surprised that his views are now referred to this way. He considered himself a social behaviorist (Strauss 1964:xix); the term symbolic interactionism was coined by Herbert Blumer in 1937, a term that even Blumer considers a "somewhat barbaric neologism" (Blumer 1969:1). However, it is the term that stuck. Although he wrote many articles, Mead never wrote a comprehensive manuscript describing his views (Morris 1934:vii). His major work, *Mind, Self, and Society* (1934), was not actually penned by him. After Mead's death, several of his students compared their class notes from his social psychology class—one of which was a stenographic copy—and they organized his views in book form to be published three years *after* his death (Morris 1934:vi). Other posthumous works were to follow, but *Mind, Self, and Society* is the most important in presenting Mead's views of socialization and social relationships and the one for which he is best remembered.

Mead took great pride in his speaking ability, and his lectures at the University of Chicago were always well attended. He instructed his students without benefit of notes. Sometimes, he would pick up an eraser from the board or a piece of chalk, hold it at arm's length, and gaze intently at it as he spoke (Ritzer 2000:342). At times, students felt more like spectators to Mead's conversation with an eraser or piece chalk than as parts of the discussion. He never gave exams. Each student was expected to write a term paper, the grade on which was the grade in the course. Some of his students were quite impressed with his approach and could not get enough of him; others, however, didn't have a clue what Mead's philosophy was really about (Coser 1971:345). While Mead never courted fame and fortune, he is now recognized as one of a small number of individuals who have made a lasting contribution to the social sciences (Coser 1971:347). In fact, no explanation of social relationships should ever neglect Mead's thoughts and ideas. He died of heart failure on April 26, 1931.

Social Relationships and Symbolic Interaction

Mead's basic objective was to explain how social order is possible by explaining how societies get inside of individuals so that they become societies in miniature. Mead stressed throughout his work that individuals do influence a society just as they are influenced by it, and his "strikingly processual view of social organization" is a counterpoint to those approaches that miss the negotiated nature of social order (Strauss 1964:xiii–xiv). In Mead's view, the individual is an active constructor of the world that he or she perceives and within which he or she acts. In fact, the title of Mead's book would have more correctly represented his views if the word "society" had come first instead of last. This would have shown the importance that Mead, the sociologist, attached to it.

The society—to put it far more simply than does Mead—is the organized set of responses that humans make to each other and to certain situations in the external world (Mead 1934:270). Humans are able to cooperate because they are able to read or infer each other's attitudes, intentions, or plans of action and then adjust to others accordingly (Meltzer 1967:7). Separate lines of behavior must be fit together by the interactants—purposely, intelligently, consciously—into some coordinated whole (Blumer 1969:8). The unique feature of human social behavior is that humans can interact with each other using symbols (or significant gestures).

A **symbol** (or **significant gesture**) is a vocal gesture (e.g., a word) or a physical gesture that stands for, or represents, something because of group agreement. The word "rabbit" stands for, or represents, a cute, furry creature, for a particular community of language users, just as moving the forefinger across the throat can mean "stop it" or "knock it off." The physical gestures used by people who are deaf to communicate with others are good examples of significant gestures. When you know what the gestures mean, you can use them to connect with others and to describe what you want to describe. A **conversation of significant gestures,** then, has the great advantage of allowing humans who use them—and only humans use them according to Mead—to share attitudes or outlooks in the context of the social or collective act. "We are calling out in the other person something we are calling out in ourselves, so that unconsciously we take over these attitudes" (Mead 1934:68–9). It is the vocal significant gesture that is especially powerful for creating a shared tendency to respond. Symbols are the basis of language, and human society requires language for its organization (Mead 1934:235).

Symbolic interaction makes it more likely that an individual, say a developing child, will **take the role of the other** or **role-take.** Role-taking is a process that was explored in great depth by Mead, and it may, in fact, be his most original and useful term. When you role-take, you mentally project yourself into the position of another and look at the world (and yourself) from that other position (Mead 1934:160–1). As a child matures and becomes both more social and more socialized, he or she continues to get better and better at taking the role of the other. The earlier days of one's life are characterized by an egocentricity in which little or no role-taking exists. However, day by day, a child gets better at projecting himself or herself mentally into the position of others. Eventually, the child will internalize these views and carry them around with him or her, sometimes for life. Some of these views will be those of the entire society, what Mead called the **generalized other** (Mead 1934:154).

What is unique about human activity is not simply that it is intelligent—nonhuman animals may have a measure of intelligence—but that it is *reflexively* intelligent (Mead 1934:92). Humans can select certain stimuli and envision certain plans of action *before* a particular course of action is selected (Mead 1934:98–9). Humans are able to construct their acts based on their anticipation of the likely consequences of those acts.

> We are finding out what we are going to say, what we are going to do, by saying and doing, and in the process we are continually controlling the process itself (Mead 1934:140).

In this way, the future (or at least expectations of it) exist in the present and help to influence the course of human relationships.

The **self** exists when individuals engage in a process of viewing themselves as social objects. We can act toward ourselves just as we act toward others; and we can act toward ourselves just as we think others would act toward us. We can blame ourselves, encourage ourselves, or hate ourselves just as we can blame, encourage, and hate other people. What is more, once self-development starts, we use our conceptions of self in constructing all our future acts. We are objects of our own experience, and we sally forth into the world with these understandings as core elements in our relationships to others and in our evaluations of ourselves. We are sensitive to the views of others—some at any rate—and we strategically comport ourselves in anticipation of their responses to us.

One day I was at a local airport to pick up a friend. I had arrived early and decided to make my way to the restroom while I waited for the plane. I approached the men's restroom, threw open the door like I was entering a saloon in the Old West (that is the way we manly men do it), and entered the place. After going in a few feet, I noticed a very long mirror, much longer than I had ever seen before in a men's restroom. A few feet more and I noticed a few tables extending from the wall. I had never seen such things before in a men's lavatory, and I wondered about their purpose. I completed my journey to the back of the restroom only to find that *someone* had forgotten to build stand-up urinals in the place. Very curious. Then this manly man realized that he had made a serious mistake: He was in the women's restroom. I turned an appropriate shade of red, and I got out as fast as I could. Even though I met nobody going in or coming out (whew!), I was still embarrassed by my mistake; even years later I feel silly for having made it. I took the role of the other, the *generalized* other, and evaluated my behavior as inappropriate. Societies and social groups—and the individuals in them—exist in action and through action and that is the way they must be understood (Blumer 1969:6).

Max Weber (1864–1920)

Weber's dictum: Humans take account of others as they meaningfully construct their actions.

A Biographic Sketch

Max Weber was born in Erfurt, Thuringia (Germany), on April 21, 1864. Even from the beginning, he was a tormented individual. At age 4 he experienced an attack of meningitis. Irreconcilable differences between his parents were to have a profound effect upon both his personality and his intellectual development (Ritzer 2000:110). Weber's father was shallow and self-indulgent, and his mother was strict and self-contained. While Max's parents appeared on the surface to be happy with each other and content in their marriage, they actually were not. His mother's strong sense of duty and responsibility, along with her strict religious views, did not fit well with his father's pursuit of pleasure and all of his political wheeling and dealing. The young Weber was powerfully affected by the inconsistencies and contradictions in his home, as well as the ongoing tension between his parents. If he chose to identify with one of his parents, he thought he was betraying the other.

Weber developed a strong curiosity about the world around him and the people in it, and he lost himself in books. Even at 14, he was able to write and speak with a measure of authority about the works of writers like Homer or Kant. During Max's teen years, his father started to exert a stronger influence upon him than did his mother. When Max entered the University of Heidelberg at 18, he joined his father's dueling fraternity, decided to major in law (as had his father), and learned how to hold his liquor. "He became as active in duelling as in drinking bouts, and the enormous quantities of beer consumed with his fraternity brothers soon transformed the thin and sickly looking young man into a heavy-set Germanic boozer proudly displaying his fencing scars" (Coser 1971:236). Remarkably, these extracurricular activities did not keep Max from his reading, and he studied not only law but also economics, history, philosophy, and theology. He passed his doctorate exam in law at Berlin and joined the bar, and he was hired there as a university professor in the law department. In 1894, he became a professor of political economics at the University of Freiburg, and one year later he left Freiburg to take a position at the University of Heidelberg. His strong work ethic and his prodigious intellect made him a powerful figure in academic circles.

In 1897, when Weber was 33, he had a major falling out with his father. His parents came to visit him in Heidelberg. He and his father got into a violent quarrel, and Max told his father just what he thought of him and of his dictatorial treatment of Max's mother. Max then threw the elder Weber out of his house. His father died about a month later, and Max held himself responsible. Max had always been sensitive and shy as a child, and it was easy for him to feel guilty for what had happened. He suffered a mental collapse that affected him for the rest of his life. He had difficulty working, and at times he could not even concentrate long enough to read. In 1903, he improved a bit and was able to write again. He was even invited to the United States to give a lecture in 1904 before a Congress of Arts and Sciences that was meeting in St. Louis in connection with the World's Fair (Bendix 1962:3).

Near the end of his life, Weber became intensely political. He wrote articles about current events, and he even considered running for political office himself. He was intolerant of injustice and strong in his defense of victims of it. He defended colleagues of his who had been discriminated against by university administrators because of their ethnic heritage or their political views. When Jewish students were ignored by German professors, Weber invited the students to his home. When anti-Semitic, fascist students in Munich insulted a Jewish student, Weber insisted on an immediate apology from the leader of the group. He had a brilliant mind and an amazing work ethic. He could write with authority on a wide range of topics, and he maintained his social conscience and determination to do and to say what was right throughout his life. His mother died in 1919; his sister Lili took her own life in 1920, leaving children whom Max and his wife planned to adopt. However, it was not to be. In June of that year, Weber developed a high fever, thought to be caused by the flu. A few days later it was identified as pneumonia, but by then, nothing could be done. Weber died June 14, 1920, at the age of 56.

Social Action

Weber's unit of analysis was the acting individual, constructing action in a specific social and historical setting, taking account of others and their orientations (Runciman 1978:3). **Social action** was the pivotal concept for the kind of sociology Weber was formulating, and an understanding of social action was decisive for sociology's status as a science (Weber 1968a:24). It exists when an individual takes account of another, constructs a meaningful act, and lets the meaning and the accounting direct the course of further activity. In other words, what makes action *social* is that it takes account of another (or others) and is oriented in its course or sequence; what makes it *action* is that it possesses subjective meaning (Weber 1947:88). Solitary prayer or behaviors oriented exclusively toward inanimate objects or toward nonhuman animals, Weber insists, are not social action because they lack the element of mutual orientation (Weber 1968a:22). Social action is also not the same thing as the similar actions of a lot of people. Just because members of a crowd open their umbrellas in a downpour does not make this act a social experience; it is not mutually oriented meaningful behavior (Weber 1968a:23).

Sociologists, Weber believed, can explain in unique ways because they can come to understand and interpret the subjective meanings that direct the course of the actions of individuals in the group (Weber 1968a:15). Understanding or **verstehen** comes from interpreting the "states of mind" of humans in terms of their motive and intent, and it also comes from comprehending the culture and its system of symbols (Weber 1947:87). "Sociology . . . is a science which attempts the interpretive understanding of social action in order thereby to arrive at a causal explanation of its course and effects" (Weber 1947:88). This understanding of the states of mind of social actors is possible because an observer can decipher inner states of others by inferring them from knowledge of social relationships and of social context. Weber's interest in subjective meaning and understanding of the inner consciousness of social actors links his sociology to the sociology of symbolic interactionists (Wallace and Wolf 1999:191).

One day I was in a grocery store. I saw a student of mine out shopping. He was pushing his young daughter—a stranger to me—around in a shopping cart while he purchased items. As I approached them, I exchanged a few pleasantries with him. Then, in my most charming manner, I asked the young child how she was. She met my kindness and concern by sitting there in stone-face silence, holding up her right fist, and extending the middle finger of her hand. Wow! I know parents are supposed to teach their children not to talk to strangers but to teach them to give the "finger" to their college professors seems a bit much. My initial interpretation, however, was not the correct one. It seems that the child had actually gotten her middle finger jammed in the shopping cart a few minutes before we met. When I asked her how she was doing, she was simply showing me her injury. Fitting social context, meaning, motive, and social action together into some intelligible whole and then coming to some causal understanding of them is what sociology is all about according to Weber.

Rationality, Bureaucracies, and Social Relationships

Weber concluded that the subjective meaning that is found in social action could be inferred the best in relationships in which a clear association exists between means and ends, between action and goals. This is why he gave such prominence in his work to an analysis of **rational action** (Eldridge 1971:53; Weber 1968a:17). "It is possible for us to understand the rational actions of individual human beings by re-living them in our own minds" (Weber 1978:389). The more rational an action is, the easier it is to understand the subjective meaning that orients it (Weber 1968a:28).

Weber analyzed the characteristics of modern bureaucracies, principally because he viewed the bureaucracy as the epitome of efficiency and rationality. In **bureaucracies,** relationships are tightly governed by written rules and regulations. Individuals are given official duties to discharge on behalf of the bureaucracy, and employees are thoroughly trained in a field of specialization. A clear chain of command or office hierarchy exists in which orders flow down and information and appeals flow up. Rules are abstract and general, while promotion and retention are based on merit rather than on favoritism (Weber 1968b:956-8). Weber was not altogether pleased by the penetration of bureaucracies into more and more areas of everyday life. With increasing rationality came an **iron cage** of bureaucracy in which boredom and routinization undercut any sense of pleasure, excitement, or fulfillment. Employees in bureaucracies are expected to follow the rules and procedures of the organization no matter what (Weber 1968b:988).

Erving Goffman (1922–1982)

Goffman's dictum: Humans manage and manipulate impressions about themselves to influence others.

A Biographic Sketch

Erving Goffman was born June 11, 1922, in Manville, a city in the province of Alberta, Canada. Very little information is available about his life other than what can be inferred from his published works. This secrecy seems to be intentional. Goffman thought his business was his own business and not open to the scrutiny of a prying public (Martin, Mutchnick, and Austin 1990:321–2). He considered himself an outsider, and he may have been one, principally because of his penetrating intelligence (Lofland 1984:17–8). He was at times a stranger in a very strange land, and he was fascinated by the impression management that he saw in everyday life among everyday people. He had a master's eye for detail, and he was able to understand and then describe social relationships in ways that nobody had ever done before (Lofland 1984:8).

Goffman was influenced by some of the symbolic interactionist themes at the University of Chicago—where he received his Ph.D. in 1953—but he was more influenced by social anthropologists than social psychologists (Ritzer 2000:364). It is impossible to read Goffman's writings without carrying away a new thought or idea about the interaction order. He was especially good at seeing through the facades that people use to manipulate and deceive others. "His insistence on taking nothing at face value can therefore and without embarassment [sic] be said to be the most empirically relevant of his legacies" (Lofland 1984:22). All who knew him agreed that he was an incredibly interesting person (Lofland 1984:28). Goffman died November 20, 1982, after a protracted battle with cancer.

Late in his life, Goffman was elected to the presidency of the American Sociological Association (in 1981). He brought his experience and his intelligence to the job and made many positive contributions to the organization. However, his untimely death made it impossible for him to deliver the presidential address that he had written, so it was published posthumously. This is an important work. Not only were these words to be his last about the interaction order, he *knew* that they would be his last, because he knew he was dying (Lofland 1984:22). His charge to sociologists was for them to stumble along as best they could and assure themselves that they were moving in a forward direction (Goffman 1983:2). It is a spirit of "unfettered, unsponsored inquiry" that sociologists have inherited from their sociological ancestors and what they have to leave to their sociological descendants. This spirit of inquiry should be used, Goffman thought, to expose the privileges and practices of those individuals (e.g., psychiatrists, police officers, government leaders, media spokespersons) who have institutional authority that allows them to palm off on others their biased views of reality and thereby reap rewards that they do not deserve (Goffman 1983:17). Goffman's explorations of the masks that we wear and the masquerades that we encounter in everyday life are an enduring contribution to the social sciences and an important part of the use of the sociological imagination to understand human relationships.

The Presentation of Self

Goffman's approach to the interaction order—called the dramaturgical perspective—is nicely presented in his first book, *The Presentation of Self in Everyday Life* (1959). The **dramaturgical perspective** compares all human interaction to a theatrical or dramatic performance. For Goffman, society is a stage and we are all actors on that stage, performing to others as we perform to ourselves. People manipulate others and engage in **impression management** all the time in order to give and sustain a particular definition of the situation. The principal or central part of any presentation, however, is the desire to give a positive view of self—or at least some view—to others. Self, for Goffman, is the *product* of a particular scene that is being played out; it has more to do with what others impute to an individual than it does with any firm or organic structure of self that lies inside of a person. Self is a dramatic effect, and the most important issue is whether a particular presentation of self will be accepted and believed by others (Goffman 1959:252–3).

An individual who is presenting a self and working to construct a particular definition of the situation—the lone performer—has to pay attention to certain details if he or she is to have any chance of success in convincing others to accept it. That is exactly why the best performers will structure every detail—how they look, what they say, their props, and their settings—to maximize the chances that their performances will be believed by practically everyone. Often an individual does not perform alone. In this situation, the performance is designed not simply to enhance some performer's self-image (although that is possible) but to reflect on an entire group as a unit and to present a definition of the situation of interest to all its members.

Goffman coined the term **performance team** or simply **team** to describe a collection of individuals who work together—if only for a short time—to present a performance (Goffman 1959:79). A team is not identical to a group. In fact, members of the team may not know each other; certainly, they do not have to like or care particularly about each other. An individual who is dissatisfied with the alignment of his or her teeth and gets them changed by an orthodontist can now count that professional as a member of the team that helped improve his or her appearance. Groups may act through force or violence to get what they want; teams do not. A team accomplishes its ends through—and only through—dramaturgical cooperation and impression management (Goffman 1959:85).

Some regions can be identified, Goffman insisted, by the role that they play in impression management. A **region** is a place that is bounded to some degree by barriers to perception, often physical ones (Goffman 1959:106). So, lectures at universities usually take place inside particular rooms, and customers at restaurants eat in particular parts of the building. It is easy to look at different organizations and bureaucracies with Goffman's imagination and recognize that offices, rooms, corridors, and floors are also regions. Even an automobile can be a region if impression management takes place in it. A **front region** or **frontstage** is the place where the performance is regularly given (Goffman 1959:107). A classroom is best viewed as a front region because that is where the action takes place. Another region exists, called the **back region** or **backstage** (Goffman 1959:112). This is a place where information or facts that would be discrepant or inconsistent with the front stage performance can be worked out and rehearsed. Back region is where the performance may be tried out prior to actual presentation out front. A professor's office serves as a back region when he or she is inside, door closed, working on a lecture. A third region is called the **outside region** (Goffman 1959:134–5), which includes any region that is not front or back.

Goffman makes it very clear that regions are not simply identified by their physical properties or qualities. A front region to one team may be a back region to another, and a front region can be easily transformed into a back region and vice versa. One evening my wife and I were giving a party. I came home from work to get ready for the event, and she told me to go in the bathroom and take a shower but not to use the towels. Very strange. It is clear, however, what the show was. The bathroom, almost always a back region in our house, was transformed into a front region for the duration of the party, so I was not allowed to use the towels too soon. Regions are social arenas, and they are defined in terms of what happens in them as much as they are by anything else. If individuals use a backstage style in a region that once was a front region, it transforms it into a back region (Goffman 1959:128–9).

Identity Spoilage

Performances are fragile affairs. It is not easy to prepare props, select regions, coordinate members of the team, and successfully manipulate impressions for audiences so that they always believe what they are being offered.

> Given the fragility and the required expressive coherence of the reality that is dramatized by a performance, there are usually facts which, if attention is drawn to them during the performance, would discredit, disrupt, or make useless the impression that the performance fosters (Goffman 1959:141).

Having members on the team who are competent and loyal can do a lot to make a performance convincing. When all the people around you—your butcher, your baker, your candlestick maker—tell your prospective in-laws what a delightful person you are, it has a ring of truth that it might not have if you are the only one singing your praises. However, a performance team is a double-edged sword. Just as more people may help to contribute to the credibility of the performance, their presence means that a greater opportunity exists for one of them to ruin it. A slip of the tongue or lack of attention to detail by *any* member of the team can have long-term consequences for everyone.

Identities may be **tarnished** (bringing a *temporary* loss of face) or even permanently spoiled (called **stigma**) by a faulty performance and poor impression management (Goffman 1963). A flawed performance can also result in a loss of jobs, a loss of partners, and a loss of property. A "kiss-and-tell" book surfaces that permanently spoils, or at least calls into question, the identity claims of a public figure, or the rumor of a sexual dalliance between a public figure and his intern receives enough corroborating evidence to know that they were more than just friends. In these cases, little can be done of a dramaturgical nature to recoup the losses and to fix the damage that has been done to self-concept and personal identity. The discredited individuals must wait and see if time does heal all wounds and if members of the public do have short memories.

Conclusions

Many of the unit-ideas that are now at the core of sociology emerged in response to the exaggerated efforts to psychologize or individualize social events (Hughes, Martin, and Sharrock 1995:9). Comte's dictum indicates that societies do exist as units that can be scientifically understood in terms of integration (social statics) and change (social dynamics). Marx's dictum indicates that the driving force of social change is conflict between classes of individuals who are trying to survive in a place where survival is never guaranteed. The way of life of a society is not a simple product of natural evolution; some people in a society make decisions and pursue lines of activity that have an impact on everyone else. Durkheim's dictum indicates that the whole is more than the sum of its parts and that social facts exist and they cause other social facts. Mead's dictum and Weber's dictum help us to understand how societies get in us and how we are able to act together to create and sustain an interaction order. Goffman's dictum reminds us that masks and masquerades—the deliberate management of impressions—are a central part of social life. These social theorists achieved their understandings of society through application of the scientific method and, especially, the use of logic and observation to answer questions about social relationships. In addition to the scientific method, they used imagination and intuition to develop sketches of society that can serve as a source of inspiration to us all (Nisbet 1966:18–20).

Chapter Two at a Glance

- The growth of the social sciences made it possible to develop explanations of human behavior that were based more on observation and logic than on hunches or suppositions.

- Early sociologists used science to help them explain and predict human behavior, and they believed that human nature and social nature were inseparable.
- Early sociologists believed that humans were constituted by social experiences and their lifelong relationships to others.
- Social transformations like industrialization, political revolution, and urbanization encouraged social scientists to think about the nature of human relationships, groups, and societies.
- Prominent U.S. sociologists were harassed by agents of the Federal Bureau of Investigation for radical and un-American activities when, in fact, sociologists were actually fulfilling their professional responsibility to take nothing in a society for granted and to call into question what other people might overlook.
- Comte's dictum: Social units can be understood by a scientific analysis of their patterns of integration and change.
- Marx's dictum: Humans construct and reconstruct social forms as they act together, and they themselves are changed in the process.
- Durkheim's dictum: The whole is more than the sum of its parts.
- Mead's dictum: Humans become societies in miniature as they internalize the perspectives of others.
- Weber's dictum: Humans take account of others as they meaningfully construct their actions.
- Goffman's dictum: Humans manage and manipulate impressions about themselves to influence others.

Glossary

altruistic suicide a type of suicide correlated with too-high levels of social integration

anomic suicide a type of suicide correlated with too-low levels of social regulation

anomy a state of deregulation or normlessness where individuals become too self-centered to have a sense of shared destiny and a common moral direction

back region or **backstage** the place where the elements of impression management are tried out and rehearsed

biological metaphor comparing societies/social groups to biological organisms in order to make better sense of these social units

bourgeoisie the class that owns the forces of production; the "haves" or capitalists

bureaucracies large and complex organizations that are constructed to accomplish tasks efficiently and effectively; rules and regulations exist in bureaucracies, along with a division of labor, a hierarchy of authority, and a great amount of impersonality

class consciousness the recognition by members of a class of what they have in common and their willingness to further their collective interests through revolutionary action

collective conscience the body of beliefs and sentiments that holds people together

conversation of significant gestures a distinctly human way of interacting that is based on the use and understanding of symbols

division of labor societies and groups apportion the necessary and important tasks among different specialties and positions in order to maximize the chances that they will be done well

dramaturgical perspective a way to understand social relationships by comparing them to a theatrical performance

egoistic suicide a type of suicide correlated with too-low levels of social integration

false consciousness the acceptance of *bourgeois* ideas by members of the *proletariat* as right and true and the failure to overthrow the existing social order through revolutionary action

fatalistic suicide a type of suicide correlated with too-high levels of social regulation

forces of production the technological abilities of a people and the social relationships that evolve around the creation (or collection) of the goods and services that sustain human life

French Revolutions of 1789 and 1848 wars that upset the prevailing social order and called into question the way that property was distributed and owned

front region or **frontstage** the place where the impression management regularly takes place

generalized other the viewpoint of the entire society or community, internalized in self

impression management the activities of a lone individual or a collection of individuals to present a particular definition of a situation to others

Industrial Revolution the transformation of societies and social relationships produced by the partial replacement of human and animal power by the power of machines

iron cage bureaucracies become so confining that all members of them can do is to follow the rules and regulations without question

outside region any region that is not serving as a front or back region

performance team or **team** individuals who work together to manipulate

impressions and present a performance to others

proletariat the class that does *not* own the forces of production; the "have-nots" or laborers/workers

rational action a clear and knowable relationship exists between means and ends or action and objectives

region physical locations that are important to the success of dramaturgical performances; front, back, and outside regions exist

relations of production the legally supported differences in the ownership of property, including the ownership of the forces of production

role-taking or **taking the role of the other** mental projection into the position of another

scientific explanations the construction of theories of human relationships, the logical deduction of hypotheses, and the collection of data that allowed social scientists to answer questions about social life

self the process of viewing one's self as an object

social action takes account of others and is meaningfully constructed

social dynamics the multitude of forces that change and transform a society

social facts social constructions that attain an exteriority to individuals and then constrain collective and individual behavior

social identities humans identify with some categories and positions more than with others, a social process that connects us with some individuals and separates us from other individuals

social institutions ongoing behaviors and the shared understandings regarding them, organized around important social tasks in major sectors of social life like the family, economy, education, religion, and politics

social integration people's identification or association with social groups; too little or too much social integration can provoke a specific type of suicide according to Durkheim

social regulation the degree of control imposed on individual desires by social factors; too little or too much social regulation can provoke a specific type of suicide according to Durkheim

social sciences the branch of science that explains and helps to predict human experience by using the methods of science, particularly controlled observation

social statics the forces that integrate and stabilize a society, that is, the glue or cement of social life

society as a *sui generis* society has priority over the individuals who comprise it

sociology a social science that makes sense of human behavior and human nature by looking at societies and social relationships

stigma permanent identity spoilage

suicide the act of taking one's own life in order to end all existence; Durkheim linked suicide with social relationships

supernatural explanations the many ways that social relationships were explained prior to the growth of the social sciences; supernatural explanations are not based on observation and theory, nor do they give attention to the existence of social or physical laws

symbol (or **significant gesture**) a word, sound, or physical gesture that stands for or represents something else because of group agreement

symbolic communication human interaction almost always takes place with symbols

tarnished self temporary identity spoilage and loss of face

verstehen a method for understanding social relationships by examining social context to figure out the subjective experience of those who are responsible for the behavior

References

Aron, Raymond. 1968. *Main Currents in Sociological Thought, Volume I: Montesquieu, Comte, Marx, Tocqueville, and the Sociologists and the Revolution of 1848*, translated by Richard Howard and Helen Weaver. Garden City, NY: Anchor.

Aron, Raymond. 1970. *Main Currents in Sociological Thought, Volume II: Durkheim, Pareto, Weber*, translated by Richard Howard and Helen Weaver. Garden City, NY: Anchor.

Bendix, Reinhard. 1962. *Max Weber: An Intellectual Portrait*. Garden City, NY: Anchor.

Berger, Peter. 1963. *Invitation to Sociology: A Humanistic Perspective*. New York: Doubleday.

Blumer, Herbert. 1969. *Symbolic Interactionism: Perspective and Method*. Englewood Cliffs, NY: Prentice-Hall.

Comte, Auguste. 1968/1875. *System of Positive Polity*, second volume, containing social statics, or the abstract theory of human order. New York: Burt Franklin.

———. 1968/1876. *System of Positive Polity*, third volume, containing social dynamics, or the general theory of human progress. New York: Burt Franklin.

Coser, Lewis. 1971. *Masters of Sociological Thought: Ideas in Historical and Social Context*. New York: Harcourt Brace Jovanovich.

Durkheim, Emile. 1933. *The Division of Labor in Society*, translated by George Simpson. New York: Free Press.

———. 1938. *The Rules of Sociological Method*, 8th edition, translated by Sarah Solovay and John Mueller and edited by George Catlin. New York: Free Press.

———. 1951/1897. *Suicide*, translated by John Spaulding and George Simpson. New York: Free Press.

———. 1974. *Sociology and Philosophy*, translated by D. F. Pocock with an Introduction by J. G. Peristiany. New York: Free Press.

Eisenstadt, S. N., with M. Curelaru. 1976. *The Form of Sociology—Paradigms and Crises*. New York: John Wiley & Sons.

Eldridge, J. E. T., editor. 1971. *Max Weber: The Interpretation of Social Reality*. New York: Charles Scribner's Sons.

Geis, G. and C. Goff. 1983. "Introduction." Pp. ix–xxxiii in E. H. Sutherland, *White Collar Crime: The Uncut Version.* New Haven, CT: Yale University Press.

Goffman, Erving. 1959. *The Presentation of Self in Everyday Life.* Garden City, NY: Doubleday Anchor.

———. 1963. *Stigma: Notes on the Management of Spoiled Identity.* Englewood Cliffs, NJ: Prentice-Hall.

———. 1983. "The Interaction Order," American Sociological Association, 1982 Presidential Address. *American Sociological Review* 48:1–17.

Hinkle, Jr., Roscoe, and Gisela Hinkle. 1954. *The Development of Modern Sociology: Its Nature and Growth in the United States.* New York: Random House.

Hughes, John, Peter Martin, and W. W. Sharrock. 1995. *Understanding Classical Sociology: Marx, Weber, Durkheim.* Thousand Oaks, CA: Sage.

Jones, Robert Alun. 1999. *The Development of Durkheim's Social Realism.* New York: Cambridge University Press.

Keen, Mike. 1999. *Stalking the Sociological Imagination: J. Edgar Hoover's FBI Surveillance of American Sociology.* Westport, CT: Greenwood Press.

Lofland, John. 1984. "Erving Goffman's Sociological Legacies." *Urban Life* 13:7–34.

Martin, Randy, Robert Mutchnick, and W. Timothy Austin. 1990. *Criminological Thought: Pioneers Past and Present.* New York: Macmillan.

Martindale, Don. 1960. *The Nature and Types of Sociological Theory.* Boston: Houghton Mifflin.

Marx, Karl and Friedrich Engels. 1963/1848. *The Communist Manifesto.* New York: Russell and Russell.

Mead, George H. 1934. *Mind, Self, and Society: From the Standpoint of a Social Behaviorist,* edited and with an introduction by Charles Morris. Chicago, IL: University of Chicago Press.

Meltzer, Bernard. 1967. "Mead's Social Psychology." Pp. 5–24 in *Symbolic Interaction: A Reader in Social Psychology,* edited by Jerome Manis and Bernard Meltzer. Boston: Allyn and Bacon.

Mills, C. W. 1943. "The Professional Ideology of Social Pathologists." *American Journal of Sociology* 49:165–80.

Morgan, Gordon. 1997. *Toward an American Sociology: Questioning the European Construct.* Westport, CT: Praeger.

Morris, Charles. 1934. "Introduction: George H. Mead as a Social Psychologist and Social Philosopher." Pp. ix–xxxv in *Mind, Self, and Society.* Chicago, IL: University of Chicago Press.

Nisbet, Robert. 1966. *The Sociological Tradition.* New York: Basic Books.

Peristiany, J. G. 1974. "Introduction." Pp. vii-xxxii in *Sociology and Philosophy,* by Emile Durkheim. New York: Free Press.

Ritzer, George. 2000. *Sociological Theory,* 5th ed. New York: McGraw-Hill.

Runciman, W. G. 1978. "Introduction." Pp. 3–6 in *Max Weber: Selections in Translation,* edited by W. G. Runciman and translated by E. Matthews. Cambridge, UK: Cambridge University Press.

Strauss, Anselm. 1964. *George Herbert Mead: On Social Psychology.* Chicago, IL: University of Chicago Press.

Sutherland, Edwin H. 1949. *White Collar Crime.* New York: Dryden.

———. 1983. *White Collar Crime: The Uncut Version.* New Haven, CT: Yale University Press.

Turner, Jonathan. 1974. *The Structure of Sociological Theory.* Homewood, IL: Dorsey.

Wallace, Ruth and Allison Wolf. 1999. *Contemporary Sociological Theory: Expanding the Classical Tradition,* 5th edition. Upper Saddle River, NJ: Prentice-Hall.

Weber, Max. 1947. *The Theory of Social and Economic Organization.* New York: Oxford University Press.

———. 1968a. *Economy and Society: An Outline of Interpretive Sociology, Volume I,* edited by Guenther Roth and Claus Wittich. New York: Bedminster Press.

———. 1968b. *Economy and Society: An Outline of Interpretive Sociology, Volume III,* edited by Guenther Roth and Claus Wittich. New York: Bedminster Press.

———. 1978. "Sociology and Biology." Pp. 389–90 in *Max Weber: Selections in Translation,* edited by W. G. Runciman and translated by E. Matthews. Cambridge, UK: Cambridge University Press.

The Unique Nature
of Being Human

In 1799, hunters were walking through a woods in the county of Aveyron, in the country of France. They came upon a boy who appeared to be in late childhood or early teens. If seeing a child in the woods was not startling enough, his condition certainly was (Jones and Gerard 1967:5–8). The boy was naked and remarkably dirty. As the hunters approached, he ran away from them, climbed a tree, and scrambled out on a limb. When they tried to get him down from his perch, he snarled and growled and bit and scratched at his pursuers. The boy's strenuous resistance was finally overcome by the hunters, and this real wild child was taken to a physician of some renown for his treatment of the insane, Dr. Pinel. The doctor found the child unable to talk, inattentive, incapable of imitation, defective in memory, and amoral. The boy was afflicted by periodic spasms and convulsions, and he swayed back and forth constantly. Pinel decided that the child was an "incurable idiot," and he would have nothing more to do with him. The child subsequently came under the care of a physician named Jean-Marc-Gaspard Itard, a man who did not share Pinel's pessimistic assessment of the child's prospects. Itard set about to civilize the boy.

The boy was given the name of Victor, a first step toward socializing him. The task of socializing Victor was to demand all the patience and ingenuity that the doctor had. The child was physically impaired. He did not respond when a pistol was fired next to his ear or when snuff was placed in his nose. He could squat in the snow for hours, scantily clad, with no seeming discomfort. He could even pluck potatoes out of boiling water without hurting himself. Itard was still able to get the child to prefer warmth over cold, and the doctor then used this preference to teach the child additional tasks. Victor eventually learned to dress himself and to pass the night without wetting his bed. He learned to do some reading, and he did develop a limited vocabulary. Itard could say words like "hat" or "book," and Victor would search the room until he found the named item. The going was slow and Victor never was able to do much, but clear changes occurred during the five years in which Itard worked with the child. Victor did learn to display some emotions—like sadness or happiness—and in the proper situations. He also changed from being indifferent or even hostile to the presence of others to being capable of some warmth and affection toward them.

Other cases of **feral children** (children raised in extreme isolation), few in number as they are, do suggest that basic human qualities are far from natural, and that relationships—their nature and number—have a profound impact on the course of human development. Kingsley Davis reported the case of a child named Anna, born in March 1932. She lived in horrid conditions in her early years and received very little care or attention during that time. Anna, like her older brother, had been born out of wedlock. Her illegitimacy was so upsetting to her grandfather that he would have little to do with her. Because no place could be found for her to live away from the grandfather, she was forced to stay at his house. However, she was confined to an attic-like room on the second floor because her mother did not want to upset Anna's grandfather by keeping the child around him. Anna's mother was not much fonder of the child than was the grandfather, and she made little time for her. Anna was rarely moved. Her clothes were always dirty, her bedding was filthy, and she received no training at all even in rudimentary skills. The mother fed the child enough to keep her alive, but she did not hold her or bathe her (Davis 1940:557). Anna had very few pleasures in her life.

When Anna was almost 6, word of her isolation and abuse reached authorities, and they promptly removed her from the house. She was very malnourished, with thin arms and legs and a bulging stomach. She could not walk, talk, or do anything else that required even minimal intelligence. In time, Anna did learn to perform some tasks, as well as the beginnings of relating to others. She learned to follow a few rules, string beads, and identify some colors. She learned to walk and run. She was easily agitated, but she still had a pleasant disposition. She could imitate words and carry on a simple conversation. She came to like clean clothing, and she brushed her teeth and washed her hands frequently. She tried to be helpful to others, and she developed a strong attachment to a doll that she seemed to love (Davis 1969:91). Many of the things that most of us take for granted, however, were forever out of reach for Anna. She died from hemorrhagic jaundice on August 6, 1942, at the age of 10 (or was it from neglect and deprivation?).

Another case of childhood social isolation has striking parallels with Anna's case. This girl child, named Isabelle, was discovered in November 1938 (Davis 1969:93–6). Isabelle was also born out of wedlock, and she, too, had been forced to live in isolation because of the embarrassment it caused her grandparents. Isabelle spent most of her time with her mother in a small room that was away from the rest of the family. While Isabelle's mother was far more responsible and loving than was Anna's mother, Isabelle's mother was both deaf and mute. This meant that Isabelle did not get the opportunity to learn to speak or to develop other bodily responses and abilities in the way that she should have. When she did communicate with her mother, it was through physical gestures and grunts or croaks. When she was discovered by authorities, she acted like a wild animal in her level of fear and hostility. It seemed impossible that she would ever progress very far in her social development.

Caretakers launched an intensive program to train the child. While the going was slow, Isabelle responded quickly and her advances were dramatic. She learned to walk, run, speak, write, read, sing, and count. She could retell a story after it was told to her (suggesting the presence of memory), and the size of her vocabulary increased greatly. She learned in a few years what it usually takes an average child six years to learn. By age 9, she reached the point where she could enter public schools and participate in school activities with her classmates without seeming too out of step. Isabelle's case shows that it is possible to compensate for some of the adverse effects of early social isolation if the child suffers from no disabling physical conditions and the training comes early enough to do some good. However, if social isolation is prolonged, it makes it most unlikely that a child raised in social isolation will ever be able to speak, think, feel, and act like individuals who were not isolated as youngsters (Davis 1940:564).

Isolation is one thing. When isolation is compounded with abuse, neglect, and cruelty, it shows us even more forcefully how necessary social relationships—good ones—are for human development. The child was discovered in 1970 after more than a decade of deprivation and inhumane treatment at the hands of her family members. Her name was Genie, and to understand what happened to her we must look at her family dynamics (Curtiss 1977). Her father did not want to have any children at all. Because he was such an angry and brutal man, prone to violence, his wife did all that she could to keep him happy. However, after five years of marriage, the couple started having children. The first child, a girl, cried a lot as babies are prone to do. The father was so annoyed by the noisy child that he confined her to the garage so he would not have to hear her. At the age of two-and-a-half months, she died of overexposure and pneumonia. Another child, a boy, was born the following year, but he died after only two days, from choking on his mucus. Three years later another son was born. He did not die prematurely, but he did have many developmental problems. The boy eventually went to live in the home of his paternal grandmother, and she was able to teach him things that he had not learned from his parents. Three years later, Genie was born, and she was a lively child. However, her health and developmental progress soon started to falter.

When Genie was about 2 years old, her grandmother was killed by an automobile as she crossed the street. She had left her house to her son, and he moved the family into it after her death, isolating them even more from the outside world. The situation was hellish for the young girl. Even when Genie was allowed to play in the backyard, these were times of restriction and confinement because she was almost always forced to stay in her playpen, uncared for and unsupervised. Her time inside the house was even worse. She was kept inside one of two small bedrooms near the back of the house, secured to a potty seat with a harness that her father had fashioned. There she was left, naked except for the swaddling harness, to sit day after day and night after night. All that she could move were her fingers and toes and hands and feet. Some nights she was taken from the harness but immediately placed in another restraining garment that wrapped around her so that she could not move her arms. She was then placed into a crib with wire on the sides and over the top. Genie—either harnessed or wrapped and caged—was left alone to endure the years of her life.

The extreme social isolation that Genie experienced for so many years would have been sufficient to scar her permanently. However, this was not the full measure of her abuse. In the back of the house, hungry and alone, the child would occasionally attempt to get some attention by making noises. Her father took every opportunity to punish Genie for the sounds that she made. He would in fact beat her with a stick that he left in the corner of her room if he heard her. The child learned to keep silent and to suppress all vocalizations. Whenever the father was around the child, he never spoke to her. He acted like a wild animal. He barked and he growled at her; he bared his teeth; he even let his fingernails grow long so that he could scratch her. Sometimes he would torment her by standing outside her door, growling and barking, and then, when he had scared her enough, he would leave without entering her room.

Genie had very few toys, none that were store bought. She was given an empty cottage cheese container, a wooden spoon, or empty thread spools to bang around. Two raincoats hung near her closet, and Genie was sometimes allowed to do what she wanted with them. Her room had little furniture, no carpet, no pictures on the wall, few windows, and one bare ceiling light bulb to illuminate her room.

> This was Genie's life—isolated, often forgotten, frequently abused . . . , physically restrained, starved for sensory stimulation. Thus minimally exposed to humanity, and most of that the most hideous of human behavior, Genie grew into a pitiful creature (Curtiss 1977:7).

The only food that she ever received was baby food, cereal, or an occasional soft-boiled egg. She was expected to feed herself, or she was hastily fed by some family member, usually her mother. If Genie was unable to swallow the food and spit it out, her face was rubbed in it. She often went to sleep hungry.

When Genie was approximately 13 1/2 years old, her mother and father had a violent argument. The mother convinced her husband that she would leave him unless he let her talk to her mother on the phone. Genie and her mother left the man that same day. Mother and child stayed at the maternal grandmother's home for about three weeks. Genie's mother decided to go to apply for aid to the blind. (She could not even dial a phone on her own.) With Genie in tow, she mistakenly went to the family aid building. An eligibility worker saw the child and realized that something was terribly wrong. The worker's supervisor was summoned, and they both quizzed Genie's mother. What they heard from her prompted them to call police. Genie was placed into custody, and both parents were charged with abuse. Genie was taken to a hospital where the long journey to heal her—her body and her spirit—began. On the day that the parents' trial was to begin, the father took his own life. His suicide note contained only one sentence: "The world will never understand." He was right. As hard as I try, I cannot understand how any child could be brutalized this severely by anyone.

Genie was a pitiful sight to behold. Even though she was alert and curious and explored her new surroundings in the hospital, she had been brutalized for so long that it had produced profound impairment in her development—physical, cognitive, emotional—that would not soon be reversed.

> Hardly ever having worn clothing, she did not react to temperature, heat or cold. Never having eaten solid food, Genie did not know how to chew, and had great difficulty in swallowing. Having been strapped down and left sitting on a potty chair, she could not stand erect, could not straighten her arms or legs, could not run, hop, jump, or climb; in fact, she could only walk with difficulty, shuffling her feet, swaying from side to side. Hardly ever having seen more than a space of 10 feet in front of her (the distance from her potty chair to the door), she had become nearsighted exactly to that distance. Having been beaten for making noise, she had learned to suppress almost all vocalizations save a whimper. Suffering from malnutrition, she weighed only 59 pounds and stood only 54 inches

tall. She was incontinent of feces and urine. Her hair was sparse and stringy. She salivated copiously, spitting on anything at hand. Genie was unsocialized, primitive, hardly human (Curtiss 1977:9).

The most conspicuous characteristic—and one that made Genie so different from those children who are raised in more normal surroundings—was her almost total lack of vocal ability. Except for the few words that she imitated in her first few days in the hospital and her occasional whimpering, she made no sound whatsoever, even when she was upset. She did not even make sounds when she cried. She could be seen to throw savage temper tantrums that involved spitting, scratching, physical gyrations, blowing her nose, pulling at her hair, and rubbing her face with her own snot—all in dead silence. What noises she did make came from throwing objects, stamping or shuffling her feet, or rubbing her hands against some object.

Some of Genie's most disagreeable habits reflected her ignorance of the difference between the public and the private. She salivated all the time, and she spit it out whenever and wherever she wanted—on her chin, on her clothing, or on her companions. This meant, of course, that her body was almost always covered with spit (and with whatever odors accompanied it). She blew her nose onto her clothing as well. If she became upset or angry, she would urinate in the most inappropriate of places, leaving other people to deal with the mess. At meal time, she would stuff as much food as she could manage into her mouth and wait—remember she did not know how to chew—for it to digest. If it took too long, she would simply spit the food back on her plate and begin to play with it. Sometimes she would circle the room and spit the food on *other* people's plates; she would then take whatever she wanted from theirs (she was particularly fond of ice cream and applesauce).

Genie coveted certain objects—for instance, anything made of plastic always caught her eye—and certain articles of clothing. If she saw an item she liked in the possession of someone on the street or in a store, she simply went up and grabbed what she wanted and tried to make off with it. When she took something from a stranger's shopping cart, it was bad; when she tried to make off with something a stranger was wearing, it was even worse. Her most offensive habit, however, was her persistent masturbation.

> Many of the items she coveted were objects with which to masturbate, and she would attempt to do so, regardless of where she was. She was drawn to chair backs, chair arms, counter edges, door knobs, door edges, table corners, car handles, car mirrors, and so forth; in essence, indoors and outdoors she was continually attempting to masturbate (Curtiss 1977:21).

Curtiss reported, with a great deal of relief, that Genie's masturbatory behavior was eventually eradicated, at least when Genie was in public.

Genie was eventually moved to a foster home. Curtiss described it as a warm and loving household with two teenage boys, a teenage girl, and a dog and cat. Genie had her own room, bathroom, access to a large backyard, and a foster family to provide her with care, guidance, companionship, and affection. Genie flourished in this setting, and despite the many challenges and complications that she created for those who were trying to get her to enter the social world, she did enrich the lives of those who knew and worked with her (Curtiss 1977:xvi).

In order to be—or to become—fully human, humans need a great deal of proficiency at taking account of others and forming relationships with them. Humans need to be thoroughly soaked in a social environment—master the language, learn the culture, participate in groups, establish quality relationships with others—if they are ever to be given a chance to engage in socially guided actions. Nobody can be at all familiar with the experiences of children raised in isolation—with or without additional abuse—and fail to appreciate how much humans are constituted by social experiences. The central features of being human are not natural; they must be acquired in the context of the relationships that we establish early in life and then carry on with others as we mature and develop. A unique human biology, crafted and constructed by millions of years of evolution, both complements and is complemented by our human social heritage. We humans are unique because social relationships are so pivotal for us in all that we are and all that we will become. No other living creature can make such a claim.

The Pathetic Fallacy and Anthropomorphism

The **pathetic fallacy** is the attribution of human emotions and characteristics to the forces of nature. Describing the high-velocity winds as a "vengeful" storm or empty drums as "lonely" rain barrels would be examples of this. It is easy—but wrong—to credit inanimate objects with an intention or purpose that they do not have. I once had a friend with whom I played golf. One day he got so mad at his golf club that he beat it against a tree until the club was bent in the shape of a horseshoe. I do not know the full details of his thought processes, but I suspect that he held the club responsible for his poor showing during the game. While we may all at times give human qualities to inanimate objects, it is fairly easy in our more sober moments to know that this is an error to be avoided.

Humans also are **anthropomorphic.** This means that they give human qualities to nonhuman *living* things. The word anthropomorphism comes from the Greek word *anthropos* (meaning *man/woman*) and the Greek word *morphe* (meaning *form*). So, anthropomorphism exists when animals (or other living organisms like plants) are credited with human capacities for thinking, feeling, and acting. The growing influence of Darwin's ideas about evolution meant that anthropomorphism seemed far more reasonable after his work than it did before; humans could no longer be viewed as entirely separate and independent from other living things.

Every part of Darwin's thesis is open to test. The clues—from fossils, genes or geography—differ in each case, but from all of them comes the conclusion that the whole of life is kin. This is no mere assertion, but a chain of deduction with every link complete (Jones 2000:3).

Sociobiology, the field that studies the biological basis of social behavior in both nonhumans and humans, has certainly shown to all social scientists that some relationship exists between human and nonhuman animals (Wilson 1975:547–75). **Nature** (inborn or innate characteristics) and **nurture** (learned or acquired characteristics) work together in all kinds of ways, some not entirely understood, to make a creature what it is. At the human level, nature includes reproductive systems, secondary sex characteristics, our genetic makeup, and the evolution of our bodies; nurture includes the physical environment, life experiences, social arrangements, and culture (Kennelly, Merz, and Lorber 2001:599). Characteristics of one species may be similar to characteristics of some other species because of comparable genetic factors (Lindesmith, Strauss, and Denzin 1999:37). It is no coincidence that humans are more like chimpanzees than they are like bullfrogs or that deer are more closely related to whales than they are to pigs (Jones 2000:19). Evolution is at work.

Imputing Humanness

While the pathetic fallacy is clearly a fallacy and easy to recognize and avoid, things are a bit trickier in regard to anthropomorphism. "Despite some 400 years of general agreement that avoiding anthropomorphism is desirable—and, in science, central—its definition, its causes, and even its status as an error remain in doubt" (Guthrie 1997:51). We stack the deck in favor of seeing humanness in nonhumans because of how we describe them. Because humans use a language system that was designed to describe humans in human terms, when it is used to describe nonhumans it makes them look more like humans than they are (Lindesmith, Strauss, and Denzin 1999:38). "The dog wants to go for a walk" is a statement that seems to be both harmless and correct. However, the statement is *incorrect* if it means that the animal has formulated plans and purposes and behaves with the anticipation that its actions will get it out the door. It is hard to imagine exactly how nonhuman animals could act purposefully and intentionally without having far greater cognitive and symbolic abilities than they do.

We can often see human cognition, human emotion, and human behavior in nonhuman animals—some at any rate—because they do seem to go through many of the same life events and to have some of the same experiences we do: birth, growth, hunger, weakness, sickness, and death. What is more, some animals resemble us and may even share our homes. Chimps have two eyes, two arms, two legs, and a torso, just like us, but that is just the start of the similarities.

There is no known chemical in the chimpanzee brain that cannot be found in the human brain. There is no known part of the immune system, the digestive system, the vascular system, the lymph system or the nervous system that we have and chimpanzees do not, or vice versa (Ridley 1999:29).

In fact, humans are a 98 percent approximation of chimpanzees; humans are more like chimpanzees than chimps are like gorillas (Ridley 1999:28). The closer our relationship to some nonhuman animal and the more like us it is, the greater the tendency to give it human qualities.

How can you raise an ape in a human environment, provide human experiences, and encourage human behavior, such as language acquisition or comprehension, to make the ape more humanlike, and then succeed in being nonanthropomorphic in your interpretations (Miles 1997:385)?

Individuals who live and work with nonhuman companions (like dogs) tend to believe that animals have some ability to create meaning, to define situations, to formulate plans of action, to be self-conscious, and to be able to project themselves into the positions of others (Sanders 1999:5).

Human and Nonhuman Resemblances

Nonhuman animals are capable of some things that do seem remarkable, at least for nonhuman animals. Elephants in the Namibian desert of Africa are able to find both food and water generation after generation. How can they do it? It is a harsh environment, and water is sometimes many miles away from the elephants' feeding grounds and several feet underground to boot. If they wandered around aimlessly, they would die. "But the elephants know where all the water is, where all the food is, and where all the best routes between water and food are. This knowledge is not instinct. They have learned the map of the region and passed it down through the generations" (Page 1999:71–2). Beavers build dams that seem to be far too complicated to be explained by any kind of innate programming or instinct (Page 1999:123). The great apes— chimps and gorillas at any rate—have been taught to communicate with physical signs, computers, and even to respond to the spoken words of humans. A chimp by the name of Kanzi (the ward of Sue Savage-Rumbaugh) responds very well to human speech. He can pick up objects that humans ask him to get, and he can follow directions like "Put the ball in the bowl" (Page 1999:153). He has a 90 percent accuracy rate to even strange commands like "put the soap on the apple," suggesting that he is not randomly guessing at the meaning of sentences (Deacon 1997:124).

Linden (1993) concluded in his cover story for *Time* that animals can think and maybe even lie and play politics. Alex, a one-pound gray parrot, shows an amazing adeptness with spoken questions. When a block is selected from a tray of toys and the parrot is asked to identify it ("What toy?"), Alex shoots back the word "block." He can also answer questions about a toy's composition, color, shape, and size. If he gets an answer wrong, it seems to upset him and he may say "I'm sorry" and "I'm gonna go away" (Linden 1993:55). One day, Alex was left overnight with a veterinarian. As the bird's owner (an ethologist named Irene Pepperberg) left the clinic, Alex appealed to her sense of caring by saying in his sad, little voice, "Come here. I love you. I'm sorry. Wanna go back" (Linden 1993:59). Two female dolphins, Phoenix and Akeakamai, are told through gestures from their human trainers to do something creative together.

> The dolphins break away from their trainers and submerge in the 6-ft.-deep water, where they can be seen circling until they begin to swim in tandem. Once they are in synch, the animals leap into the air and simultaneously spit out jets of water before plunging back into the pool. The trainers flash huge smiles at their flippered pupils and applaud wildly. The animals also seem delighted and squeak with pleasure (Linden 1993:53).

Kanzi the chimp and Washoe the chimp (the ward of the Gardners) both have learned to communicate in humanlike ways. Kanzi learned to use lexigrams on boards to communicate, and Washoe learned parts of American Sign Language for the deaf. We cannot know exactly what is happening in the head of a nonhuman animal when it uses gestures to communicate with humans or what it expresses about the animal's inner state. Consider Koko, a gorilla that has learned to use sign language. One day the powerful animal broke a sink in her living quarters. Without a moment's hesitation, the animal signed "Kate there bad." What was happening? Was Koko actually trying to throw the blame on Kate, a slightly built human assistant, or did Koko mean something else, if she meant anything else at all? It is still a mystery after all these years (Linden 1993:58).

Self-Recognition and Consciousness

Do nonhuman animals possess self-consciousness? Does it feel like something to be a termite, a dog, a cat, a frog, or an elephant? One of the ways that the existence of self-consciousness has been explored is through a **mirror self-recognition test (MSR).** The test is simple to perform but difficult to interpret, especially across species. A mark is put on the forehead of a test subject (it is done with human children, too) in such a way that the individual does not know it has been done. If it were a nonhuman animal, the creature would probably be anesthetized to maximize the likelihood that it had no awareness of a mark on its head. Once the animal regains consciousness, it is placed in front of a mirror, and its responses are observed. If the animal looks in the mirror and then touches its own head (not its reflection in the mirror) and tries to wipe off the mark, it seems likely that it does have some sense of body and, perhaps, even a self-concept. Human children are usually able to pass the MSR test between the age of 18 months and 2 years (Newman 2002:108). In all the experiments with chimpanzees, they show that they too can pass the test. A chimp will try to remove the mark by scratching its forehead with a finger (Page 1999:247). Self-recognition—even if we grant it to those animals that pass the MSR test—is not identical with self-consciousness, and it is possible that what seems to be an indication of self-awareness really is not (Page 1999:247).

Distinctively Human

Clever Hans was a horse that was owned by Willhelm von Osten. Hans was clever because he could do arithmetic. If he was asked what two plus two was, he would stomp his hoof until he reached four; if he was asked what three times two was, he would stomp his hoof until he reached six. Hans was not like the animals that do the "stupid pet tricks" on the late-night television or the pigs, chickens, or dogs that pound out a song on a small piano at a state fair so they look musically inclined. It seemed that Hans could actually add, subtract, multiply, and divide, and his owner had no idea how Hans could compute the numbers. After some up-close investigation, it was found that giving human abilities to the horse was unwarranted. The animal was not really figuring out the answers to arithmetic problems. All that was really happening was that Hans started hitting his hoof when he perceived his examiner making a downward movement and stopped when his examiner reversed direction. So, in the usual case, what happened was that a human would ask Hans a question and then move toward Hans's hoof to watch. Hans, in response, started hitting his hoof. As Hans neared the correct answer—according to the human who was waiting for the answer—the questioner moved his or her body to a more upright position (or simply relaxed). In response to the change of stimulus, Hans stopped hitting his hoof. This process of stimulus and response, coupled with the knowledge of arithmetic possessed by the individual who asked the question, made the whole thing work. Hans got the right answer far more often than would be expected if he were simply a dumb horse. Hans was indeed clever; he just wasn't able to do arithmetic. Is it not possible that other animals are also given credit for human abilities when actually something else is operating?

Continuity and Emergence

No doubt exists that animals—all of them—have a kinship. **Continuity** is there, and it is important. However, another aspect of evolution exists, and it is also important. It is called **emergence** or, more technically, the **theory of**

punctuated equilibria (Lieberman 1991:6). Evolutionary changes are not—and do not have to be—gradual and continuous. Levels exist, and it is possible for new processes and capacities to emerge in a species that make members of that species distinctive and unique from members of all other species (Lindesmith, Strauss, and Denzin 1999:37). "A series of small, gradual *structural* changes can lead to an abrupt change in behavior that opens up a new set of selective forces" (Lieberman 1991:8). Animals from different species move toward some of the same general end-states like food gathering, reproduction, protection, care and protection of offspring, and group cooperation. However, the *way* that these ends are achieved may be very different from species to species. Food-gathering for one animal may be primarily under the control of innate factors, while for some other animal, food-gathering strategies are learned symbolically in the context of a culture. To the proverbial visitor from Mars, little difference may be seen. However, to those in the know, the instinctual food gathering of a largemouth bass is qualitatively different from shopping at the local supermarket by a father of six children. Anthropomorphic tendencies may be based on the erroneous belief that if a nonhuman creature acts in what appears to be human ways, it must think and feel like a human, too.

Most people can accept that a line can be drawn to separate the human animal from some other species of animal. The question, however, is where should the line be drawn? Should it be drawn between humans and nonhumans, or between plants and animals, or between vertebrates and invertebrates, or between mammals and everything else? Page (1999:48–9) offers a decision rule to help us decide.

> Would you say, regarding your pet dog, "We are going for a walk down the block"? I think you most likely would. Would you say this regarding your horse? Maybe, but to me, this seems like more of a stretch, for some reason. What about you or your child's pet gerbil or parakeet? Now we're losing a lot of folks, I'm pretty sure. Your reticulated python? Very few of us are comfortable with "we" in this case. An oyster? That's where I draw the line!

This "we" rule is far from perfect, because humans feel close to their pets no matter what they are. Some people would use "we" in regard to a horse or a pot-bellied pig and not in regard to a dog or cat. It is also true that some animals have been given human qualities—elephants, dolphins, parrots, pigeons, turtles, bees—that would rarely be included in the category "we."

The Anthropomorphic Fallacy

Anthropomorphic interpretations are often rooted in what Davis (1997:336) calls the logical error of **affirming the consequent.** Being aware of this error will help us to keep our thinking straight about some things that get hopelessly confused in discussions of animal cognition and consciousness. Here is the way it works. An antecedent (the first event in a chain of events) and a consequent (the second event) are tied together into a statement. For example, the antecedent "If you are a good person," is followed by the consequent "you will give to charity." As stated, this statement is true. Good people do give to charity. However, the logical error comes when the consequent is *affirmed* and used to prove the truth of the antecedent. In other words, it is a false statement that because you give to charity, it means you are a good person. You might give to charity for lots of reasons other than being a good person. Politicians are famous for donating to popular causes primarily because it makes them look good and helps to garner votes.

Thinking and consciousness may make it possible for a creature to do something smart and reasonable, but that doesn't mean that a creature that does something smart and reasonable is doing it because of thinking and consciousness (an example of the error of affirming the consequent). "When I think, I scratch my head" may be true while "Because I scratch, I think" is not. Lots of reasons can be found for scratching the head from dandruff to scalp irritation (Davis 1997:336–7). Complex inner processing in a nonhuman animal and highly efficient behavior are both possible without any consciousness, thinking, or self-awareness. An **instinct**—which requires no ability to think, reason, or know—can make it possible for a creature to adapt perfectly to its environment and act in highly intelligent and sensible ways, especially if the environment changes little over time (Davis 1997:340).

What looks like thinking and knowing may actually be neither. A nonhuman animal may appear to know when it really does not. Clever Hans learned to respond in a rather automatic fashion to certain stimuli that made it *appear* that this horse was actually able to do arithmetic, a very demanding and a very *human* task. If this type of direct learning can make horses look more human than they are, it can do the same for other creatures. In **direct learning** (as opposed to symbolic or cultural learning), a creature's responses are associated—either through its own activities or through the manipulation of some human trainer—with reinforcers that are either positive and rewarding or negative and punishing. To teach a dog to sit, the dog's sitting movements must be associated with something positive and its failure to sit must be associated with something negative. Responses that are positively reinforced tend to be repeated, and those that are negatively reinforced tend to be eliminated (Deutsch and Krauss 1965:79–80). It may take a while for a creature to learn a new way of behaving (depending on its level of intelligence and features of the learning process), but given enough time and training, practically any creature can learn to repeat those responses on command for which it has been positively reinforced and to avoid those for which it has been negatively reinforced.

Direct learning and instinct are factors that carry us a long way toward understanding the seemingly human abilities of nonhuman creatures. When those are inadequate to explain what is happening, we may need to use some restricted notion of thinking and knowing. It is certainly true that nonhuman inner processes exist that are beyond the description of humans and that a huge ravine of mutual incomprehension exists between humans and other animals. If we wonder what is on the mind of a migratory bird that makes it possible for it to reach the solar icecap, we are probably traveling down a blind alley. No one knows how the navigational system works (Page 1999:63). My bet is that the birds do not know either. Similar behaviors in different species do not mean necessarily that the same cognitive processes are operating.

> . . . if I were to get on my hands and knees and start barking along with my dogs, would I be truly barking in the sense that they are? No (Page 1999:91).

Nonhuman animals may accomplish what they do through mechanisms that are unique to them and that can neither be described nor understood by humans in human terms, just as no animal can really understand what a "first date" is all about or "being stood up."

The Human Revolution

The story of human evolution is constantly being written and rewritten, and a great deal is unknown and, perhaps, unknowable. However, it is still possible to draw on what is known to construct a reasonable account of what happened to make us what we are. About eight million years ago in eastern Africa, a geological event occurred that caused the area that is now called the Rift Valley to sink, accompanied by the rising of a line of peaks on its western rim.

> . . . the original extensive region was divided into two, each possessed of a different climate and vegetation. The west remained humid; the east became ever less so. The west kept its forests and its woodlands; the east evolved into open savanna (Coppens 1994:91–2).

This change in the structure of earth's crust divided the common ancestor of both chimps and humans into two subgroups, one to the east on the savanna and one to the west in the woodlands. Members of one group adapted to the drier and cooler environmental conditions of eastern Africa and eventually developed into humans; the western descendants adapted to the humid, foresty environment and developed into chimps. This **East Side Story** is a convincing explanation for the strange fact that chimps and humans are very close in molecular structure but are never found together in the fossil record (Coppens 1994:91).

Humans were forced to adapt to savanna living where special skills were needed and new threats—from predators especially—existed. As a result, human body size and physical structure changed. Humans developed and then improved upon an upright stance, and they diversified their food preferences and diet from one that was strictly vegetarian to one that was broader and more opportunistic (Coppens 1994:95). They started to eat more meat, even though plants remained important supplements in their diet (Wrangham, Jones, Laden, Pilbeam, and Conklin-Brittain 1999:570). The human brain changed its structure and its size, partly as a result of increased nutritional contributions of an omnivorous diet. A larger and more complex brain was to change the course of human development profoundly. Greater mobility, along with greater curiosity and inventiveness, led to the migration of humans from eastern Africa to the rest of the planet. We humans have distinct qualities and skills that may have been initiated by adaptations to the environment in which we found ourselves, but those human qualities and skills changed our relationship to the world in which we lived in dramatic ways.

Bipedal Locomotion

One of the most remarkable things that we humans do—and one of the most profound—is that we walk upright on two legs (**bipedalism**). Some other animals can do this, too, but not with the same level of proficiency and dedication (Wilson 1975:547). Our human ancestors were walking upright approximately five million years ago (Johanson and Edey 1981), and a great deal of mystery (and controversy) surrounds why they were. Bipedalism might have represented the extension of the knuckle-walking abilities of our nonhuman ancestors into the human realm. If you have ever seen a gorilla move, then you have seen knuckle-walking. This huge animal uses the backs of its hands to support its bulk as it propels itself along the ground with its hind legs. Knuckle-walking is a good method of moving around when the terrain is rough and a creature only must travel for short distances (Ridley 1999:31). Our early human ancestors probably did not knuckle-walk often—remember that they had to travel efficiently on open plains—but they did inherit certain physical features that would have made it possible for them to do so. The climbing, hanging, and swinging abilities of our tree-dwelling primate ancestors might also have set the stage for upright locomotion when the time and conditions were right.

> Pre-bipedal locomotion is probably best characterized as a repertoire consisting of terrestrial knuckle-walking, arboreal climbing and occasional suspensory activities, not unlike that observed in chimpanzees today (Richmond and Strait 2000:384).

One thing is fairly certain: Bipedal locomotion preceded things like extensive tool use, substantial increases in brain size, the development of culture, and the ability to use language.

An animal—any animal—is a lump of living matter that must be able to do many things if it is to survive and to have offspring. In order to survive, an animal must be able to find food to eat and water to drink. If it is to leave part of itself for future generations, it must be able to mate and reproduce. In order to have chances of eating and reproducing, it must be able to move, and move efficiently. It must be able to protect itself from threats posed by environmental changes and from threats of animal predators. Even the constantly mutating microorganisms inside a creature's body pose a substantial threat to it (Ridley 1993).

> Despite our cultural complexity, we humans must solve the same ecological problems as all other organisms in order to survive and to reproduce. That is, in any environment, individuals must extract sufficient resources to survive and to reproduce in competition (sometimes cooperative) with others, both among our own and different species (Low 2000:12).

The common ancestor of apes and humans was, in all likelihood, a potentially erect animal. It may very well have felt comfortable both in the trees and on the ground. Its relatively large brain, binocular vision, climbing and swinging ability, short spine, and dexterous hands may have prepared it for existence on the ground, but none of these traits tells us why a creature that had never before moved erectly started to do so. Maybe hunting was easier for an upright biped, or maybe upright posture made it easier for a creature to see danger in time to avoid it. Maybe all the best food was high on the trees—easier for an upright creature to reach—or maybe food had to be carried back to camp for others to eat. Erect posture might have evolved as a sexual display (Jones 2000:321). Bipedalism was associated with other developments: increased use of hands and arms (e.g., for using tools), further changes in the human brain, the creation of language and culture, and enhanced ability to create and sustain social relationships.

The geological changes that transformed eastern Africa into open savanna, of course, affected the availability of food and protective cover. These changes also made existence riskier. Some primates undoubtedly stayed with the diminishing forests as long as they could. This is where they felt comfortable and where the food was. Others, however, had to move frequently in open country and travel from one grove of trees to another in search of food and water (Hockett and Ascher 1964:140). Life on the ground was not like life in the trees. Entire bands or troops were on the move, which may have offered some protection (strength in numbers), but probably not enough to compensate for increased visibility and vulnerability of members of the group. Large, ferocious, four-footed animals were always on the prowl, and all of them were dangerous when they were hungry.

A new skill that was of tremendous survival value was the ability to carry things. Hands and arms were no longer totally occupied with climbing, so the carrying function that was traditionally done by the mouth could be transferred to them. What was carried? Water, most certainly, and also weapons (both for defense and for attack), as well as food and perhaps even tools. Carrying may also have had substantial psychological effects in that it may have promoted both the development of memory and foresight (Hockett and Ascher 1964:141). An animal that lugs an item around with it for any period of time or distance has a distinct advantage. If the animal is smart, it will certainly learn to remember what the item is best for and be able to use it on subsequent occasions. Carried items could also be used to reinforce group solidarity, because they could be brought to others and shared with them. Improvements in carrying ability and bipedal locomotion went together (Hockett and Ascher 1964:141). It would be far less likely for a creature with something in its hands to drop to the ground and start to shuffle along on all fours.

Brain Changes

A dramatic change in sensory capacities came about approximately 65 million years ago when the neocortex developed on top of older brain structures in the primate brain. The evolution of the neocortex, especially the visual cortex, made it easier to perform complicated motor tasks, allowed greater sensitivity to sensory data, and integrated perception, thought, and action in highly efficient ways (Maryanski and Turner 1992:38). The **neocortex** is the part of the brain that is most closely associated with thinking and in being able to respond to an ever-changing environment with correct responses (Lieberman 1991:21). The visual system became the primates' principal sense (Maryanski and Turner 1992:49). Visual acuity and the evolution of the visual cortex meant that a creature could visually monitor its own behavior and construct purposeful actions in response to changes in the external environment.

> This dramatic change in the nature of sensory input made the primates a cortical step removed from most other mammals. What began as an increasing dominance of the visual organ over the olfactory in information processing was to culminate in the capacity to represent the world symbolically and use language (Maryanski and Turner 1992:47).

The early primates lived in a three-dimensional world. They had the ability to monitor visually that world, which, in turn, modified their brain structures. Changes in brain led to a greater reliance on learning and memory, which eventually led to more flexible and intentional behavioral responses (Maryanski and Turner 1992:50).

A crucial leap in the size of the human brain occurred between 2.5 million and 1.6 million years ago, a factor that probably gave our human ancestors the edge over close rivals, both human and nonhuman. Part of the reason may have been the demands of a more complex social division of labor, the advantage of being able to plan ahead or to integrate sensory data more effectively, and the increasing size of human culture and the new demands of tool use (Taylor 1996:49). However, the principal and most fundamental event that is responsible for human brains and, therefore, much of human progress is the human capacity for rapid vocal communication (Lieberman 1991:9). Language and culture select for bigger brains (Hockett and Ascher 1964:146), it is true, but they also select for a different *kind* of brain. Pathways and connections in the brain that are used frequently become stronger, while those that are not used either disappear or start to perform different functions. An animal that uses language and that shares cultural information with others is inadvertently restructuring its own brain.

The Origin of Symbolic Interaction

The first use of a **symbol** by some way-back ancestor was to have profound effects on the entire course of human development. Symbolic interaction impacted human cognition, emotion, and behavior, while it increased the ability of humans to construct the world within which they lived. The human brain is remarkable because it makes possible the existence of a human mind, and the human mind is a direct consequence of the use of words (Deacon 1997:321–2). Our closest nonhuman relatives, as intelligent and humanlike as they are, lack both the brain systems and the vocal structures to produce anything close to human speech. Humans have specialized brain structures that allow them to engage in rule-governed movement of lungs, tongue, and lips to make human speech possible. They are also able to understand the speech of others, as well as to understand the words that they themselves utter. Speaking is complicated business!

> Human speakers usually estimate the length of time it will take to produce all the words of the sentence they *intend* to speak when they inhale before speaking. The volume of air breathed in is proportional to the length of the intended sentence. First the duration of each word must be computed; then the durations of all the words that compose the sentence must be added to one another. . . . The "preprogramming" necessary to control the muscles that regulate the airflow and air pressure that determine the melody or intonation of the sentence also involves taking into account whether we are upright or reclining, jogging and conversing with a friend, the amount of fluid in our stomach, and linguistic factors—whether we are asking a yes/no question or emphasizing part of the sentence that we *intend* to speak (Lieberman 1991:108).

Wow! Lieberman (1991:82) must be close to the mark when he concludes that rapid, precise vocal communication was the engine that produced the modern human brain.

While the first humans probably did use hand gestures to communicate with one another about the environment, our more immediate human ancestors reached a point where this method of communicating was replaced with the spoken word. Manual sign language makes it practically impossible to use the arms and hands for carrying if they are needed for communicating, too. The advantages of speech far outweigh the disadvantages, and speech certainly did contribute to the evolutionary fitness of speakers (Lieberman 1991:38–9). "There is a deadly snake behind that tree" is a declaration that would be highly functional from the standpoint of survival for any creature that could utter it. In fact, comprehensible speech allowed the effective transmission of any piece of useful knowledge, from how to start a fire, to how to build a wheel. Speech would have made food gathering, defense, water collection, hunting, and the rest of life's activities more efficient and, perhaps, more enjoyable.

A minimum requirement for human vocal language is the existence of a brain and other physical structures that make it possible for us to voluntarily control our vocalizations (Lieberman 1991:106). While we might utter sounds that are involuntary (as when we hit our thumbs with a hammer), or say things when we are angry that we wish we had not, the essence of human speech is that we can consciously construct complex thoughts and then verbalize them to others (or even aloud to ourselves). Maryanski and Turner (1992) identify two sets of environmental pressures that encouraged the development of speech. First, on the open plains of the savanna, where sound traveled easily and little protection existed, random sounds and emotional outbursts would have scared potential prey away and drawn attention of hungry predators (Maryanski and Turner 1992:60–1). So, silence—or at least the ability to remain silent when the situation demanded—was golden. Selection pressures must have made it more likely that the individuals who would survive would be the ones who were able to suppress random vocalizations even when they were excited or upset (Maryanski and Turner 1992:61). It is but a short leap to the voluntary control of vocal sounds. Second, the advantages of group living made human speech more likely. Because human social bonds are not programmed into us at birth, they must be built and reinforced through symbolic interaction (Maryanski and Turner 1992:67). Conversation is a principal way that we humans generate feelings of solidarity among ourselves (Lindesmith, Strauss, and Denzin 1999:82).

The human brain continued to enlarge from 1.6 million years ago until about 150,000 years ago (Taylor 1996:7). One factor that contributed to human brain development was the invention of the baby sling (Taylor 1996:46). This harness, in all probability made first by females from animal tendons, allows a young child to be carried by the mother in ways that will not interfere too much with her daily activities. The baby sling allowed human mothers to give birth to underdeveloped children who could then mature and learn during an extended period of physical helplessness and almost total dependency, close to a nurturing adult. The mother's walking movement would help to organize the infant's responses while it calmed the child. This would make it possible for the child to grow, directing his or her energies toward adjusting to, and learning from, the outside world and the people in it.

Because we can use symbols so fluently—Deacon (1997:340–1) suggests calling us *Homo symbolicus*—we possess a remarkable ability. Language allows a flexible but precise response to a constantly changing world of people, places, and things.

> As many scholars have noted, human language is creative; its rule-governed syntax and morphology allow us to express "new" sentences that describe novel situations or convey novel thoughts (Lieberman 1991:81).

Our symbolic system is the lens through which we interpret the world and with which we relate to others and even to ourselves. No matter what nonhuman animals do or can do, no matter how humanlike they appear, and no matter how extensive the vocabularies that they are taught, the fact remains that these creatures can do whatever these creatures are "supposed" to do *without* benefit of language. Nonhuman creatures do not need language in order for them to be what they are. Humans do. Talk is at the very heart of social interaction, and it contributes in countless ways to the creation of social order (Boden 1990:247). It is a principal reason that we are so unique (Goffman 1981). In fact, our refined ability to communicate with symbols is something that certifies our humanity more clearly than any physical trait we possess (Deacon 1997:341).

Conclusions

One of the unique features of human experience is that our thoughts, feelings, and behaviors are influenced by the actual, imagined, or implied presence of others (Allport 1985:3). Children raised in social isolation, or those who are neglected or abused, show clearly—and tragically—the power of social relationships to make or unmake human beings. Unless we have the opportunity to acquire an appropriate amount of information from our environment and our social heritage, the distinctive features of what it means to be human will not be ours. Victor, Anna, Isabelle, and Genie all had the potential for full membership in society, but for reasons over which they had little control, that was not to be.

Humans project human qualities onto both inanimate forces and nonhuman animals. The first type of attribution, called the pathetic fallacy, is easy enough to recognize for the error it is. However, a second type, called anthropomorphism, is trickier. Do nonhuman animals think, feel, and act consciously and self-consciously? While overlap or continuity exists between members of different species, what is most impressive is the great divide between humans and everything else. We have many characteristics that make us unique.

Our evolution millions of years ago in eastern Africa set the physical foundation for the human revolution. Important emergents were our bipedalism, changes in the size and structure of the brain, our ability to use vocal speech, the use and transportation of tools, and the creation of culture and its assortment of symbols. Our most impressive feature as humans is our extensive network of social relationships. Many factors worked together to make it possible for our human ancestors to transform the environments in which they lived, which, in turn, produced further changes in how our ancestors evolved. They relied more and more on visual cues and transferred many important functions to the neocortex of the brain. The evolution of language and symbols allowed them to respond to changing situations with precise and flexible responses. The emerging symbolic abilities lessened the need for instinctual responses to environmental conditions, and cultural learning became a central part of human development. Humans are the result of millions of years of distinctive evolution, and we can symbolize, think, and feel in unique ways.

Chapter Three at a Glance

- In order to be—or to become—fully human, humans need a great deal of proficiency at taking account of others and forming relationships with them.
- The disabilities of children raised in social isolation show how necessary social relationships are for human development.
- While similarities exist between humans and nonhumans—important ones—what is more impressive are the profound differences, especially the human abilities to form social relationships and to interact symbolically.
- The start of humanity in eastern Africa millions of years ago required our ancestors to adapt to life on an open savanna.
- Our human ancestors became proficient at bipedal locomotion, experienced changes in the size and structure of the brain (especially the evolution of the neocortex), created both tools and cultures, and invented systems of communication based almost entirely on symbols.
- The many developments of the human revolution made us not only unique creatures but uniquely capable of both creating and being created by social relationships.

Glossary

affirming the consequent a logical error that, when applied to nonhuman animals, makes them look more humanlike than they really are

anthropomorphism giving human qualities for thinking, feeling, and acting to nonhuman things

bipedalism (bipedal locomotion) walking upright on two legs

continuity the similarities that exist between members of different species due to evolution

direct learning an animal's responses that are positively reinforced tend to be repeated and those that are negatively reinforced tend to be extinguished

East Side Story the hypothesis that humankind originated in eastern Africa as a result of changes in the structure of the earth's crust that transformed it into an open savanna

emergence (theory of punctuated equilibria) new processes and capacities appear in a species that make members of it distinctive and unique from members of all other species

feral children children raised in social isolation who have had little opportunity to acquire the distinctive traits of humanness

Homo symbolicus a descriptor for our species that emphasizes the fact that we are able to create and use symbols, a more important criterion of humanness than any physical trait that we possess

instinct an inborn act that makes it possible for a creature to adapt perfectly to its environment and to act in what appear to be highly intelligent and sensible ways

mirror self-recognition test (MSR) use of a mirror to see if a creature will rub off a mark on its forehead from seeing its reflection

nature innate or inborn characteristics; at the human level it includes reproductive systems, secondary sex characteristics, genetic makeup, and the evolution of the body

neocortex the dorsal part of the cerebral cortex that gives humans the capacity for advanced thought processes and for the use of symbols

nurture learned or acquired characteristics; at the human level it includes the physical environment, life experiences, social arrangements, and culture

pathetic fallacy the attribution of human emotions and characteristics to the forces of nature, for example, an "angry" storm

sociobiology a theoretical perspective that explains both human social behavior and culture as a product of biological factors

symbol a word, sound, or physical gesture that stands for or represents something else because of group agreement; symbols help to humanize us and contribute to human evolution

References

Allport, Gordon. 1985. "The Historical Background of Social Psychology." Pp. 1–46 in *Handbook of Social Psychology, Volume I*, 3rd edition, edited by Gardner Lindzey and Elliot Aronson. New York: Random House.

Boden, Deirdre. 1990. "People Are Talking: Conversation Analysis and Symbolic Interaction." Pp. 244–74 in *Symbolic Interaction and Cultural Studies*, edited by Howard Becker and Michal McCall. Chicago, IL: University of Chicago Press.

Coppens, Yves. 1994. "East Side Story: The Origin of Humankind." *Scientific American* 270:88–95.

Curtiss, Susan. 1977. *Genie: A Psycholinguistic Study of a Modern-Day "Wild Child."* New York: Academic Press.

Davis, Hank. 1997. "Animal Cognition Versus Animal Thinking: The Anthropomorphic Error." Pp. 335–47 in *Anthropomorphism, Anecdotes, and Animals*, edited by Robert Mitchell, Nicholas Thompson, and H. Lyn Miles. Albany: State University of New York Press.

Davis, Kingsley. 1940. "Extreme Social Isolation of a Child." *American Journal of Sociology* XLV:554–65.

———. 1969. "A Case of Extreme Isolation." Pp. 88–96 in *Readings in Social Psychology*, edited by Alfred Lindesmith and Anselm Strauss. New York: Holt, Rinehart and Winston.

Deacon, Terrence. 1997. *The Symbolic Species: The Co-Evolution of Language and the Brain*. New York: W. W. Norton & Company.

Deutsch, Morton and Robert Krauss. 1965. *Theories in Social Psychology*. New York: Basic Books.

Goffman, Erving. 1981. *Forms of Talk*. Philadelphia: University of Pennsylvania Press.

Guthrie, Stewart Elliott. 1997. "Anthropomorphism: A Definition and a Theory." Pp. 50–8 in *Anthropomorphism, Anecdotes, and Animals*, edited by Robert Mitchell, Nicholas Thompson, and H. Lyn Miles. Albany: State University of New York Press.

Hockett, Charles and Robert Ascher. 1964. "The Human Revolution." *Current Anthropology* 5:135–68.

Johanson, Donald and Maitland Edey. 1981. *Lucy: The Beginnings of Humankind*. New York: Simon and Schuster.

Jones, Edward and Harold Gerard. 1967. *Foundations of Social Psychology*. New York: John Wiley & Sons.

Jones, Steve. 2000. *Darwin's Ghost: The Origin of Species Updated*. New York: Random House.

Kennelly, Ivy, Sabine Merz, and Judith Lorber. 2001. "What Is Gender?" *American Sociological Review* 66:598–605.

Lieberman, Philip. 1991. *Uniquely Human: The Evolution of Speech, Thought, and Self-less Behavior*. Cambridge, MA: Harvard University Press.

Linden, Eugene. 1993. "Can Animals Think?" *Time* 141:54–61.

Lindesmith, Alfred, Anselm Strauss, and Norman Denzin. 1999. *Social Psychology*, 8th edition. Thousand Oaks, CA: Sage.

Low, Bobbi. 2000. *Why Sex Matters: A Darwinian Look at Human Behavior*. Princeton, NJ: Princeton University Press.

Maryanski, Alexandra and Jonathan Turner. 1992. *The Social Cage: Human Nature and the Evolution of Society*. Stanford, CA: Stanford University Press.

Miles, H. Lyn. 1997. "Anthropomorphism, Apes, and Language." Pp. 383–404 in *Anthropomorphism, Anecdotes, and Animals*, edited by Robert Mitchell, Nicholas Thompson, and H. Lyn Miles. Albany: State University of New York Press.

Newman, David. 2002. *Sociology: Exploring the Architecture of Everyday Life*, 4th edition. Thousand Oaks, CA: Pine Forge.

Page, George. 1999. *Inside the Animal Mind*. New York: Doubleday.

Richmond, Brian and David Strait. 2000. "Evidence That Humans Evolved From a Knuckle-Walking Ancestor." *Nature* 404:382–4.

Ridley, Matt. 1993. *The Red Queen: Sex and the Evolution of Human Nature*. New York: Penguin.

———. 1999. *Genome: The Autobiography of a Species in 23 Chapters*. New York: HarperCollins.

Sanders, Clinton. 1999. *Understanding Dogs: Living and Working with Canine Companions*. Philadelphia, PA: Temple University Press.

Taylor, Timothy. 1996. *The Prehistory of Sex*. New York: Bantam.

Wilson, Edward. 1975. *Sociobiology: The New Synthesis*. Cambridge, MA: Belknap Press.

Wrangham, Richard, James Holland Jones, Greg Laden, David Pilbeam, and NancyLou Conklin-Brittain. 1999. "The Raw and the Stolen: Cooking and the Ecology of Human Origins." *Current Anthropology* 40:567–94.

Socialization
Becoming a Society in Miniature

William James, a philosopher who turned his intellect to understanding some of the principles of psychology, hypothesized that on the day of one's birth, the world is a bloomin', buzzin' confusion. Of course, we will never know if he is right, but it is hard to be at all familiar with newborns and not to think James was close to the mark. Upright posture presented unique opportunities and challenges for humans, but it also created a dilemma, at least for mothers. It sculptured the pelvis very badly for childbirth exactly at that point in time when brains were increasing in size and so were heads. What to do? Evolutionary pressures made it more likely for children to be born at earlier ages when the head was smaller and could still fit through the birth canal more easily. Human babies of long ago probably developed inside their mothers for at least twelve months, but natural selection eventually made it better for a woman to give birth at nine months when the baby's head was still small enough to fit through the pelvic bones (Duham, Myers, Barnden, McDougall, and Kelly 1991:123). The fact that a human baby rotates as it slides down the birth canal is another plus in allowing large heads to fit through small openings (Taylor 1996:46). A human baby's brain weight is only about 30 percent of the adult weight, and it increases in size for about eighteen months after birth inside a skull that allows the brain room to grow (Taylor 1996:46–7).

The birth of a child offered an opportunity for other people to get involved, which may have increased the solidarity of the group. These individuals could assist the new mother by verbally guiding her through labor and by helping her physically to get the baby down the birth canal and into the outside world (Taylor 1996:49). They also could help her by sharing her pain and by helping her to make sense of some of the mysterious or even frightening events that she was experiencing—her water breaking, her bleeding, and her painful contractions. The infant was born into a group with both a relational system and a culture, factors that were bound to have immediate and far-reaching consequences for the child. Because a human newborn is so dependent and helpless, a great deal of attention and care from others is necessary if the child is to grow and develop.

In the Beginning: Nature and Nurture

A unique human biology, crafted and constructed by millions of years of evolution, both complements and is complemented by our human **social heritage** (a society's structure of institutional arrangements, shared understandings, and patterns of interaction). Human babies come into the world physically, mentally, and emotionally underdeveloped but with great potential for learning the essentials of group life and for adapting to others (Taylor 1996:48). Most of the characteristics that make us most human are acquired in the context of our relationships to others, and relationships—their nature and number—have a profound impact on the course of one's development (Douglas and Ney 1998).

What Is Socialization?

Socialization refers to the social experiences by which individuals develop their human abilities while they learn the way of life of their society (Macionis 2001:115). It is the process of social interaction within which an individual acquires the social heritage and develops a self, self-concept, or personhood. The term socialization replaced the word **education** in discussions of child development, and it was more than a semantic substitution. The study of socialization is concerned with what is learned and how, when, and why this happens in the context of social relationships in which the child is an *active* participant. Any view of a newborn as passive and submissive in the socialization process, carried very far at all, is a woefully inadequate view of the nature of things (Danziger 1971:14). A newborn has a great deal of impact on others, even on the day of the child's birth, and he or she both influences and is influenced by others in a lifelong process of learning (Corsaro and Eder 1995:428). If the world that a child initially enters is a bloomin', buzzin' confusion to him or her, it is also true that day by day, week by week, month by month, and year by year, the confusion and the chaos are reduced as a developing child acquires more and more information about the world.

Who Rocks the Cradle?

Deciding who or what exactly is responsible for our actions is risky business. **Hume's fork** (named in honor of David Hume, the Scottish philosopher) shows the nature of the dilemma: Either our behaviors are determined, in which case we are not responsible for them, or our behaviors are random, in which case we are still not responsible for them (Ridley 1999:309). Then who or what is? At one time it was an article of faith that parents have the most powerful and direct influence on what their children become. The family was the cradle of socialization, and the parents were the hands that rocked the cradle. However, Harris called this view into question in her analysis of the nurture assumption and its relevance for explaining why children turn out the way they do. She concluded that what is learned in the home is pretty much irrelevant when the child sallies forth into the outside world.

> Although the learning itself serves a purpose, the *content* of what children learn may be irrelevant to the world outside their home. They may cast it off when they step outside as easily as the dorky sweater their mother made them wear (Harris 1998:13).

People in environments outside the home do play a role in personal development, a role that may sometimes—most times, according to Harris (1998:52)—supersede the role of parents. However, let us not throw all common sense out the window, especially when it fits much of our own experience. Parents are important agents of socialization.

Research cannot pick up all the direct and indirect ways that a child is influenced by learning experiences, then separate those from biological and genetic factors, and then determine the amount of interaction that exists between the two. A developing child impacts the forces that impact him or her, and that child may pick and choose from parents' instructions what seems most relevant, important, or useful. Parents may work to teach their children to be different from them (as in immigrant parents encouraging their children to assimilate to a new society), or parents may give mixed messages to their children. This hardly means that children are unaffected by their parents and have thrown off their parents' instructions like "dorky sweaters." It might even be possible for children to learn their values from parents but learn how to express these values from peers (or vice versa).

We all have to be like our parents in many ways because our parents are like us. How could research fail to measure it? We may be less like our parents at some point in our lives—perhaps when we are out dancing or dating—but when we have children of our own, we find that we have become the parents that our parents were. Our peer groups consist of people who are similar to us, and they may be more in tune with the latest trends in a way that our parents are not. However, being trendy is not the end-all of socialization. Parents can influence who we pick to be our friends and what we think of the friends we pick; our peers, of course, can influence how we view our parents. We should avoid blaming parents for things over which they have little control (Cohen 1999:59), it is true, but we certainly should not miss their influence in our lives. Parents have lasting effects on their children and how they develop (Amato and Sobolewski 2001:915–6; Cunningham 2001:193–5; Stacey and Biblarz 2001:177–8).

We have many different **statuses** to occupy and **roles** to play, and we may pick and choose which ones are most important. We may even decide that none of them is to be taken too seriously. Humans are fully capable of creating and modifying their roles in a process of **role-making** (Turner 1962:21–2). We may struggle—sometimes greatly and sometimes not so greatly—against the prevailing forces of control and conformity. We may select our statuses, some at any rate, and then decide how to play the accompanying roles to a great extent. A given individual may *make* the role of "student" in such a way that it is different—at least is some ways—from how other students manage the role. Socialization is a *process* that is ongoing and dynamic, and the self is created and re-created in each social situation that an individual enters (Berger 1963:106). We often plod along in our same old ways because we know what we are and know how we should act (memories of things past); other people may have memories of us that also make it more difficult for us to leave the path of tradition and conformity. However, at any point, we may resist socialization pressures and *make* our roles into something new and different. This is not necessarily a bad thing. The socialization process can be destructive if it transforms spontaneous, lively children into tense and emotionally insecure adults (Bell and McGrane 1999:289).

Key Emergents in the Social Process

While the things that we bring to the world—**reflexes** and **drives,** for example, or our upright posture or brain size—certainly help us to customize our socialization experiences, it is our relationships to others in our lives that account for what we are. In the early days of life, the developing child is characterized by a high degree of **egocentricity** in which he or she is separate and apart, wrapped up in his or her own point of view (Piaget 1932:26). One day I heard my second-born when she was just a baby crying in her room. I rushed in and found her in her crib, standing rigidly at attention, holding a large handful of her own hair tightly and painfully. I went to her and loosened her fingers, releasing her hair, and she stopped crying immediately. I'm pretty sure I know what happened. She was opening and then closing her fingers into a fist, got near her hair, and accidentally got a clump of it in her hand. She then stood there, in pain, waiting for someone to save her from her own egocentricity. This egocentered view of the world must be overcome if a child is ever to become a responsible member of the group.

Imitation and Object Permanence: The Early Years

One of the first things that nudges a child away from egocentricity is his or her **imitation** of others. Meltzoff and Moore (1977) reported the results of experiments that they did with very young children (12 to 21 days old). The children were presented with three facial gestures by an adult male: (1) tongue sticking out, (2) mouth wide open, and (3) lips protruding. The results were clear and convincing: Infants even this young were able to imitate facial expressions. Tests on infants who were 6 weeks old suggested that they, too, could imitate facial gestures they saw like sticking the tongue out of the *side* of the mouth; they could still reproduce these gestures twenty-four hours later (Meltzoff and Moore 1994). Hauser's summary statement about the available research on infant imitation seems close to the mark.

> . . . subsequent experiments demonstrated that infants from a wide variety of cultures are capable of facial imitation, that the capacity appears in newborns (as young as 42 minutes old!), and that it can be elicited even when there is a delay between the initial facial display by the experimenter and the first opportunity to reproduce the gesture by the infant (Hauser 1997:353).

We must remember that studies of infant imitation are controversial. For example, an infant will stick the tongue out when a pencil is moved toward the child's face, so maybe what appears to be an imitation of an adult's facial expression is really just a reflexive action (Hauser 1997:353). It is not always clear which one of an infant's responses qualifies as imitation and which one does not (Kugiumutzakis 1999:43). However, it does seem likely that imitation is an innate capacity for humans and something infants use in their very first interactions with other people (Meltzoff and Moore 1999:9–10).

Imitation is not a singular ability, for the imitation of gestures may be different from the imitation of vocal sounds (Nadel and Butterworth 1999:3).

Very early in life, a human child becomes capable of **echolalia**. This exists when a child is able to imitate and babble back vocal sounds of others. A child might hear the word "mama" or "papa" and be able to echo it back in the correct way. In the beginning of a child's life, the imitation that exists is probably not for the purpose of creating an emotional bond or for identifying with other people. Because these imitations can appear so soon after birth (within 42 minutes), it is likely that the mechanism of their action resides in a child's brain systems that are organized to allow a child to imitate in some way (Trevarthen, Kokkinaki, and Fiamenghi 1999:131). These first efforts at imitation occur without benefit of thinking, knowing, intent, or purpose. However, more mature imitation is based on learning and the ability to project one's self—no matter how slightly—into the position of another.

When my second-born was a child, I stood in front of her and placed my forefinger over my lips in the classic gesture for "stay quiet, you sweet young thing." She looked at me and immediately imitated me . . . , well, sort of. What she did was to stick her finger *into* her mouth. Her behavior was almost certainly a response to my gesture, a form of imitation, and because of who she was and some of the other things that she could do, I am almost certain that she was starting to become aware of me and my view of things. It is just that she did not get it exactly right. This **incipient role-taking** (Meltzer 1972:9) is one of the most important processes in nudging a child away from his or her egocentricity and toward being able to empathize with others (Lieberman 1991:142).

One of the first, and most important, cognitive emergents in the life of a child is called the **object concept** or **object permanence.** This is the intuitive sense or notion that objects and people have a permanence across space and across time. Our understanding of this cognitive ability was provided by Jean Piaget, the highly acclaimed and influential Swiss child psychologist (who was trained as a biologist). What he learned about object permanence or the object concept came from his direct observation of his three children as they developed (Piaget 1954:3–96).

In the early days, weeks, and months of life, when an object is removed from a child's point of view, the child acts as if it no longer exists (because it really does not). Out of sight is out of experience. Take your finger and move it in front of an infant's face, and the child may follow it with his or her eyes. However, the instant your finger is out of sight, it is out of experience, and the child moves to looking at, or playing with, something else. Things that are placed in such a way that a child can see, smell, taste, touch, or hear them may have a direct and immediate impact on the child. However, once they are removed, they cease to have any impact whatsoever. If a favorite toy—say a rattle—is hidden under a handkerchief, a child may make no effort to lift the cloth and retrieve the toy. Why? Piaget concluded that it was because an object concept or object permanence had not yet developed. Young children do not look at objects as adults do. Whereas adults look at objects as things that have substance and that exist with permanent and constant dimensions, children do not view the world that way (Sugarman 1987:148).

By the age of 2, most children have developed object permanence. When object permanence is established, objects can be hidden from the child's view (say, in a pocket or under a handkerchief), and the child searches for that which he or she cannot see, smell, taste, touch, or hear. Things out of sight (or taste, touch, smell, or sound) are no longer out of experience. When my granddaughter was young, I set her on my lap, facing away from me. I held a playing card in front of her face and started to move it behind her until she could see it no longer. The instant it was out of sight, she lost interest in the activity. However, when she was older and we played with the card, she would turn her head back and forth, looking for the card that she could no longer see. Piaget would hardly be surprised at her behavior. Piaget and Inhelder believe that object permanence develops in children through a process of **sensorimotor integration** as they relate to objects and people in their environment (Piaget and Inhelder 1969:3–12). A child grasps a toy and looks at it. The child then moves the object and receives a different mental image of it. In time, the object becomes all the ways that the child can act on it, and it is a *very* short mental leap to the intuitive notion that objects have a permanence across time and space (Piaget 1954:42).

Object permanence has important consequences for a child's further social development. It alerts a child to the fact that a world exists that is separate from his or her knowledge of it, reducing some of the confusion and the chaos. It nudges a child away from egocentricity, while it helps to stimulate the development of memory. Because of object permanence, the child is no longer tied so directly and immediately to the world of sights, sounds, tastes, touches, and smells. The child lives in a world of objects and people that have a permanence and a durability even when they are not around the child. A child can start to be aware of things that he or she cannot directly perceive and remember things long after they are gone from view. Object permanence is a process that evolves slowly over time and that sets the foundation for further social, cognitive, and emotional development.

The Symbolic Organization of Experience

The Categorical Attitude.   Both imitation and object permanence are of great value for setting the early foundation for the acquisition of the social heritage. These help to prod the child away from egocentricity and toward being more aware of others and sensitive to their views. However, we would not get very far in our social development if we did not learn to use and understand language and the symbols on which it is based. Language use develops during what is called the **categorical attitude,** and it has two principal parts (Lindesmith, Strauss, and Denzin 1999:73–4). The first part of the categorical attitude is the realization that things can be named. This exists when names are associated with those objects that have become a more permanent part of the child's life. A child learns, for example, that "popcorn" is that fluffy, white stuff making all that noise and that "water" is that wonderful, cool something flowing out of the faucet. The second part of the categorical attitude comes when the child realizes that named objects can be placed into larger and more inclusive categories like "animal," "plant," "person," or "thing."

The categorical attitude is not simply the naming and categorizing of objects. What it is really is the *realization* that things can be named and categorized. It would be possible for a child to name an object, even correctly, without realizing that things have names. How? Either through imitation (echolalia) or through some kind of direct learning that does not require knowing or understanding to work. Children can associate words with corresponding objects before they realize that names exist and certainly before they can place named objects into categories. It would also be possible for a child to realize that things have names but be unable to name things well enough to be understood by others. A child might say "peetoe" to refer to a favorite pillow, but only close family members will know what that word means. The child still understands, however, that a word exists and that it can be used to refer to that soft, cushy thing upon which he or she sleeps. When one of my daughters was a child, she got very upset with me. She looked me right in the eye and declared me to be a "bingbonk." To this day, decades later, I am not sure what I was being called, but I *am* sure it was not something good. My child had already started to develop the categorical attitude even though she was unable to voice a word that would have made sense to me.

It is during the naming phase that a child first uses a **symbol.** Before this, whatever words a child used were said because of imitation or simple learning. With the arrival of the first part of the categorical attitude, however, the child realizes that *this* particular sound, gesture, or word stands for, or represents, something *because* people around the child want the child to use the same word that they use. A child uses the word "water" to refer to that cool stuff in the glass because that is what other people do. Now the child knows that words exist and that they can be used to refer to objects, people, situations, and experiences in his or her life. The categorical attitude is about understanding something that was not understood before.

The cognitive milestone of learning to categorize emerges sometime during the second year of life (14 to 18 months) in the usual case (Lieberman 1991:145). A good example of thinking in categories is found with the concept of money. Get a wallet, remove a dollar bill from it, and hold the wallet and the dollar bill next to a quarter. The quarter and dollar are both named objects that belong to the category "money." Both of them are different from the named object "wallet." Curiously, however, the dollar looks and feels more like the wallet than it does the quarter. Wallets and dollars are shaped generally alike; they are both soft and pliable; they are even found together. So why are dollars and quarters in the same category when dollars look a lot more like wallets than they do quarters? Categorical thinking allows us to group things together that we want to group (or in ways demanded by others), distinguish one category from others, and see the world as orderly. Money may come and money may go (and it gets there in a hurry), but the *category* of money has a certain permanence and orderliness to it. This categorical thinking helps to reduce a great deal of the confusion and chaos of the world.

> When someone tells you that the item on the counter is a fruit, you immediately know a great deal about it. You know that it is a plant, that it can be eaten, and that it probably tastes sweet (Lieberman 1991:144).

Once we have mastered higher-order concepts like number, weight, length, and color, we can use them to think about anything we like, from bedknobs to broomsticks. Without categories, we would be unable to think in advanced or sophisticated ways (Lindesmith, Strauss, and Denzin 1999:75).

Speech, Language, and Displacement.   A child's acquisition of language is a richly textured developmental process (Hauser 1997:318). Children enter the world prepared to learn a human language (Deacon 1997:102) and both to make sounds and to respond to the sounds of others. Within hours of birth, human newborns seem to display a stronger preference for their mother's voice than for the voices of other women, their father's voice, or nonspeech sounds (Hauser 1997:320). They soon develop the ability to select from the acoustic stream of sounds some of the more important ones and then respond to them (Hauser 1997:324).

In the usual case, understanding of words comes before their production by a couple of months as it seems that youngsters understand talk before they can enter into the conversation themselves (Hauser 1997:338). When human newborns do start making sounds, they are not words. Infants cry, grunt, shriek, squeal, squeak, and coo. As with all forms of human communication, an early stage exists in which the sounds are reflexive and meaningless; the child emits them because the child can. However, at some later point, the child uses the same (or comparable) sounds and vocalizations voluntarily and with purpose and intent. Even cries have this capacity.

> The earliest cries appear to be completely involuntary, driven by the limbic system. As cortical structures mature, however, cries can be voluntarily produced and used to manipulate the behavior of potential caretakers (Hauser 1997:327–8).

Separation calls are emitted by young mammals from many species when they are apart from their mothers. This may be one of the reasons that mammals have a middle ear and reptiles do not. It allows them to hear softer or quieter sounds because the bones of the middle ear (hammer and anvil) serve as amplifiers (Lieberman 1991:20).

Babbling (e.g., "mamamama" or "dadadada") is an important form of communication for the newborn, and of all the baby's noises, it is the one that most clearly qualifies as a precursor of speech. Babbling helps children to develop into speaking individuals because it allows them to realize that they can actually make vocal sounds (Hauser 1997:331). Babbling also gives other members of the group an opportunity to reward and echo back children's sounds to encourage and influence children's acquisition of language. Not much interaction can take place around a child's utterance of a grunt or a coo. However, when a child says "mama," "dada," or some other comparable sound, a whole bunch of responses—most highly pleasurable from the standpoint of the child—are directed at him or her. This reinforcement may be all the more reason for the child to continue to babble in more purposeful ways on future occasions.

When adults speak to infants they will use a simplified form of speech, at least much of the time. This type of speech has been dubbed **motherese** (Newport, Gleitman, and Gleitman 1977:112), but with the emergence of so much co-nurturing, it should probably be called **parentese** or maybe even **caretakerese.** Regardless of what it is called, it is an interactive event in which the child's utterances are rephrased or restructured especially for him or her. For example, a child might say something like "my be tired," and the parent will rephrase it into "yes, you are tired." While this "ese dialogue" may help a child learn language, it is not essential for language acquisition (Hauser 1997:332). It may be little more than a way to get a child to obey adult commands *right now* or to interact with adults, and not a way to turn the child into a gifted speaker (Newport, Gleitman, and Gleitman 1977:130).

Once children realize that things have names and that names are associated with objects, people, situations, and experiences, they acquire new words at a rapid pace. All studies of language development show that at about 18 months children experience a "naming explosion" during which they become interested in naming objects and people, and their vocabulary increases substantially (Lieberman 1991:145). Children learn a complex rule system and an extensive vocabulary at a time in their lives when they cannot even handle simple arithmetic or some basic motor skills (Deacon 1997:103). Some children learn to speak in an intelligent way before they can even open a door with a doorknob, do a somersault, or ride a tricycle.

> The acquisition of a child's first language is one of the mysteries of human life. Although children need years of schooling to learn arithmetic, geometry, or history, they effortlessly acquire the ability to use a system of communication that learned scholars cannot adequately describe (Lieberman 1991:127).

This paradox of knowing a complex system of rules (**syntax**) and the meanings of many words (**semantics**) before one could ever have formally learned a complex system of rules and word meanings has led some linguists to conclude that children are born with a universal grammar and that language must be instinctual (Chomsky 1986:12). How else could young children who are not particularly proficient in other aspects of their lives be able to learn something as complex and demanding as language?

The reason children can become such proficient or skilled language users so early in life may have more to do with the structure of languages themselves than with the existence of some language instinct in children's brains. The most successful languages are the ones that are arranged in such a way that they are as learnable as possible by children and at the earliest possible ages (Deacon 1997:137). Children's brains do not possess some innate knowledge of language structures. What is really happening is that language evolves to embody children's predispositions (Deacon 1997:109).

> Human children appear preadapted to guess the rules of syntax correctly, precisely because languages evolve so as to embody in their syntax the most frequently guessed patterns. The brain has co-evolved with respect to language, but languages have done most of the adapting (Deacon 1997:122).

The human inborn bias toward learning language is simply that we can recognize and learn quite early in life the logic behind symbolic reference (Deacon 1997:141). Even those chimps that have learned some of the fundamentals of language use learned them early in life in a relatively spontaneous and unstructured way. Kanzi, one of the most successful chimpanzee language users around, learned language while climbing on his foster mother (Matata) or clinging to her while *she* was being given a full language education. She never learned the fundamentals of language use but Kanzi did (Deacon 1997:125).

A child acquires symbolic meanings by learning what particular sounds, words, or physical gestures will do in terms of how others respond; eventually, these sounds, words, or physical gestures come to evoke in him or her the same response that they have evoked in others. The child is able to complete mentally the act that his or her overt gesture stands for or represents, because he or she has learned what effect the gesture has had on others (Rose 1962:15). At the heart of **symbolic learning,** then, is the ability to take the role of others and look at the world—and one's own self—through their eyes. New meanings are added to old ones, and old meanings are discarded or transformed. As children mature and get more proficient with symbols, they are able to learn with greater speed and ability. During peak or critical periods, a child may learn a great deal of new information about self and others; at other times, much less is learned.

One of the more valuable things about a language system is that it allows displacement to a remarkable degree (Hockett and Ascher 1964:139). **Displacement** exists when humans are able to refer to people, objects, situations, and experiences that are not physically or immediately present. When displacement exists, it means that symbols exist in conversation but the actual things symbolized do not have to be present. In fact, the things symbolized do not have to exist in physical space at all, because symbols can symbolize the imaginary. Symbols can be evoked voluntarily in a moment's notice to name, describe, and classify things. It is through this ability that language users are able to separate themselves from the concrete and immediate world of the here and now. Symbols allow humans to travel *together* in their imaginations to anywhere or any time they want.

Human language gives us a spectacular way to displace. Not only does language make it easier for us to recall some of the past experiences that we have had because we can symbolize them and hold them in our memory, it allows us to refer to these images and share them with others whenever we want. "Let me tell you what I did on my sixteenth birthday" is a statement that opens the door to a discussion of experiences from long ago. Even if non-human creatures do seem to have an ability for some type of displacement, it is certainly an unusual event and not dependent on the existence of symbols. By holding symbolic representations of people, places, objects, and experiences in our individual and collective memory, it actually creates these things and gives them a permanence and durability.

The categorical attitude in both its naming and categorizing phases is an emergent of historic dimensions in the life of an individual. Building upon imitation, direct learning, and object permanence, the categorical attitude provides not simply a new way of communicating but also a new way of reacting to one's self (Maynard and Whalen 1995:155–7). Once symbols are part of us, we no longer—and never will again—respond to the world directly; we respond to our symbolic representations of it. When humans start to use symbols to communicate with others, it makes it much easier for them to express to others what they intend to do, while they figure out others' intended plans of action. This symbolic interaction nudges children even further away from their egocentricity, while it helps them to refine their abilities to project themselves mentally into others' positions (or **role-take** or **take the role of the other**). Symbolic interaction, role-taking, and displacement are remarkable abilities, abilities that are correlated with other things that make humans so distinctive.

Mind and Self Are Twin Emergents

New words give birth to new thoughts, and thinking in terms of categories gives a new way of relating to others, to the world, and even to one's self.

> Thought is not merely expressed in words; it comes into existence through them. Every thought tends to connect something with something else, to establish a relation between things. Every thought moves, grows and develops, fulfills a function, solves a problem (Vygotsky 1986:218).

Children who are bilingual seem to be better at cognitive tasks than are children who are monolingual (Lieberman 1991:146–7). One reason may be that learning a language (or languages) activates or stimulates those areas of the brain involved with cognition (Lieberman 1991:148). If our wish is to understand how humans think and develop, it is necessary to pay close attention to the existence of symbols and their role in human cognition (Douglas and Ney 1998:54; Lindesmith, Strauss, and Denzin 1999:88). **Mind** is basically an internalized conversation of meaningful gestures (Mead 1934:156).

When children think and solve problems, one of the things that they do is to use private, self-directed speech that is really the internalization of speech that they have learned from others (Vygotsky 1978:27). Young children learn their most important skills not entirely on their own but from more accomplished instructors. One day my granddaughter was determined to climb a ladder in the backyard. However, unlike an ordinary ladder, this ladder went up from the ground at a 90-degree angle. It's a tough climb for anyone, especially for a young child. She started up the ladder and made it to the second rung (Vygotsky would call her activity "independent performance") and then stalled: She thought she could go no farther. At that point I showed her where to put her hand so that she could pull herself up and reach the top rung (Vygotsky would call my help of the child "assisted performance"). She reached the top successfully, but then she could not get down. I again showed her where to place her hands and feet (and I supported her in her downward journey but not so much that she would think I was doing it for her). The message from Vygotsky's work is that a child should be given enough room to grow. If children are assisted by adults no more than necessary, they will stay with the task longer, and they will learn a whole lot more (Gonzalez-Mena and Eyer 1997:123). It practically goes without saying that adults should help to organize children's experiences by talking to them while they are assisting them. This is one important way that children develop thinking (or inner speech).

The human capacity to act with purpose and intent, to channel behaviors deliberately and self-consciously, requires a sense of self. **Self** exists when a human is making indications to himself or herself and viewing one's self as an object. We must remember that self is really a *process*, not a concrete object or body organ. We are tempted to think of the self as something tangible and concrete when in fact it is continually created and re-created during interaction (Hewitt 2000:84). We remember things that we have done in the past (and others can remember them, too), and these self-images may be present to exert a powerful effect on what happens and on further understandings of self. Part of self is an image (or image*s*) of what we want to be in future relationships; we then construct and monitor our behaviors in ways that will fit that particular image and help us to become what we want to become (Carver and Scheier 1998). The process of self involves imaginings of how we look to others, and the evaluations and self-feelings that those imaginings generate in what has been called a **looking-glass self** (Cooley 1902). The self at any particular moment is a process of imagining how we look to others and filtering those perceptions through any previous imaginings of self that we possess (Gerth and Mills 1953:85).

Self, Mead instructs, has two discernible phases. He referred to one phase of self as the **I** and the other phase as the **me**. The word "I" describes the more spontaneous, impulsive, or even creative aspect of conduct. Every act has an element of "I" to it. The word "me" refers to that phase of self in which individuals are using their internalization of the attitudes or views of others to judge or evaluate themselves. So, an adolescent male is attracted to an older woman. He sees her lifting some heavy bags. In order to be of some help he says, "you shouldn't lift those because you might rupture your spleen." After she leaves, he hits himself on the forehead with his open hand, because he realizes that he has probably said the wrong thing to impress her and to get into her good graces. In this instance, the teenager shifted from his "I" to his "me" in constructing this series of actions. He initiated a conversation and then projected himself mentally into the woman's position and evaluated his words from her standpoint. In some of Mead's writings, he insisted that "I" starts the act and "me" directs it; we don't even know what we have done until the happening passes into our "me," and we can then be aware of it for the first time (Mead 1934:174). In actuality, a reciprocal relationship exists between these two phases of self, and the "I" both calls out the "me" and responds to it (Mead 1934:178).

The dialogue between the "I" and "me" is easier to see in young children who have not yet completely internalized it. One day when my first-born was still a child she was eating her breakfast cereal all by herself in the kitchen. I was in another room, eavesdropping on her. I heard her say something in her normal tone of voice like "I don't want all this cereal," seemingly to nobody in particular. Her voice then lowered in pitch, and she said in a very commanding voice, "Eat your cereal, you doe doe" (that is pronounced like the name of the extinct bird). She returned to her normal voice, stated to nobody in particular that she would finish the food, and continued with her meal. For the life of me I cannot imagine where she learned the word "doe doe," but I do understand the rest (and so would Mead). She was vacillating from one phase of self to another. I imagine that even today, years later, she does something similar but her dialogue between "I" and "me" now takes place privately and a whole lot quicker. The "I" and "me" are at the core of Mead's views, because he needed to have a place for both conscious responsibility and creativity (Mead 1934:178).

Play, Games, and Self-Development

All mammals play (Lieberman 1991:18), and human beings are no exception. Young children engage in a great deal of boisterous play, such as running around the house screaming and turning somersaults again and again. This kind of play may be fun and probably fulfills a variety of needs, but it does not have serious implications for self-development. However, some play does. It gives children an opportunity to take the role of others and to view themselves from their standpoint (Mead 1934:150). It is during play that a child develops the I–me dialogue and acquires a concrete understanding of a very abstract idea, that is, the attitudes of others toward one's self.

Mead writes of the **double** (Mead 1934:150). This is a "thing-like" self that seems to have an existence independent and separate from the child. The closest approximation to this "double" in the life of children is the imaginary and invisible friend that many of them have. A pretend companion actually helps a child to organize his or her responses by calling out in another that which he or she calls out in himself or herself. Play helps a child to learn the difference between the ordinary world and the world of pretend and imagination (Vygotsky 1978:93).

During the **play stage,** Mead (1934:150–2) insists, children **play at** different **roles** like firefighter, police officer, mother, father, teacher, or even cartoon characters like Scooby-Doo. Mead used the words "play at" to remind us that the children are doing things that are pretend for them; a child cannot really be a police officer or a teacher. However, pretend does not mean unimportant. It is during play that a child gets good at the *mental* process of role-taking by *physically* moving from one status and role to another. This movement drives the point home to the child that he or she can be many things, while it gives the child different vantage points for viewing himself or herself. During the play stage, children start to hone their role-taking skills and they start to construct self. The young daughter who says "hi, I'm 6 and I'm pretty" is revealing a lot about herself and, more important, about her relationships to others. The important feature of playing at roles is that children are developing a capacity for a shared tendency to respond to happenings. Children reach a point where the responses that they call out in themselves are similar to the responses that they have called out in others (Mead 1934:150).

Role-taking (mental projection into some other position) is something that a child only gets good at with maturation and with richer socialization experiences. When role-taking does occur for the first time, it is in reference to **specific others.** Part of what makes up that "other" is highly idiosyncratic and individualized ("*my* dad does not like me to watch cartoons"), and part of it reflects the institutionalized role that the other plays (parents do not like children to watch too much television, especially when they should be sleeping). Most of the specific others in a young child's life are also **significant others.** These are individuals who have a powerful impact on a child's life. A parent or a teacher is a significant other; an individual who delivers mail to the child's home or who sells the child a ticket to a movie is not. One of the most consistent things about role-taking during the early years is its inconsistency. A young child is not very good at role-taking. He or she may mentally take on the role of some specific other but then abandon it quickly and take a new role in imagination for a while. This quick flight from one role to another is one of the principal reasons that children take years to develop an integrated sense of self that transcends particular people and particular relationships. Children do not know for sure what they are nor how they are supposed to act because they pick up and abandon different roles very quickly and without much rhyme or reason.

Eventually, an individual will accumulate enough relational experiences (and become a proficient enough role-taker) that he or she develops a clearer and more consistent sense of self; this individual will come to value certain images of self (and the relationships based upon them) more than others. Individuals will search for, and try to establish relationships with, **confirming others** (Gerth and Mills 1953:86–7). These are individuals who help people to further the self-images that they have of themselves and are trying to present to others. Friends are often "best" friends precisely because they will confirm or support each other's self-assertions and claims about personal identity. The search for, and connection with, confirming others—and the avoidance of **disconfirming others** (individuals who sabotage one's efforts at self-presentation)—is a lifelong process. In fact, in the absence of a sufficient number of confirming others, individuals may very deliberately and very thoroughly manage impressions about themselves in order to get other people to view them the way that they want to be viewed (Goffman 1959).

The final stage in the development of self is what Mead called the **game stage** of socialization (Mead 1934:152). Its arrival—at about age 7 in the usual case—signals the emergence of a different way of thinking about others and about one's self (Mead 1934:152). With more experience, maturation, and practice, we reach the point where we are capable of taking the role of a different kind of "other," an other that is more abstract and extensive, called the generalized other. The **generalized other** is the view or perspective of the entire society or community, internalized in self. While a child may still mentally take the role of some specific other (or significant or confirming other), he or she can also take the role of the generalized other, which combines many different positions or views into an integrated whole. The individual then uses this general viewpoint to judge and evaluate his or her own conduct and attributes. Now the individual really is a society in miniature. He or she has figured out the views and attitudes of a large number of individuals and figured out the relationships among them (Mead 1934:151).

Play is something that we can do alone with very little planning. A game, however, coordinates the activities of a number of people according to a system of rules. Mead (1934:154) used the game of baseball to illustrate gaming and the generalized other, and it is a good example. To play baseball as a game it is essential for players to understand the generalized other of the "team" (and perhaps fans, coaches, and viewing public) and use that generalized view when deciding how to play the game or even what to do during any given play of the game. When you are playing shortstop and you pick up that ground ball hit in your direction, you quickly take the role of the team (generalized other) and then the individual playing at first base (specific other). Only then do you throw the ball to get out the runner.

One summer I was one of the coaches on a girls' softball team. The players ranged in age from 9 to 12, and Mead's writings helped me to interpret some of the things I saw that summer. Softball requires a lot of different physical skills like running, throwing, catching, and hitting. Some of the children, of course, were better at these skills than other members of the team. However, more difficult to see but every bit as important were differences in the children's abilities to role-take and to learn and follow rules. The older children were far better at gaming than were the younger ones and far more committed to it. On game day, the younger children would have been just as happy to have gotten together with their friends in the outfield and picked up bugs with their gloves. This kind of "play," however, is not what the "game" of softball is all about (or what their parents and coaches *wanted* it to be about). Mead was using baseball to make an important point about socialization. In the game of life, we must each take account of many other individuals and internalize their attitudes if we are ever to develop properly and to relate to others with any proficiency (Mead 1934:154–5).

The game stage represents the passage in the life of the child from taking the role of specific others in play to taking the role of the generalized other in games, which is responsible for the full development of self-consciousness (Mead 1934:152). For the individual, the internalization of the generalized other promotes a unity in self that would be impossible without it (Mead 1934:155). The child "knows" who he or she is in a more general and universal sense, and he or she is not so dependent on the particular views of specific others. You do not get along with the first-base coach? Fine. The rest of the team thinks you are the best thing since sliced bread, so you are far less concerned with the view of that particular coach. The game stage sets the foundation for a more mature and sophisticated way of thinking by making it possible for the child to experience a richer inner conversation of gestures (Mead 1934:156).

Children under the age of 7 have trouble with the **principle of conservation** (Piaget and Inhelder 1969:97–100; Sugarman 1987:118–9). If two identical glasses are filled with the same amount of water and a child is asked if they hold the same amount, he or she will say that they do, which is true. If the water from one of the glasses is poured into a shorter but wider glass, the young child will think that the shorter glass contains less water, which is not true. The child concludes that the water level is lower in one glass so it contains less water, period. The fact that the child saw the water poured from glass to glass makes no difference (Piaget and Inhelder 1969:98). A child who does not understand the principle of conservation does not understand that the quantity of water in one glass does not change by being poured into a different-sized glass (or that the number of checkers in a row does not change by making the row longer or shorter). With the arrival of the game stage—and what Piaget called the **concrete operational stage** of cognitive development—comes the principle of conservation. The child understands higher-order properties like length, weight, volume, and the like, properties that allow him or her to perceive the world and to think about it in more correct ways.

Starting at age 12, a child must clear one more cognitive hurdle. The child must learn to think in abstract, hypothetical ways, called formal thought by Piaget and Inhelder (1969:132). During the **formal operational stage,** the individual learns to be able to think about what might happen and to predict that certain changes are more likely to produce some outcome rather than others. The first few years of life prepare a child for thinking by making it possible for him or her to select objects, plan how to use them, and carry this plan out on a regular basis. Later, the individual's thought is affected dramatically by the social environment, especially a society's language, intellectual values, and cultural rules (Piaget 1950:156). Each new cognitive emergent is crafted onto prior personal developments and accomplishments until the child is able to think correctly and effectively without any props whatsoever. For Piaget, the ability to think abstractly without dependence on the concrete world was the Superbowl of cognitive development. The internalization of rules by a child and a self-conscious determination to follow the rules out of feelings of respect, and not external compulsion, set the foundation for future social development (Piaget 1932).

Sex, Gender, and Socialization

The early years in the life of any child are the period of what sociologists call **primary socialization.** These are the years when a child learns to role-take, to speak, to name, to categorize, to displace, and so on. The lessons that children start to learn about themselves and others during primary socialization are elaborated, modified, or even reversed by subsequent socialization experiences during the stage of **secondary socialization.** Sociologists emphasize that learning about self and others does not stop with primary socialization; socialization is a lifelong process of changing and becoming.

An important part of the social construction of self is the development of gender, a relational event or process that starts during primary socialization and continues throughout life. While **sex** is principally about biological placement as male or female, **gender** is about attitudes and feelings in regard to masculine and feminine. Sex reflects the operation of chromosomes and body chemicals (testosterone or estrogen) on the development of anatomical structures (ovaries, testes, uterus, scrotum, vagina) and the emergence of secondary-sex characteristics (distribution of body hair, breast development, voice pitch). Gender, however, refers to the psychological aspects of being masculine or feminine, as well as the social statuses, roles, and cultural prescriptions or proscriptions for acting, thinking, and feeling in sex-appropriate ways.

While it may be correct in some general sense to look at sex as some-thing you are or possess, this is a far less satisfactory view of gender. Gender is continually constructed and reconstructed, made and transformed, in the con-text of our relationships to others (van den Wijngaard 1997:117). Gender is not a "thing" that a human has as much as it is a constellation of actions that one *does* in anticipation of the actual or imagined reactions of others. When we do gender, we do it in front of other people, and our gender displays are regu-larly evaluated by others who are in a position to encourage or to discourage them (Kimmel 2000:106). Gender is actively and interactively constructed by people in their daily encounters with one another (Deaux and Major 2000:83; Kennelly, Merz, and Lorber 2001:600; Kimmel 2000:106; Miller and Costello 2001:595).

Because most young children prefer to play with same-sexed friends and playmates, this usually creates some gender-specific interaction patterns for them, along with some distinctive social activities (Maccoby 1998). Boys do seem to play together in larger groups, characterized by more aggression and competition, often organized around team sports (Corsaro and Eder 1995:432). Girls are more likely than boys to engage in play activities like jumping rope, dressing up, dancing, or singing. These activities have fewer rules, are less com-petitive, and are more difficult to conceptualize in terms of who wins and who loses (Lever 1978:472–9). According to most evidence, boys tend to be more aggressive than girls, and this difference emerges early in life (Maccoby and Jacklin 1974). The play of boys and girls may reflect this difference in levels of aggression, at least a bit.

Gender differences may come to look more natural than they really are, and far more constricting than they have to be (Kimmel 2000:154). More similarities than differences exist between boys and girls, and males and fe-males are more like close neighbors than residents of different planets (Kimmel 2000:16). Girls and boys do interact with one another, and they do play together all the time. Girls' play is also characterized by conflict and com-petition, and it shares many similarities with boys' play (Thorne 1986:170). Girls, too, enjoy team sports. Children—both boys and girls—do spend a fair amount of time in activities that do not belong to one sex more than the other: modeling with clay, working on computers, playing in sand, frolicking on schoolyard equipment, listening to music, riding tricycles or bicycles, swim-ming, painting, or helping their teachers. The *belief* that males and females re-ally are very different—or must be—may initiate a host of social processes to keep them separate and different from each other (Martin 1998:509). We may be nudged, pressured, or even ruthlessly coerced to get us to follow prevailing gender rules and to play gender-appropriate roles (West and Zimmerman 2000:139). We all become gendered in a gendered society (Kimmel 2000:16).

Children use gender as a cognitive organizer, starting early in life, and gender develops into an important lens that children use to perceive and evaluate each other, as well as themselves. By age 3, the average child knows what sex he or she belongs to but still has little understanding of what it all means (Frieze, Parsons, Johnson, Ruble, and Zellman 1978:126). When my first-born was about 3, I asked her to tell me whether she was a boy or girl, and she easily classified herself as female. Then I asked her what she wanted to do when she grew up. She told me that she wanted to grow a mustache. Hmmmmmm. It took many more years for her to develop a clearer sense of what it means to be a female and, by contrast, a male. Children learn about masculine and feminine by imitating others and eventually by identifying with members of their own sex and gender.

It will take years for the average child to understand that sex and gender do have a permanence that does not change automatically along with hair length, voice pitch, clothing style, or gait. Immediately after my first-born told me of her desire to grow hair on her lip, I asked her to tell me the difference between boys and girls. She informed me that boys have short hair and girls have long hair. I pressed her. "You mean if I let my hair grow longer than your mother's hair, it will make me a girl?" She replied, "Yes, daddy," surprised that I hadn't figured out something so obvious all by myself.

> Children are aware of their own sex by three. But . . . these same children are not yet able to identify the sex of others, nor are they convinced that gender is a constant trait of the individual. It is not until five or six that they have accepted the permanence of gender (Frieze, Parsons, Johnson, Ruble, and Zellman 1978:126).

The older a child becomes, the more committed he or she is to his or her own gender and the more resistant he or she is to any pressure to change it. Individuals receive information throughout their lives—subtle and not-so-subtle—about how to be "proper" males and females. Peer groups, especially, offer important lessons about gender and gender differences.

During adolescence, teenagers move from the influence of families, at least a bit, and become more involved with secondary relationships at school and at work. A **democratic parenting style**—in which parents are receptive to input from their children and are willing to explain the rationale behind parental decisions and expectations—seems to be the one that creates the most well-adjusted teenagers. Democratic parenting promotes a greater sense of independence among children, while it maximizes feelings of cohesion and closeness between parents and their offspring. This parenting style also promotes greater academic achievement and self-confidence in children and reduces their temptation to associate with deviant peers (Corsaro and Eder 1995:434).

Most teenagers report that they feel good about their future job prospects and think that one day they will land jobs that are both high-paying and enjoyable. However, they will not all get the rewarding, high-paying jobs that they covet (Booth, Crouter, and Shanahan 1999). A principal reason is that some adolescents spend more time than other adolescents in a state of **disengagement.** This is an unfocused state for the teen during which he or she is doing neither work nor play. This disengagement not only fosters low self-esteem in these teenagers, it accounts in part for their generally lower occupational and educational accomplishments. Parents who are able to instill in their children a sense of engagement are able to counter many of the adverse effects of economic disadvantage (Csikszentmihalyi and Schneider 2000).

For most teenagers, friendships increase during adolescence and the norms of the youth culture attain increased importance. **Youth culture** provides important lessons about how to interact with members of the opposite sex as well as with people from different ethnic and racial groups (Corsaro and Eder 1995:438). It also provides information about interpersonal relationships, personal worth, and how to get along in a fast-paced world. Adolescents actively work together to construct the situations in which they live and to choose those relationships and roles that work the best for them. Teenagers will eventually grow up and join the adult world with all its pushes and pulls and start to transmit the social heritage—its system of action and culture—to new members of the society. What goes around really does come around!

Conclusions

Children come into a world that for them is a bloomin', buzzin' confusion. However, day by day, week by week, month by month, and year by year, the confusion and the chaos are reduced as children come to approximate more mature ways of acting, thinking, and feeling. While a child brings things to the world—reflexes and drives, for example—that certainly help to customize socialization experiences, it is a child's relationships with others that account for what he or she becomes. Some of the most important emergents in the social process are imitation, object permanence, language use, role-taking, mind, and self. Imitation nudges a child away from his or her egocentricity a bit, while object permanence gives the child the understanding that objects exist even when they are out of sight. Language—naming and categorizing—makes it possible for a child to describe happenings in the outer world, as well as inside of his or her own body. When naming is coupled with the ability to mentally project into the position of another (role-take), it sets the foundation for the twin emergents of both mental activity (mind) and personhood (self).

Socialization experiences make it possible for an individual to organize symbolically the world in which he or she lives. An important feature of this symbolic organization of experience is the internalization of the viewpoint of others, first specific others, and then a generalized other. Through the involvement with play and games, a child develops the ability to act spontaneously (the "I") and also to judge or evaluate his or her own action (the "me") as selfhood develops. Further cognitive development comes with the principle of conservation, where a child realizes that matter is neither created nor destroyed, and the stage of formal thought, where an individual can think in abstract, hypothetical ways. Individuals eventually acquire even more of the social heritage as they learn about gender and form relationships outside the home at school and at work. Eventually they will pass on the culture and system of action to others.

Chapter Four at a Glance

- The immaturity and receptivity of human newborns makes socialization a necessary and important process for all human development.
- Many agencies help to socialize a child, paramount among them is the family.
- With sufficient maturation and socialization, humans reach the point where they are able to make their own roles as they interact with others.
- The initial years of a child's life are characterized by egocentricity and immature thought processes.
- A child will start to imitate others and then will develop the object concept or object permanence in which he or she has the intuitive notion that things exist even though he or she cannot perceive these things directly.
- A child eventually learns that things can be named and categorized (called the categorical attitude), and this sets the foundation for language acquisition and symbolic speech.
- Mind and self emerge together in the social process.
- A socialized individual moves from responding to specific others to responding to the entire society in the form of a generalized other.
- An individual learns to use rules, which helps to replace immature playing with more advanced gaming.
- Gender becomes an important cognitive organizer for viewing self and others, and it is continually constructed and reconstructed throughout life.
- Participation in a youth culture not only helps its members learn to be adolescents, it prepares them for movement into adult statuses and roles.

Glossary

categorical attitude (1) the realization that things can be named is followed by (2) the realization that named things can be placed into categories like "money," "dogs," or "fruit"

concrete operational stage the stage of cognitive development that goes from approximately age 7 to age 12 during which a child learns more advanced ways of thinking, but he or she still relies upon the presence of concrete props in order to think correctly

confirming others individuals who will support—or actively assist—in one's presentation of self

democratic parenting style parents and their offspring are more like partners, and children are actively involved in creating and applying the rules that govern their own behavior

disconfirming others individuals who sabotage, undermine, or forcefully contradict one's efforts at self-presentation and impression management

disengagement when adolescents are involved in neither work nor play; a period of drift and lack of direction

displacement the ability to refer to people, objects, situations, and experiences that are not physically or immediately present

drive an organic tension that directs activity but does not determine it (e.g., hunger or sex)

double an invisible or imaginary friend that helps a child to organize his or her responses by offering an "entity" whose position can be taken

echolalia children's parrotlike and senseless repetition of words or phrases uttered by people around them

education an older term to describe the process of acquiring the social heritage; it was supplanted by the term socialization because the term education made the child seem more passive and helpless than he or she really was

egocentricity a child's experience early in life in which he or she is separate and apart, wrapped up in his or her own point of view

formal operational stage the stage of cognitive development, starting at about age 12 and continuing throughout life, in which an individual is capable of thinking in very abstract and hypothetical ways, called formal thought

game stage an individual becomes proficient at role-taking and responds to rules and internalizes the generalized other, that is, the view of the entire society

gender the psychological and social characteristics that are considered most appropriate for males and females

generalized other the viewpoint of the entire society or community, internalized in self

Hume's fork either human behaviors are determined, in which case we are not responsible for them, or our behaviors are random, in which case we are still not responsible for them (named in honor of David Hume, the Scottish philosopher)

I the spontaneous or impulsive phase of self that starts or initiates the unorganized part of a social act

imitation children's copying or modeling of both actions and words of people around them

incipient role-taking a child's first and immature efforts at role-taking

looking-glass self imagining how we look to others, evaluating those imaginings, and then experiencing self-feelings in regard to the evaluation and imagination process

mind mental processes; inner conversation with symbols; the organization of brain processes through language; the process of making symbolic indications to one's self

me the phase of self that organizes or directs a social act; it relies upon the existence of the organized set of attitudes of others, internalized in self

motherese/parentese/caretakerese an interactive event in which the child's utterances are rephrased or restructured especially for him or her by adults in the child's vicinity

object concept/object permanence the intuitive notion that objects have a reality or existence even when they can no longer be perceived directly by the child

play at a role when children pretend to be something that they cannot really be like a firefighter, a race car driver, a beauty queen, or an astronaut

play stage youngsters start projecting themselves mentally into the position of some specific other (e.g., mom, dad, imaginary other) and use this viewpoint for self-construction and self-evaluation

primary socialization the development of self and the mastery of social skills during the early years of life

principle of conservation realization that physical matter is neither created nor destroyed, particularly through changing the shape of an object (e.g., a ball of clay) or from pouring liquid from one glass into another that is shaped differently

reflexes involuntary and largely automatic muscular or glandular responses that occur when appropriate nerves are stimulated, for example, sneezing, blinking, grasping, sucking, vomiting, shivering

role(s) the customary ways of acting, thinking, and feeling by occupants of a status; the role of college student is to study, attend class, and learn

role-making humans actively construct and reconstruct their roles in a process of making and remaking them

role-taking or **take the role of the other** mental projection into the position of another, an experience that acquaints a maturing child with multiple perspectives and nudges him or her away from his or her egocentricity

secondary socialization the processes of self-development that extend, modify, and transform the experiences of the early years and what has been learned during primary socialization; socialization is a lifelong process

self the process of viewing one's self as an object and then acting, feeling, and thinking in accord with what is imagined

semantics learning the meanings of words and how they are to be put into sentences to convey a desired message

sensorimotor integration the first stage of cognitive development, lasting from birth until about age 2, during which a child learns that objects have a permanence across time and space

sex an individual's placement into the biological category of male or female

significant other an "other" who is important or influential in one's life (e.g., the *specific* other "father" is probably also a significant other)

social heritage a society's structure of institutional arrangements, shared understandings, and patterns of interaction that members of a society use to give meaning and substance to social life

socialization the lifelong process of acquiring the social heritage and learning the way of life of a society, which creates an individual's self-concept and transmits both culture and systems of action from one generation or group to another

specific other an individualized or particularized "other" who is taken account of in interaction

status(es) the position or positions individuals occupy like student, son, daughter, southerner, liberal, author, clamdigger, or circus clown

symbol a sound, word, or physical gesture that stands for something else because of group agreement; a child must learn to use the symbols that others use

symbolic learning learning to act through symbolic instruction and by taking the role of others and identifying with them rather than from the immediate distribution of positive and negative reinforcers

syntax learning how to speak and write in grammatically correct ways so that the words, phrases, clauses, and sentences fit together properly

youth culture the development of shared understandings and social relationships focused on the age-specific experiences, needs, and interests of youth (e.g., how to find jobs, how to dress in fashionable ways, how to get along with others, and how to dance)

References

Amato, Paul and Juliana Sobolewski. 2001. "The Effects of Divorce and Marital Discord on Adult Children's Psychological Well-Being." *American Sociological Review* 66:900–21.

Bell, Inge and Bernard McGrane. 1999. *This Book Is Not Required*, revised edition. Thousand Oaks, CA: Pine Forge.

Berger, Peter. 1963. *Invitation to Sociology: A Humanistic Perspective*. Garden City, NY: Anchor.

Booth, Alan, Ann Crouter, and Michael Shanahan, editors. 1999. *Transitions to Adulthood in a Changing Economy: No Work, No Family, No Future?* Westport, CT: Praeger.

Carver, Charles and Michael Scheier. 1998. *On the Self-Regulation of Behavior*. Cambridge, UK: Cambridge University Press.

Chomsky, Noam. 1986. *Knowledge of Language: Its Nature, Origin, and Use*. New York: Praeger.

Cohen, David. 1999. *Stranger in the Nest: Do Parents Really Shape Their Child's Personality, Intelligence, or Character?* New York: Wiley.

Cooley, Charles Horton. 1902. *Human Nature and the Social Order*. New York: Scribner's.

Corsaro, William and Donna Eder. 1995. "Development and Socialization of Children and Adolescents." Pp. 421–51 in *Sociological Perspectives on Social Psychology*, edited by Karen Cook, Gary Alan Fine, and James House. Boston: Allyn and Bacon.

Csikszentmihalyi, Mihaly and Barbara Schneider. 2000. *Becoming Adult: How Teenagers Prepare for the World of Work*. New York: Basic Books.

Cunningham, Mick. 2001. "Parental Influences on the Gendered Division of Housework." *American Sociological Review* 66:184–203.

Danziger, Kurt. 1971. *Socialization*. Baltimore, MD: Penguin.

Deacon, Terrence. 1997. *The Symbolic Species: The Co-Evolution of Language and the Brain*. New York: W. W. Norton & Company.

Deaux, Kay and Brenda Major. 2000. "A Social-Psychological Model of Gender." Pp. 81–91 in *The Gendered Society Reader*, edited by Michael Kimmel with Amy Aronson. New York: Oxford University Press.

Douglas, Mary and Steven Ney. 1998. *Missing Persons: A Critique of Personhood in the Social Sciences*. Berkeley: University of California Press.

Duham, Carroll, Frances Myers, Neil Barnden, Alan McDougall, Thomas Kelly with Barbara Aria. 1991. *Mamatoto: A Celebration of Birth*. New York: Penguin.

Frieze, Irene, Jacquelynne Parsons, Paula Johnson, Diane Ruble, and Gail Zellman. 1978. *Women and Sex Roles: A Social Psychological Perspective*. New York: W. W. Norton.

Gerth, Hans and C. Wright Mills. 1953. *Character and Social Structure: The Psychology of Social Institutions*. New York: Harcourt, Brace & World.

Goffman, Erving. 1959. *The Presentation of Self in Everyday Life*. Garden City, NY: Doubleday Anchor.

Gonzalez-Mena, Janet and Dianne Widmeyer Eyer. 1997. *Infants, Toddlers, and Caregivers*, 4th edition. Mountain View, CA: Mayfield.

Harris, Judith Rich. 1998. *The Nurture Assumption: Why Children Turn Out the Way They Do*. New York: Free Press.

Hauser, Marc. 1997. *The Evolution of Communication*. Cambridge, MA: MIT Press.

Hewitt, John. 2000. *Self and Society: A Symbolic Interactionist Social Psychology*, 8th edition. Boston: Allyn and Bacon.

Hockett, Charles and Robert Ascher. 1964. "The Human Revolution." *Current Anthropology* 5:135–68.

Kennelly, Ivy, Sabine Merz, and Judith

Lorber. 2001. "What Is Gender?" *American Sociological Review* 66:598–605.

Kimmel, Michael. 2000. *The Gendered Society*. New York: Oxford University Press.

Kugiumutzakis, Giannis. 1999. "Genesis and Development of Early Infant Mimesis to Facial and Vocal Models." Pp. 36–59 in *Imitation in Infancy*, edited by Jacqueline Nadel and George Butterworth. Cambridge, UK: Cambridge University Press.

Lever, Janet. 1978. "Sex Differences in the Complexity of Children's Play and Games." *American Sociological Review* 43:471–83.

Lieberman, Philip. 1991. *Uniquely Human: The Evolution of Speech, Thought, and Selfless Behavior*. Cambridge, MA: Harvard University Press.

Lindesmith, Alfred, Anselm Strauss, and Norman Denzin. 1999. *Social Psychology*, 8th edition. Thousand Oaks, CA: Sage.

Maccoby, Eleanor. 1998. *The Two Sexes: Growing Up Apart, Coming Together*. Cambridge, MA: Belknap Press of Harvard University Press.

Maccoby, Eleanor and Carol Jacklin. 1974. *The Psychology of Sex Differences*. Palo Alto, CA: Stanford University Press.

Macionis, John. 2001. *Sociology*, 8th edition. Annotated Instructor's Edition. Upper Saddle River, NJ: Prentice-Hall.

Martin, Karin. 1998. "Becoming a Gendered Body: Practices of Preschools." *American Sociological Review* 63:494–511.

Maynard, Douglas and Marilyn Whalen. 1995. "Language, Action, and Social Interaction." Pp. 149–75 in *Sociological Perspectives on Social Psychology*, edited by Karen Cook, Gary Alan Fine, and James House. Boston: Allyn and Bacon.

Mead, George H. 1934. *Mind, Self, and Society: From the Standpoint of a Social Behaviorist*. Chicago, IL: University of Chicago Press.

Meltzer, Bernard. 1972. "Mead's Social Psychology." Pp. 4–22 in *Symbolic Interaction: A Reader in Social Psychology*, 2nd edition, edited by Jerome Manis and Bernard Meltzer. Boston: Allyn and Bacon.

Meltzoff, Andrew and M. Keith Moore. 1977. "Imitation of Facial and Manual Gestures by Human Neonates." *Science* 198:75–8.

———. 1994. "Imitation, Memory, and the Representation of Persons." *Infant Behavior and Development* 17:83–100.

———. 1999. "Persons and Representation: Why Infant Imitation Is Important for Theories of Human Development." Pp. 9–35 in *Imitation in Infancy*, edited by Jacqueline Nadel and George Butterworth. Cambridge, UK: Cambridge University Press.

Miller, Eleanor and Carrie Yang Costello. 2001. "The Limits of Biological Determinism." *American Sociological Review* 66:592–8.

Nadel, Jacqueline and George Butterworth. 1999. "*Introduction*: Immediate Imitation Rehabilitated at Last." Pp. 1–5 in *Imitation in Infancy*, edited by Jacqueline Nadel and George Butterworth. Cambridge, UK: Cambridge University Press.

Newport, Elissa, Henry Gleitman, and Lila Gleitman. 1977. "Mother, I'd Rather Do It Myself: Some Effects and Non-Effects of Maternal Speech Style." Pp. 109–49 in *Talking to Children: Language Input and Acquisition*, edited by Catherine Snow and Charles Ferguson. Cambridge, UK: Cambridge University Press.

Piaget, Jean. 1932. *The Moral Judgment of the Child*, with the assistance of seven collaborators. Translated by Marjorie Gabain. New York: Harcourt, Brace and Company.

———. 1950. *The Psychology of Intelligence*, translated by Malcolm Piercy and D. E. Berlyne. London: Routledge and Kegan Paul.

———. 1954. *The Construction of Reality in the Child*. Translated by Margaret Cook. New York: Basic Books.

Piaget, Jean and Barbel Inhelder. 1969. *The Psychology of the Child*, translated by Helen Weaver. New York: Basic Books.

Ridley, Matt. 1999. *Genome: The Autobiogra-*

phy of a Species in 23 Chapters. New York: HarperCollins.

Rose, Arnold. 1962. "A Systematic Summary of Symbolic Interaction Theory." Pp. 3–19 in *Human Behavior and Social Processes: An Interactionist Approach*, edited by Arnold Rose. Boston: Houghton Mifflin.

Stacey, Judith and Timothy Biblarz. 2001. "(How) Does the Sexual Orientation of Parents Matter?" *American Sociological Review* 66:159–83.

Sugarman, Susan. 1987. *Piaget's Construction of the Child's Reality*. Cambridge, UK: Cambridge University Press.

Taylor, Timothy. 1996. *The Prehistory of Sex*. New York: Bantam.

Thorne, B. 1986. "Girls and Boys Together . . . But Mostly Apart: Gender Arrangements in Elementary School." Pp. 167–84 in *Relationships and Development*, edited by Willard Hartup and Z. Rubin. Hillsdale, NJ: Erlbaum.

Trevarthen, Colwyn, Theano Kokkinaki, and Geraldo Fiamenghi Jr. 1999. "What Infants' Imitations Communicate: With Mothers, with Fathers and with Peers." Pp. 127–85 in *Imitation in Infancy*, edited by Jacqueline Nadel and George Butterworth. Cambridge, UK: Cambridge University Press.

Turner, Ralph. 1962. "Role-Taking: Process versus Conformity." Pp. 20–40 in *Human Behavior and Social Processes: An Interactionist Approach*, edited by Arnold Rose. Boston: Houghton Mifflin.

van den Wijngaard, Marianne. 1997. *Reinventing the Sexes: The Biomedical Construction of Femininity and Masculinity*. Bloomington: Indiana University Press.

Vygotsky, Lev. 1978. *Mind in Society: The Development of Higher Psychological Processes*, edited by Michael Cole, Vera John-Steiner, Sylvia Scribner, and Ellen Souberman. Cambridge, MA: Harvard University Press.

———. 1986. *Thought and Language*. Cambridge, MA: The MIT Press.

West, Candace and Don Zimmerman. 2000. "Doing Gender." Pp. 131–49 in *The Gendered Society Reader*, edited by Michael Kimmel with Amy Aronson. New York: Oxford University Press.

5

Relationships in Public
(the Wider Society)

Dr. Martin Luther King, Jr., was a co-founder of the Southern Christian Leadership Conference (SCLC), an organization dedicated to the nonviolent fight against racism, prejudice, and discrimination. In April 1968, he had gone to Memphis, Tennessee, to support black garbage collectors who were out on strike. Tragically, he was shot and killed on April 4 by James Earl Ray, a white drifter and escaped convict. Ray pleaded guilty to the crime and was sentenced to ninety-nine years. (Ray died in prison.) King's final resting place is near Ebenezer Baptist Church in Atlanta, Georgia. His headstone reads: "Free at last, free at last, thank God Almighty, I'm free at last."

People across the world mourned King's passing, and they responded with both anger and anguish. One of the individuals who was powerfully effected was Jane Elliott, a third-grade teacher at Riceville Elementary School in Riceville, Iowa. It was National Brotherhood Week, and she was preparing a lesson on Native Americans for her class, thinking about the murder in Memphis. An idea came to her. She had to do something to make her students understand some of the forces that were tearing the country apart. Ms. Elliott decided to initiate an incident of discrimination herself, but what could she use? Her students were all young, all white, all Christian, all from a rural part of the country, and all from the same general socioeconomic background. She could have used their sex, because she had both boys and girls in her classroom, or some body characteristic like weight, height, or hair color. She could have simply divided the class by flipping a coin and placing the "heads" in one group and the "tails" in another. She decided, however, to use the color of the children's eyes. The blue-eyed children would be separated from the brown-eyed children. Ms. Elliott built upon the existing differentiation between blues and browns to construct a system of inequality or stratification.

The first thing that Jane Elliott did was to create an **ideology** that benefited the blues more than the browns. (Ideology is beliefs or statements that benefit one group more than others—even while they may seem fair and unbiased—thereby helping to justify and reproduce the stratified or unequal social order.) She told the class that she herself had blue eyes and so did George Washington (a claim that capitalized on the children's respect for Washington and for her). She also reminded her class of some of the failings of brown-eyed people. One young boy who refused to be convinced that brown-eyes were inferior to blue-eyes was reminded that his father, a brown-eyed man, once kicked him. Ms. Elliott told the boy that blue-eyed parents do not kick their children. She wrapped things up by telling her students that blue-eyed people are better, smarter, and more well-mannered than brown-eyed people. The ideology that she created both described and justified the specialness of blue-eyed youngsters.

While the existence of ideologies helps us to understand why some groups do better than others, the fact is, ideologies are not enough. Few people will believe for long that blue-eyed children are better than everyone else just because someone, even a well-respected authority figure, says so. Ms. Elliott knew this as well as anyone. She had to do more to make her students believe that blue-eyed individuals were best. She identified resources that were valuable to her students such as where they could sit in class (the most fun seats were in the front), how much food they could take at lunch, how long they could stay out during recess, and who could play with whom. She then gave all the "goodies" to the children with blue eyes. They were allowed to move to the front of the room; they were allowed to go to lunch first and return for seconds; they were given an extra five minutes at recess; and they were allowed to play on the schoolyard equipment. She made brown-eyed kids wear cloth collars so that everyone could recognize them from a distance, and they were told that they were not allowed to play with blue-eyed children.

What was the outcome of this teacher-imposed system of social inequality? The children were divided in ways that they had never before been divided, and some of them were receiving rewards for something that they had never before been rewarded. Within a short time—a very short time—what had been a model class turned into a collection of nasty little third-graders. Anger, name calling, fights, stereotyping, prejudice, discrimination, scapegoating, unhappiness, embarrassment—you name it—they were all common in this third-grade class. For example, two boys were fighting during recess. When Ms. Elliott asked them why fighting occurred, she was told that some boys were calling other boys a "dirty" name. When she asked what it was, she was told it was "brown-eyes." Ms. Elliott reminded her students that brown-eyed youngsters had always had brown eyes but they had never before been criticized for it. These third-graders were too young and immature to understand that the structure of inequality in their classroom was directly and powerfully affecting how they viewed each other and how they viewed themselves.

Stratified Relationships in a Stratified World

One of the most basic—and consequential—features of human relationships is that they are characterized by a great deal of stratification and inequality. We rarely, if ever, relate to others—certainly not in our more anonymous relationships in public territories—as whole persons. Our public lives are characterized by **doubly dissimilar encounters.** These are interactions between people who differ not only in regard to some nominal category like sex, race, or even eye color, but also in regard to valuable resources like money, power, and status (Ridgeway, Boyle, Kuipers, and Robinson 1998:334). Dissimilar encounters make it more likely that people in a society will incorrectly conclude that people who have a great deal of money, power, or status must be worth more than individuals who do not (Webster and Hysom 1998:356). In fact, no direct correlation exists between worth and rewards. It is very possible for occupants of some status to make significant contributions to a society (e.g., parents, firefighters, teachers) but not receive a lot of money, power, and status for their contributions. Other people may do far less and receive far more for it.

In Jane Elliott's class, the children were transformed into blues or browns and evaluated accordingly, but it is even more true in the world outside of Jane Elliott's classroom. Individuals may zero in on our sex, gender, skin color, age, or ethnicity and deal with us exclusively in terms of one of these traits. Statuses that we occupy (e.g., son, firefighter, judge) are part of what we are and how we are treated by others, some of which are **ascribed,** rather than **achieved,** and therefore largely beyond our control. The rewards that we receive and the quality of our lives are a reflection of what these statuses mean to others (Tilly 1998). What is easy to forget, but so important to remember, is that a system of stratification or inequality is thoroughly social and relational (Koggel 1998:10). Groups of people must fixate upon certain traits, categorize them, evaluate them, construct rewards and attach them to certain statuses but not to others, and pass on to others a belief system that justifies and perpetuates the whole enterprise. If groups change in what they find admirable, then the stratification system changes, too (Jasso 2001:107–8).

Understanding Social Inequality

Social stratification is a system of *positional* inequality in which rewards are attached to statuses, and anyone who occupies a particular status will receive certain rewards and lack others. Whoever is the President of the United States—male, female, black, white, brown, yellow, gay, straight, Italian, Irish—will receive certain rights and duties, along with a definite place in the hierarchy of a society. Likewise, whoever is the "village idiot" will also have rights and duties, along with a position in the stratification system. It is true that talent, hard work, and determination are required to become famous and successful in many—maybe most—human pursuits, and it would be wrong to act as if variations in individual success and failure have nothing to do with individual factors. However, we must also remember that the structure of opportunity and the way that rewards are allocated can only be thoroughly understood by examining the network of relationships that exists at a particular place and time (Knapp, Kronick, Marks, and Vosburgh 1997). We can understand some of what it takes to become a professional basketball player and what makes these athletes different from, say, social workers. However, a scrutiny of the skill and determination of basketball players on the one hand and social workers on the other is not going to tell us why one group receives multimillion dollar salaries and the other group does not.

Sociologists divide **social rewards** into three categories of privilege, power, and prestige. **Privilege** refers to money, land, or other valuables in a society. In a slave-owning society, privilege might mean the number of slaves that a plantation owner has, while in a seafaring society, privilege might include an individual's boats, fishhooks, and oars. In Jane Elliott's class, one privilege was the occupancy of the best seats in the room. **Power** refers to the ability or capacity to get what one wants when one wants it despite opposition or interference. Ms. Elliott had more power than her students because she told them when they would wear collars (and when they would do their arithmetic problems). **Prestige** refers to the degree of respect or status that occupants of a position enjoy. The prestige of blue-eyed kids rose along with increases in their privilege and power.

While the resources or rewards that are hierarchically arranged are valuable and pleasurable in their own right—privilege, power, and prestige can produce enormous pleasure, pride, and other psychological gratifications for those who have them—they are also the means for getting additional privilege, power, and prestige. Hunters may be able to capitalize on their ability to find and catch food, which increases both their power and their prestige. They might reach the point where they have a say in almost every decision that affects the life of the group. If they can pass their hunting abilities on to their offspring, then hunters' ability to hunt will allow them to experience a quality of life generation after generation that can only be dreamt of by candlemakers, chimney sweeps, and clamdiggers. This tendency for privilege, power, and prestige to cluster together is known as **status consistency,** and it is found in all societies (Lenski 1954). While stratification of some sort is universal, the specific way it is constructed is not (Salzman 1999:42). At one place and time, eye color is the most important determinant of how one is treated, while at some other place and time, hunting ability or the ability to catch fish is what matters most.

An important question—a very important question—is "Why social inequality?" In principal, it would be possible to have social differentiation without moving to the next step of social evaluation and ranking. Blue-eyed youngsters could be recognized as *different* from brown-eyed ones without treating blue-eyed kids as better than everyone else. Why reward professional wrestlers so handsomely when nurses, teachers, police officers, and firefighters are not treated as well? Theoretical explanations of inequality are many, often elaborate, and quite complicated, but we can grasp the basics by examining two contrasting views of social stratification, the structural-functional view and the conflict view. These two theories help us to see and understand things that would be impossible to see and understand without them.

Structural-Functional Theory.   **Structural-functional theory** is based on one fundamental claim: The unequal distribution of scarce resources (and the hierarchical arrangement of positions that it creates) is necessary and beneficial. Social inequality increases the chances that the best people will fill the most important positions, while it makes it more likely that people of lesser ability will discharge their responsibilities without feeling overly angry or resentful. This system of differential rewards motivates while it stabilizes, integrates, and coordinates. Abundant rewards must exist, structural-functional theory maintains, in order to get the best people in the most important positions and keep them there, faithfully discharging their duties for the betterment of society.

Davis and Moore (1945), popularizers of the structural-functional approach, proposed that two basic factors explain the system of stratification and the ranking of any position in it. The first factor is the functional importance of a position. Certain positions are more valuable and central to the lifeblood of a society—physicians, for example, or architects—and these are the positions that we must do all we can to get conscientiously occupied by the best people. The second factor is the scarcity of people to fill a particular position. Some positions require a special kind of individual with exceptional talents like drive, determination, and intelligence. High degrees of privilege, power, and prestige will go to those positions that are the most important and that also require personal abilities and individual accomplishments that are in short supply. Not just anyone has what it takes to be a judge, a physician, an astronaut, or an architect. The Davis and Moore position is a carrot-and-stick argument, with the emphasis on carrot. It helps us to understand why certain positions are ranked higher than others. It also helps us to understand why people who measure success in terms of privilege, power, and prestige might work so hard to attain a social position that promises an abundance of all three.

It is not hard to see some of the problems with the structural-functional approach. Functional importance cannot be defined objectively, separate from the way that privilege, power, and prestige are distributed. Why do professional basketball players make so much more money than the President of the United States, U.S. Supreme Court judges, physicians, or teachers? It is silly and insupportable to claim seriously that athletics is functionally more important than running the country, deciding upon the law of the land, healing the sick, or teaching the young. The prosperity of the super rich cannot really be due—or not due entirely—to their exceptional merit and outstanding contributions to U.S. society (Hacker 1997). Another problem is that good people do not always occupy the most important positions. What we see, of course, is a range of talent and dedication among people who occupy the same general type of position. Some attorneys are hard-working, intelligent, and dedicated to the law and to their clients; others, however, are little more than ambulance chasers, using the law for their own personal enrichment. Some teachers spend so much time working at school that it is amazing that anyone could labor so hard and so long for so little money; other teachers, however, keep the same materials on their bulletin boards year after year, and they are out the door at the end of the school day almost as fast as their students are. Some people take great pride in their jobs and work at them very hard regardless of what it means to them in terms of money, power, and prestige.

Conflict Theory.   A contrasting view of stratification is **conflict theory.** Conflict theorists generally agree that social inequality does more harm than good in a society. Whereas structural-functionalists see social stratification as beneficial for a society, conflict theorists see exploitation, alienation, and misery for the many and happiness for the few as the inevitable correlates of social inequality. Rather than guaranteeing that the most important positions are occupied by the best people, conflict theorists believe that inequality only guarantees that those people who are lucky or ruthless enough to get more than their share of money, power, and prestige will use these to extend their influence over a society. Conflict theorists think that while power and privilege are not necessarily earned, these valuable resources do stack the deck in favor of whoever has them. Social rewards can even be left to one's descendants, who will themselves benefit from resources that they had no hand at all in earning.

Some competition to attain scarce resources is beneficial for a society and even for the individuals who must compete for scarce resources and desired positions (as Davis and Moore claim). If we were all guaranteed both equality of opportunity and equality of outcome, why work to improve ourselves? Why stay home on the weekend to master algebra or to learn the history of the Civil War if we would do as well without it? Much like the athletic team in which many individuals train longer, try harder, and improve themselves more because they are competing for a limited number of slots, people in a society may work harder and achieve more because of the existence of social rewards that go more heavily to some positions than to others. However, conflict theorists remind us that whatever good a system of stratification does to encourage and reward merit is easily perverted. The playing field is rarely level, and fair competition easily becomes "capitalism with a vengeance" (Schur 1969:187). This is an allegiance to the values of profit, competition, and individualism that is so intense that it provides incentives and rewards for behaviors that are neither desirable nor inevitable, even in a basically capitalistic society (Coleman 2002:193). Capitalism can become too capitalistic.

Global Inequality

If it is true that people in a society are interdependent, it is true that *societies* are, too. It may be stretching a point to claim that all humans live together in a global village, but it certainly is true that what happens in one part of the world can have effects—sometimes profound ones—for people in other parts (Kogut and Walker 2001). Economic relationships among the world's societies are becoming more extensive and integrated (Bradshaw and Wallace 1996:26), and regional alliances (e.g., Organization of Petroleum Exporting Countries) are constantly being formed and reformed. The spread of market relationships throughout the world means that the language of money is becoming a universal language (Bradshaw and Wallace 1996:26). Political structures, however, continue to become more and more fragmented, and the global move is toward ethnic and racial separation and increasing levels of conflict (Bradshaw and Wallace 1996:35–6). Just as the students in Jane Elliott's class fought among themselves on the basis of eye color, so do citizens of the world fight among themselves based on the color of their skin and the content of their culture.

Modernization Theory.   One popular explanation of global inequality is called **modernization theory.** Modernization theory focuses on elements *within* a society to explain a society's state of development like the level of technology and the work ethic of its members. It holds underdeveloped countries and their citizens responsible for their low levels of development. As an explanation of global inequality, this theory is both tautological and ethnocentric. However, it does offer some concrete advice to countries that want to modernize. Underdeveloped countries must industrialize so that enough food is produced for citizens to eat, a quality education is within reach of the uneducated, and the unemployed can get the jobs that they need. These changes will eventually create a new kind of society in which deferred gratification, hard work, and punctuality will be the dominant psychological and cultural characteristics. This will then make it possible for more freedom, new civil rights, increased trade and commerce, greater democracy, and greater social equality to grow and flourish. In a nutshell, modernization theorists insist that in order to become modern, a society must develop modern institutions, modern cultures, and modern people (Bradshaw and Wallace 1996:40–4).

World-System Theory.   **World-system theory,** by contrast, does not directly blame poor countries for being poor, at least not in terms of internal institutional structures or personality traits of their citizens. World-system theorists believe that the lesson of history is that people at the top exploit people at the bottom. Modern, rich, developed countries like the United States, Japan, or the United Kingdom—called core countries—are prosperous and powerful because they have exploited and used unmercifully all that poorer countries in the periphery and semiperiphery—mostly in Latin America and Africa—have to offer (Wallerstein 1974). "The heart of the world-system theory is its explanation of the *exploitative process* that has enabled core countries to retain their wealth and power at the expense of peripheral and semiperipheral nations" (Bradshaw and Wallace 1996:45). If wealthy nations in the core are the sellers, they set the price. If they are the buyers, they still set the price (Braun 1997:142). The world climate is so supportive of international capital that it has caused a substantial shift of wealth from the poor and working classes of the world to the world's richest and most prosperous ones (Feagin 2001:2). Nations from the core have gone into semiperiphery and periphery nations in search of raw materials, a cheap and accommodating labor force, land, a stable political system, tax advantages, interest-free loans, and an unregulated market system (Cowie 1999). World-system theory blames international capitalism, the profit motive, and a nation's position in the global pecking order for its level of social development.

A bonus from world-system theory is that it casts light on a key player on the world stage, the **multinational corporation** (a company that operates in two or more countries at the same time). Multinationals have no loyalty to any country, even the ones in which these businesses are located, and they will go wherever they can to make the most money and to find the most supportive business climate (Bales 1999). This often means that deals are made—some legal and some not so legal—between corporate representatives from the core and business executives, government representatives, and military leaders in countries outside of it. Corporations do all that they can to shape the environment in whatever ways they can to maximize their chances for the accumulation of wealth and influence (Prechel 2000). The few are enriched in these noncore countries while the many continue to live their lives in abject poverty (Braun 1997:157). The objective of multinational corporations is, quite literally, to keep countries outside the core as dependent, as helpless, and as poor as possible.

Any effort by countries outside the core to become more self-reliant and independent by starting their own businesses or controlling their own economic destiny is fought by multinationals, often with the support of U.S. military power and U.S. foreign policy. While multinationals may come to an area with the promise of abundant jobs and higher wages for local laborers, the promise is always greater than the delivery. Even when some new jobs are available and wages do rise, this is only true in the short run. Dominance of a country by multinationals produces long-term financial disaster for most of its citizens.

> When firms enter countries in the periphery by opening new industrial facilities, there is an initial growth spurt. Yet long-run economic stagnation, unemployment, and increasing poverty all come in the end for the majority of the population (Braun 1997:164).

Modernization, *if* it is accomplished through foreign assistance and investment, will do little to help most of the population in nations in the periphery and semiperiphery (Alderson and Nielsen 1999:627; Jenkins and Scanlon 2001). Multinationals always take out of a country in profits more than they put into it in investments and assistance to host populations (Braun 1997:160). What penetration by multinationals does accomplish is a slowing of economic development, injury to the quality of life of most of the citizens, and increases in political instability and unrest (Bradshaw and Wallace 1996:51).

In the mid-1900s, the principal cause of global income inequality was the existence of intense differences *between* nations in their income levels. Some countries had grown richer while other countries had grown poorer. However, global income inequality changed in a fundamental way in the closing decades of the twentieth century. From 1980 to 1995, the between-nation income inequality decreased while income inequality *within* nations went up steadily (Goesling 2001:751–2). In other words, within a nation, the rich got richer and the poor got poorer, but the income inequality between nations fell. The greatest inequalities, however, still exist between nations, not within them (Goesling 2001:757).

Inequality in the United States

Inequality in the United States can be better understood by remembering that the U.S. economy is segmented or divided into parts or sectors, and people in one part do better than people in a different part. Just as some nations are in the core and some are not, so it is true that within any *particular* society certain positions are more central—and more highly rewarded—than other positions (Grodsky and Pager 2001). The **primary labor market** contains those jobs that are characterized by high pay, pleasant working conditions, chances for advancement, job security, the availability of interesting and important work, and unionization. The **secondary labor market** contains those jobs that are characterized by low pay, little mobility, poor working conditions, rapid turnover, few benefits, and no unionization. Income, mobility patterns, and quality of life of workers are directly dependent on their positions in the labor market. The advantage of spotlighting the labor market instead of workers' abilities and characteristics (or **human capital**) is that it directs attention to the relationships among a large number of people in the creation of social inequality.

The primary labor market is the locus of power and privilege in a society. Firms in this sector may in fact set their own prices and they may be largely beyond the traditional economic forces of supply and demand. This is especially true if a **shared monopoly** exists, a situation in which four or fewer firms control 50 percent or more of a particular market. So, if most of the books that you buy come from Allyn and Bacon, HarperCollins, Sage, and Prentice-Hall, then a shared monopoly exists. If most of the vehicles that drivers in the United States own come from General Motors, Ford, and Chrysler, then the automobile industry is a shared monopoly, too. It is most likely in a shared monopoly for prices to rise even while demand does not. The reason is that members of a shared monopoly are able to maximize their control over the market by controlling prices, establishing entry barriers, and producing extensive advertising. An individual's income and quality of life has a great deal to do with the segment of the economy within which he or she works (Hodson and Kaufman 1982; Hurst 1995:263). Women, minorities, and the young are disproportionately found in the secondary labor market with its poorer working conditions and lower earning power.

Social Mobility.   **Social mobility** refers to movement from one position to another by an individual, group, or even an entire society in terms of privilege, power, or prestige (or all three). As a process, social mobility includes that $.10 per hour raise or moving into a corner office with a window, the one that everyone wanted but only one was lucky enough to get. To bring some order to the chaos, sociologists use a number of terms to describe some of the patterns of social mobility that might otherwise be difficult to see and understand. **Horizontal or geographical mobility** refers to movement from one position to another with little or no increase or decrease in the levels of privilege, power, and prestige. This type is far less important than a contrasting type called **vertical mobility**. This is movement from one position to another with increases in privilege, power, or prestige (upward vertical social mobility) or decreases in these valuable resources (downward vertical social mobility). A further distinction is drawn between intragenerational social mobility and intergenerational social mobility (Marshall 1997:3). In **intragenerational social mobility,** the movement of an individual during his or her career is compared to people like him or her. An individual who wins the lottery and becomes a multimillionaire overnight has experienced intragenerational mobility. With **intergenerational social mobility,** however, the point of comparison is the movement of entire generations. If you and all your friends are doing better than your parents and all their friends, then what has occurred is upward intergenerational social mobility. In **open societies**, a lot of people are moving, both up and down, and they are achieving or losing greatly in terms of privilege, power, and prestige (Sorokin 1959). In **closed societies,** people are little different from their parents in terms of what they have or what they do.

Social mobility may refer to changes in the relative standing of communities, occupational groups, organizations, societies, or positions, and not simply the movement of some lone individual upward or downward. The gold coast might over time be transformed into a slum, and areas of quiet prosperity at one point in time become areas of grinding poverty at some other point in time. Poor nations improve their lot and once-wealthy nations no longer are. If one day having blue eyes is a good thing and the next day it is not, then what we have is a change in the relative positions of entire categories and not simply some individual "rags-to-riches" story. We must remember that a great deal of social mobility can coexist with extensive social inequality (Blau and Duncan 1967). If an individual thinks that he or she can go from rags to riches, then this individual may feel no bitterness about another's successes and be far more accepting of high levels of inequality.

Industrialized democracies are characterized by a great deal of mobility, both upward and downward. One reason is that a high premium is placed on skill, experience, and knowledge, so talented people can advance up the social ladder irrespective of their class background (Lipset and Bendix 1959). An individual's characteristics or human capital—intelligence, academic performance, drive, ambition—do play a role in his or her successes or failures and corresponding mobility patterns (Sewell, Haller, and Ohlendorf 1970). However, **structural mobility** also exists. It results from changes in the number of positions in a society (Stark 2001:243). An increase in the number of high-level positions will, of course, produce some structural mobility in the upward direction, just as decreases in the number of high-level positions, coupled with increases in the number of low-level positions, will produce structural mobility in the downward direction. No matter how brilliant, hard-working, or talented individuals are, only nine of them will become U.S. Supreme Court judges at any one time because nine are all there are. It would be possible to create some structural mobility by expanding the number from nine to, say, twelve, but this will have a negligible impact on the well-being and quality of life of most people. Economic growth in the United States may still lead more often to jobs at Kentucky Fried Chicken, McDonald's, and Pizza Hut than at IBM or Exxon (Schwarz 1997).

Durable Inequalities. It certainly is possible to accumulate abundant re-sources by inventing a better mousetrap, cornering the market on old mouse-traps, working hard at a high-paying job, making sound investments, or luck. However, a substantial amount of wealth is handed on from generation to generation. If you want to maximize the chances that you will be rich, the thing to do is to be born into a wealthy family (Collins and Yeskel 2000:60). The offspring of the truly wealthy find that the deck is already stacked in their favor (Lucas 2001). They benefit directly from the abundant resources that they have access to and will one day inherit; they also benefit because life in the lap of luxury makes it easier for them to develop the kinds of outlooks, temperaments, relationships, and skills to get the kinds of jobs when the time comes to continue to receive high incomes and enviable lifestyles (Braun 1997:31).

One of the more important lessons high-status parents teach their children is the importance of getting a good education (Korenman and Winship 2000:154–62; Lucas 2001). Most research does show that additional years of schooling do increase one's earnings (Ashenfelter and Rouse 2000:99). The mastery of new skills or improvement on cognitive tests, how-ever, is only part of what schooling does and only part of the reason that edu-cation and income are positively related. Schooling also contributes to the development of incentive-enhancing preferences, preferences that employers find of great value and are willing to pay for and reward. Honesty, an identifi-cation with a firm's objectives and interests, selflessness, and a future rather than present orientation are all examples of incentive-enhancing preferences that employers find in short supply and look for in their workers (Bowles and Gintis 2000:125). Intelligence and mental ability are important in producing success at school (Herrnstein and Murray 1994), it is true, but so are other things. Parents' income, parents' occupational status, encouragements for aca-demic success from teachers and parents, and the scholastic accomplishments and goals of peers all play a role in one's school success and patterns of social mobility (Hauser, Warren, Huang, and Carter 2000:225).

A study of social mobility among individuals with a working-class back-ground who entered the upper-middle class world of the university to work as professional sociologists and college professors identified the principal reasons for their upward movement (Grimes and Morris 1997). They were smart and dedicated students in their early educational years, and they were encouraged and supported by their parents and their teachers for their academic accomplishments and successes. Their parents taught them to respect hard work, and they learned to work hard at whatever they did, school included (Grimes and Morris 1997:61). They were also able to take advantage of the expanding opportunities to enter a college or university to get the education and training that they needed to move upward; at some other time they might not have been so fortunate (Grimes and Morris 1997:81–101). Individuals who are born into a family with parents who teach the value of hard work and who encourage their offspring to "reach for the stars" are likely to find that they have learned what it takes to get ahead. Family background, a family's economic resources, and the interactions and encouragements that are found between parents and their offspring all do affect offsprings' mobility patterns, educational advancements, and occupational successes (Mare and Tzeng 1987:2; Mare and Tzeng 1989:112).

One social change that has important implications for mobility patterns is that more and more children are being raised by *grandparents*, usually the grandmother, and in a substantial minority of cases, the grandmother is doing it without assistance from the biological parents (Giarrusso, Silverstein, and Bengston 2001:257). "Between the years 1980 to 1990, the number of children in the United States living with their grandparents or other relatives increased by 44 percent, and in a third of these homes, no parent was present" (Cox 2000:3). These grandparent-headed households are more likely than other types of family units to be receiving public assistance, to be poor, and to lack health insurance (Cox 2000:4). This means that the grandparents may find it difficult to give abundant *economic* resources to their dependent children; however, they may very well be able to offer a cornucopia of emotional support, encouragement, and moral direction. As grandparents become central figures in the upbringing of grandchildren, the grandparents' role in social mobility will become far more important (Thomson, Minkler, and Driver 2000:22).

Social mobility—up or down—can produce many difficulties and contradictions for individuals who leave one socioeconomic class and move into another, one for which they are generally unprepared in terms of skills, temperaments, and general resources. Having money—even a great deal of it—is not the only requirement for entry into the upper levels of a society, and having only money does not guarantee a satisfactory adjustment to a new position. Socially mobile individuals may be caught in a kind of middle ground between their class of origin and their class of destination, feeling alienated and a part of neither (Grimes and Morris 1997:18).

The Dangers of Inequality.   In the last quarter of the twentieth century, family income grew at the top of the income distribution and fell at the bottom. In other words, the income of the "haves" went up while the income of the "have nots" stagnated or fell (Danziger and Reed 2000:2). Even the bona fide economic recovery of the 1990s—a recovery that produced the lowest unemployment and inflation rates in thirty years and elevated living standards across the United States—had a negligible impact on reducing family income inequality (U.S. Census Bureau 1999:xv). The earning power of males is the single largest component of family income. From 1979 to 1997, male workers at the top of the income distribution earned more and more, while male workers at the median and below earned less and less. What was true for men, was also true for women: ". . . the college/non-college wage gap among adults aged 25 to 64 is at least as high among women as among men in both full-time and combined part-time/full-time samples" (McCall 2000:251). Highly skilled, experienced, and educated workers are making real wage gains and those without skills, experience, and education are making real wage losses. Increases in global competition, an abundance of immigrant labor, the disappearance of labor unions, and the use of temporary workers are factors that have hit the hardest on workers at the low end of the income distribution (Gustafsson and Johansson 1999). Divorces, separations, and births out of marriage have increased the number of single-parent households, which tend to have lower incomes than households with more than one earner. The tendency for men and women with high earnings (and earning power) to marry each other, thereby increasing the prosperity of a particular household even more, further widens the gap between low-income and high-income households (Weinberg 1996).

The economic prosperity of the late 1990s in the United States did not produce good times for all, and the divide between the very wealthy and everyone else is growing dangerously wide.

> Inequality has grown, with the rising tide lifting up only the yachts while the smaller boats rock in the wake. Unlike the post-World War II years, when economic growth was shared more equitably, there has been a dramatic pulling apart in the last twenty years between the small number of haves and everybody else (Collins and Yeskel 2000:7).

A growing number of individuals in the middle class are experiencing increased feelings of insecurity and vulnerability as they find that the cost of living is rising much faster than their incomes. Many people are working very hard, but they are facing growing economic uncertainty (Collins and Yeskel 2000:4; Shirk, Bennett, and Aber 1999; Tropman 1998). Not only are their paychecks buying less and less, they live without health insurance, retirement benefits, and job security. Health care costs are spiraling upward, as are the costs of a college education. A power shift has occurred in the United States. The power of big corporations and wealthy families has increased dramatically (Keister 2000), while countervailing forces like unions and political parties have become less influential in social life. The rich get richer while the poor sink further and further away.

A thriving economy, sustained over a long period of time, is an absolute must if social inequality is to be reduced. Workers' skill and motivation certainly matter, as do governmental regulations regarding affirmative action, discrimination, and sexual harassment, but without successful and sustained growth, little else will do much good (Bluestone and Harrison 2000). Rising productivity makes it possible for business firms to increase profits without increasing prices, and as stocks soar in value, inflation drops (Bluestone and Harrison 2000:17). Sustained and equitable growth should be our objective, not the creation of economic and political systems that make it possible for those who have so much to continue to enrich themselves so handsomely (Collins and Yeskel 2000:9). Inequality can be reduced through policies that encourage full employment, the growth of the manufacturing sector, widespread unionization, increases in the minimum wage, abundant educational opportunities, and containment of the adverse effects of globalization.

The Gendered Society

Gender is the constellation of traits and characteristics that members of a society use to identify masculinity and femininity. Gender differences between males and females are less biologically determined than they are socially constructed, and most gender differences are actually an *effect* of a society's system of gender inequality, not a cause (Kimmel 2000:xi; Ridgeway and Correll 2000:110). For example, more males than females have jobs in engineering and the physical sciences. A common explanation for this disparity is that males are just better at mathematics, a crucial requirement for admission to jobs in engineering and science. However, gender differences in math ability are small and getting smaller all the time. What is actually happening is that shared beliefs about both gender and mathematics encourage both males and females to search for different kinds of careers, leading to the underrepresentation of females in math-based professions (Correll 2001:1695). Gender is continually and actively constructed and reconstructed, defined and redefined, in our encounters with other gendered individuals; gender is what we *do* in our encounters with others, not something that we have (Kimmel 2000:106).

Each individual has some control over his or her gender identity, but each individual must construct it in a **gendered society** that is pervaded by complex and socially based understandings about what it means to be masculine or feminine. Males and females share far more similarities than they do differences, and they are closer to each other than either of them is to anything else like trees, mountains, or kangaroos (Rubin 1975:179). This similarity may be difficult to recognize, because none of us lives in a gender-neutral social world. Families, schools, political parties, workplaces, churches, synagogues, and play groups are themselves gendered to a greater or lesser degree, so each of us becomes gendered in a preexistent gendered society (Kimmel 2000:16). Once gender differences are constructed and institutionalized, they become expected and easier to see as natural, essential, or biological. These social constructions of difference, then, are used to reinforce the belief in the essential nature of gender differences in the first place (West and Zimmerman 2000:139–40). Gender differences actually blunt our awareness of all the natural *similarities* that exist between the sexes (Rubin 1975:180).

Women's status in the United States has gone up during the last 150 years, and greater equality now exists between the sexes than ever before (Crompton 1999; Jackson 1998; McCammon, Campbell, Granberg, and Mowery 2001:53). However, gender is almost always an important factor in social relationships. Its presence can influence people's activities in a variety of ways even when it is not supposed to be the focus of attention (Ridgeway and Correll 2000:112). This is apparent in the gender segregation that exists in the world of work and in the differences in salaries between "male" and "female" jobs, especially in large organizations (Nelson and Bridges 1999). Women may be overlooked for central positions in the upper levels of an organization. If they cannot be excluded completely, they may still find their upward movement slowed as they are kept in menial positions for long periods. Women may reach a certain occupational level, but then they can go no higher no matter what they do. They may have all the skill and determination that they need, but they still do not reach the top because they bump into a **glass ceiling,** which is as impenetrable as it is hidden (Lorber 2000:272–8). Women may be viewed as only suited for certain kinds of jobs like those dealing with health, education, and welfare (Lorber 2000:271) and denied access to a countless number of other jobs that are considered inappropriate for them.

At one time, employed women would quit their jobs to give birth to their children and raise them. Nowadays, more and more young mothers continue to work, either doing the best they can to manage the jobs they held before they gave birth or taking part-time jobs (Stier, Lewin-Epstein, and Braun 2001). Women dominate the temporary work force, and temporary employment is usually defined as "women's work." A principal justification for the segregation of women in the temporary work force is that they actually benefit from it because they can coordinate more easily their family responsibilities with the demands of work. However, temporary work is not particularly flexible—temps must still accommodate to their bosses—and the belief that women benefit from it may be nothing more than a way to justify the low pay and lack of benefits that temps receive (Rogers 2000).

Women may be channeled into the **mommy track,** a career track that is supposed to make it easier for them to manage family responsibilities while accepting lower pay and restricted opportunities for advancement. Discriminating against employed women or female job applicants because they are married, pregnant, or parents is illegal in the United States, but this does not mean that discrimination against women with children and family responsibilities has disappeared (Lorber 2000:278–80). When women can only take jobs that will allow them to manage family responsibilities and the demands of young children, they must forego the higher pay, faster promotion, and better benefits of jobs *outside* the mommy track (Adams and Tancred 2000). A "wage penalty" does seem to exist in which pay is lower for working women with children, and each and every child that a woman has lowers her pay even more (Budig and England 2001). While some of the wage penalty is caused by women being tracked into less demanding or mother-friendly jobs, most of it is not. Of far greater importance are the fewer years of experience of women who take time off from work to raise a family, employer discrimination against working women, and the lowered productivity of working mothers because they are tired or distracted (Budig and England 2001:213–9).

If women are at a disadvantage in professions and occupations that are considered inappropriate for them, the same is not true for men. While women in nontraditional professions may bump against the glass ceiling or get channeled into the mommy track, men in nontraditional professions (e.g., nursing, social work, elementary school teaching, or librarianship) actually benefit from the existence of a **glass escalator** that propels them to the top (Williams 2000). While some men may refuse to enter nontraditional professions in the first place, fearing that they may be the target of derisive comments or the butt of jokes, those men who do take the chance often find that their careers are helped by their gender. They are regularly given fair, if not preferential, treatment in hiring and promotion decisions (Williams 2000:305–7).

Race and Ethnicity Matters

As important as gender is for understanding the prevailing systems of inequality, it cannot be separated from other dimensions of stratification like race, class, ethnicity, age, and the like. For the sake of simplicity, we might speak of the influence of gender or race, but individuals do not relate to others, or even to themselves, only in terms of their gender *or* their race *or* their class (Cotter, Hermsen, and Vanneman 1999:434). Analysis of just one of these dimensions, taken out of context, simplifies and distorts the real-world experiences of real individuals. Individuals may be rewarded for having a constellation of socially desirable traits, just as they may be punished for having a constellation of socially devalued traits. For example, African American and Hispanic women are discriminated against for being both female and nonwhite; Asian women, however, are not as penalized for the color of their skin (Cotter, Hermsen, and Vanneman 1999).

Racism is a complex system of difference and domination with many dimensions to it (e.g., institutionalized norms, racist humor, cultural symbols, patterns of interaction). Central to it, however, are the institutionalized practices and routinized understandings that keep nonwhites out of those positions that offer the greatest amount of privilege, power, and prestige (Memmi 2000:32–8). The racist system has less to do with the color of an individual's skin than it does with the economic, political, cultural, and social structures within which people of different skin colors relate to one another. It was not really eye color that accounted for the happenings in Jane Elliott's class, even though that is how it might have looked. Eye color was really just part of a system of rules, relationships, and rewards that led to difference and domination. Ethnicity and race are important factors in the construction of human relationships in most societies and especially in the patterns of inequality (Bean and Bell-Rose 1999; Petersen 1997). **Ethnicity** is a socially created category that lumps people together because of the presumption they share a cultural heritage or ancestry. **Race** is a socially created category that lumps people together because of the presumption that they have inherited similar biological traits or physical characteristics like skin color or shape of the eyes.

A German named Johann Blumenbach developed the first typology of race in the 1700s. He believed that light-skinned individuals were biologically superior to all other races, so whites were placed at the top of his typology. This ranking of white Europeans at the top and Asians, Africans, and other non-Europeans lower in the hierarchy appeared so natural to him that it was beyond dispute (Johnson, Rush, and Feagin 2000:96–7). This blueprint of race was an important lever in whites' domination of nonwhites, and it continues even today to keep groups separate (Gilroy 2000). "This hierarchical scheme was primarily a means to legitimate European systems of slavery and colonization, where skin color was accepted as a marker for one's location in the 'natural' order" (Johnson, Rush, and Feagin 2000:97). This hierarchy came to have far more social power than it deserved in the formation of relationships between people with different skin colors, physical appearances (hair texture, nose shape, eye shape), and cultural traditions (Rodriguez 2000).

Stereotyping (an image of an entire category of individuals that is negative and inaccurate) of racial and ethnic groups is pervasive, and prejudice and discrimination are facts of life for minority groups in the United States. Members of some groups will hold **prejudices** (attitudes of dislike or contempt) against members of other groups and even engage in acts of **discrimination** (acts based on arbitrary criteria like sex or race that interfere with the ability of members of some group to participate fully and fairly in a society). Stereotyping, prejudice, and discrimination affect police activities, employment opportunities, educational successes, health care, and routine interactions between members of subordinate and superordinate groups in public territories. However, social meanings of race and ethnicity change all the time. For example, Italians and the Irish were once viewed as inferior by white Americans because of their skin color. As the Italians and the Irish assimilated to U.S. society and became more powerful, they became "whiter" in the eyes of white Americans, and they were far less likely to be discriminated against because of skin color (Johnson, Rush, and Feagin 2000:97). Humans are actually shades of one color—brown—and racial hierarchies were constructed primarily to make human oneness more difficult to identify (Johnson, Rush, and Feagin 2000:107).

The Social Reality of Crime and Deviance

The tendency to differentiate individuals and then to arrange those recognized differences into a hierarchical arrangement leads to a further—and important—social construction called social deviance. (**Social deviance** is usually defined as departure from a norm that produces interpersonal or group reactions designed to discourage any further rule breaking.) In a highly stratified society, some individuals will conclude that it is okay for them to look out only for themselves, which can make them fully prepared to hurt, kill, rape, rob, or steal from others, or to destroy what other people have if they see some benefit in it. Property crimes can be committed as a response to social inequalities (Beattie 1995:120), but so can violent crimes like robbery, rape, assault, and murder. In an institutionalized system of difference and domination, it is likely, if not inevitable, that self-interest, greed, and egocentricity will proliferate, sentiments that are not conducive to high levels of social solidarity or to compassion and concern for others. Social stratification also encourages some groups to label the behaviors, attributes, or beliefs of other groups as unacceptable, improper, or dangerous. Naming, defining, and stigmatizing are significant events in the social construction of deviance and crime (Becker 1963); "normal" and "stigmatized" are not persons as much as they are perspectives on persons (Goffman 1963:138). We must pay close attention both to social forces that construct action in the first place and then to those evaluations and judgments of action that transform social differences into deviance and crime.

Crime, Deviance, and Inequality

Social inequality that is glaring and based on factors like race or ethnicity over which people have little control is the kind most likely to cause acts of violence (Blau and Blau 1982:119). Judith and Peter Blau's (1982) analysis of metropolitan structure and violent crime was one of the first to establish a direct link between economic conditions in the United States and levels of violent crime. They concluded that high rates of murder, forcible rape, robbery, and aggravated assault were the "cost" we pay for maintaining social inequality. Social inequality created enduring conflicts, which led to high rates of predatory violence (Blau and Blau 1982:117). The feelings of frustration and resentment experienced by people who can see others with great riches that they themselves know they can never get can lead to criminal violence (Fox and Levin 2001:21–3).

> Brutal conditions breed brutal behavior. To believe otherwise requires us to argue that the experience of being confined to the mean and precarious depths of the American economy has *no* serious consequences for personal character or social behavior. But this not only misreads the evidence; it also trivializes the genuine social disaster wrought by the extremes of economic inequality we have tolerated in the United States (Currie 1985:160).

You cannot have secure and orderly communities if you also have an economic system that condemns some people to misery and degradation while visibly enriching others (Currie 1989:18). The experience of being humiliated or shamed is a powerful stimulus to human violence (Gilligan 1996:223).

Constructions of Violence

Violence is a term that is used to refer to a range of acts, some intentional and some not, that cause physical harm to others (Chasin 1997:4). One form of violence is **interpersonal violence.** An identifiable person (or persons) intentionally kills, maims, rapes, or in some way harms another (or others). Even when violence does not lead to a loss of life and limb, it can still be injurious by causing depression, suicidal thoughts, and apathy among its victims (Hagan and Foster 2001). Sometimes violence is little more than a form of **wilding,** in which the perpetrators hurt and destroy others because they think it is fun. Those who are responsible for wilding violence usually display a smugness about their terrible crimes, and they experience no remorse over them (Derber 2002:2–3). Some violence is little more than a response to a pervasive sense of boredom and idleness (Levin and Fox 2001:18). Another type of violence is more structural. **Structural violence** results from the routine operations of parts of a society, but particularly its system of stratification (Chasin 1997:4). Structural violence is found whenever people are injured or killed by lack of opportunity and a scarcity of necessary resources. Structural forms of violence may be deadlier than all forms of interpersonal violence taken together, and poverty may be the deadliest form of all (Gilligan 1996:191–208).

The United States is organized in such a way that the damage done by the powerful to the powerless is concealed or explained away, but the damage done by the powerless to everyone else is exaggerated (Box 1983:5; Shelden 2001). The term **offensible space** (Hagan and Peterson 1995:27) refers to an area in which the police see threats around every corner—real or imagined—and they actively initiate investigations of suspicious activities or directly confront suspicious citizens. The more time individuals must spend in offensible space, the more visible to police they and their activities are, and the greater the chances that they will be stopped or even arrested. This selective enforcement sends out the message that the worst threats to our collective and individual well-being come from lone, ruthless predators, while it offers a convenient scapegoat to blame for some of our social problems. What this does is to blunt our awareness of the pervasiveness of structural violence, and it serves to legitimate and reproduce the status quo with all its dangers and disparities in privilege, power, prestige, and opportunity (Reiman 2001:4).

It is true that interpersonal violence is a real threat, and we should all be thankful when the number of murders, rapes, assaults, and robberies goes down. However, we do not want to allow ourselves to be bamboozled into thinking that the kinds of criminals and crimes that our criminal justice system deals with are necessarily the greatest threats to our collective and individual well-being.

> I argue . . . that the failure to reduce crime substantially broadcasts a potent *ideological* message to the American people, a message that benefits and protects the powerful and privileged in our society by legitimating the present social order with its disparities of wealth and privilege and by diverting public discontent and opposition away from the rich and powerful and onto the poor and powerless (Reiman 2001:5).

The fear of crime and criminals, reasonable in so many ways, can still be played upon and manipulated in order to justify the expansion of the criminal justice system and the increased surveillance and control of powerless individuals (Chambliss 2000). Some individuals can do what they want and get away with it, free from harassment and control, while other individuals certainly cannot (Box 1983:6).

Violence has a social reality that is constituted in a fundamental way by the claims that are made about it. We must understand how acts and events are defined as violence in the first place and separated from other things, things that may be as harmful and destructive.

> . . . we define a social act as violent when we recognize and understand it as an attempt by one or more people to force their dominance over others. The question is who holds the lenses to the action so that its reflection appears to us as violent (Brownstein 2000:168).

Definitions of major forms of deviance tend to develop and grow in specific locations or arenas in a society like mass media, government, legal organizations, medicine, and religious institutions (Hilgartner and Bosk 1988). These definitions (and claims based on them) tell us how much violence there is, where it is found, who the victims and victimizers are, and what we must do to protect ourselves from it (Brownstein 2000; Cerulo 1998). Some new crimes are identified and worried about only for a while (e.g., freeway violence), while others are far more enduring and become part of the standard discourse about what plagues us (e.g., stalking or shootings in schools).

New crimes are likely to endure as permanent features of the social landscape when they become the object of concern of the **iron quadrangle,** a constellation of (1) experts, (2) the government, (3) political activists, and (4) media representatives. These four sectors or arenas can mutually reinforce each other's interest in the promotion of new crimes (Best 1999). This may lead to the creation of a **moral panic,** where fears and reactions are exaggerated out of all proportion to the degree of the threat (Cohen 1972). A moral panic is characterized by a pervasive sense of dread, coupled with a strong feeling of righteousness and the determination to do something, often of a punitive nature, to make things right (Goode and Ben-Yehuda 1994:31–2; Thompson 1998). No human action, even a dangerous one, occurs in a social vacuum, and moral panics are always a product of many things in addition to the presence of a dangerous act (Burns and Crawford 1999:156–8). A moral panic is most likely to evolve and develop when antagonists (e.g., conservatives and liberals) put aside their differences and work together to create a quick consensus on what is most troubling and how to deal with it most effectively (Jenkins 1998).

Whether something gets defined as a type of crime or deviance in public arenas is related to general selection principles like the level of competition between different public arenas, the scarcity of their resources (money, time, and compassion), the need for drama and novelty in public arenas, the dangers of saturation, cultural preoccupations with certain themes or problems, and the political climate (Hilgartner and Bosk 1988:58–66). In general, the more central an arena is (in terms of the size of its audience or the number of its resources), the greater the pressure for it to carry the newest, hottest, or trendiest type of social deviance. Unless the carrying capacity of public arenas is expanding for some reason, the rise of one issue will be associated with the fall or at least neglect of others. The less trendy deviance is up for grabs, and other people in less central arenas may take advantage of it for a while. They may "own" the issue and be able to tell other people what must be done about it to make things right (Gusfield 1981). A troubling condition becomes a social problem at the point that people think something can be done about it and a public problem when they expect a government to control or correct it (Burstein and Bricher 1997).

Crime and Legitimacy

Social changes in the United States have periodically created a crisis in institutional legitimacy that spilled over into the production of crime waves. Legitimacy of social institutions is a rough indicator of how respected conventional society is and how well members of a society follow rules and submit to demands of authority figures (LaFree 1998:6). To the extent that most of the people most of the time view institutional norms as legitimate and reasonable, then most people will follow them without much thought or consideration. Widespread agreement exists that rules are morally right and politically just. However, when the legitimacy of institutions declines, proper behavior does not occur automatically and people may feel freer to avoid the institutional prompts and break the rules. "In short, as the hold institutions have over individuals declines, institutional effectiveness in controlling crime is correspondingly weakened" (LaFree 1998:78).

Violence exists in crime-prone communities partly because of the erosion of central institutions in these areas (Levine and Rosich 1996:15–6), which lowers the **collective efficacy** of community residents (Sampson and Raudenbush 1999:612–3). When collective efficacy is high, it makes it more likely that members of a community will support one another and work together to maintain order in public spaces, factors that decrease the rates of violent crime (DeLeon-Granados 1999; Gould 1999; Sampson and Raudenbush 1999:624). People who live in places characterized by disorder and disadvantage—especially if they feel powerless to control the forces that are affecting them—tend to have high levels of mistrust and low levels of neighborhood cohesion and interdependence (Ross, Mirowsky, and Pribesh 2001:571–3).

Violent crime went down in the United States in the 1990s, and this was a most welcome occurrence. Lives were saved and injuries avoided (Currie 1999:4). However, some misunderstanding exists in regard to the reasons for the drop. The decade of the 1980s was a period in the United States of "getting tough" on crime. A concerted effort was initiated by politicians, police agencies, and the prison establishment to legitimate and then implement extensive prison terms, especially for drug crimes, increased police patrol, and the punishment rather than the rehabilitation of criminals (Mauer 1999). The only criminal justice policies that had much hope of garnering enough support to become official policy were those that seemed punitive enough to get rid of the threat of violent crime (Gest 2001:41–62). The "get-tough" approach of the 1980s probably did have some impact on bringing crime down in the 1990s (Blumstein and Wallman 2000; Currie 1999). However, too much credit has been given to tougher policing and harsher prison sentences and too little to the deeper institutional forces that played a far greater role in reducing the levels of violence (Currie 1998a; Currie 1999). The most important factor was the extraordinary economic boom in the United States in the last decade of the twentieth century. This caused unemployment to drop and pulled people into the labor force who would otherwise have never gotten the opportunity. They developed a stake in conformity, directed their energies toward more lawful pursuits, and stayed away from criminogenic settings and involved themselves more completely in the world of work (Currie 1999:13).

The worst of the violence has passed, at least for awhile. However, the United States still has higher rates of violent crime than other developed nations (Hagan 1994:23), high rates of imprisonment by international standards, and longer prison sentences for those who are caught and convicted than do most other industrialized nations (Walker 2001). Two different worlds exist in regard to predatory violence: the world of U.S. minority poor and the world of everyone else (Currie 1998b). Racial differences in violent death are so large that they parallel the influence of gender (males kill and are killed more than females) and of age (teenagers and young adults are more likely to kill and be killed than are the middle-aged or the elderly). The death and injury in minority neighborhoods from violence has not decreased appreciably even though more and more minority men, especially those with black skin, and increasingly more minority women (largely because of their involvement in drug crimes), are being put behind bars (Currie 1998b:103). Economic prosperity in the United States has not been shared equally by all Americans, and this affects powerfully U.S. patterns of violent crime (The Milton S. Eisenhower Foundation 1999:10). Poverty is endemic in the United States, and it is deeper, blacker, and browner than it has ever been before, and more concentrated in the cities (Harris 1998:18; Harris and Curtis 1998:2).

Conclusions

This chapter examined some of the social dimensions of our more public relationships. Interactions with others, especially strangers in public territories, are characterized by extensive social divisions that are translated into social evaluations and stark inequalities. These inequalities characterize the relationships between different countries of the world, as well as each and every country in the world. Modernization theory explains the position of a particular society in the global system of stratification in terms of characteristics of that particular nation; world-system theory looks at the exploitative relationships between core countries and those outside of the core. The structural-functional view of stratification explains hierarchical arrangements in terms of the functional importance of positions and the scarcity of qualified people to fill them. An opposed view, conflict theory, looks more at the struggle between groups with different amounts of privilege, power, and prestige in determining who has resources and who does not.

The interests and resources of multinational corporations are central features in understanding global inequality, as well as patterns of upward and downward social mobility for us all. Nations are not totally powerless when confronting the power and influence of multinationals, and citizens acting together can influence *up to a point* economic policies and practices in their countries (Doremus, Kelley, Pauly, and Reich 1998; Starr 2000; Weiss 1998). Even members of a powerful monopoly can be threatened by competition from new businesses with better goods and services or more effective or slicker advertising campaigns (Baker, Faulkner, and Fisher 1998:173).

The United States is characterized by a dual-labor market. It is split into a primary labor market, which contains the best jobs in terms of pay and promotion, and a secondary labor market, which contains those jobs characterized by low pay and poor working conditions. Income, mobility patterns, and quality of life of workers are directly dependent on their position in the labor market. Industrialized democracies are characterized by a great deal of mobility, both upward and downward. One reason is that a high premium is placed on skill, experience, and knowledge, so talented people can advance up the social ladder irrespective of their class background (Lipset and Bendix 1959). An individual's characteristics or human capital—intelligence, academic performance, drive, ambition—do play a role in his or her successes or failures and corresponding mobility patterns (Sewell, Haller, and Ohlendorf 1970). However, structural mobility also exists. It results from changes in the number of positions in a society (Stark 2001:243). Ascriptive forces operate to affect patterns of mobility, and an individual's gender, race, and ethnicity work together to determine how he or she is treated by others.

Social differentiation and social inequality spill over into the social construction of crime and deviance. In a stratified society, some individuals are encouraged to commit violent acts, and other individuals are encouraged to dramatize these dangerous acts and brand them as more harmful than they really are. The United States is organized in such a way that the damage done by the powerful to the powerless is concealed or explained away, but the damage done by the powerless to everyone else is exaggerated. The fear of crime and criminals is used to justify the expansion of the criminal justice system and the increased surveillance and control of some groups by other groups. Some groups can do what they want and get away with it, while other groups cannot.

The declines in U.S. violence in the 1990s were real, and lives were saved. However, a misunderstanding of the reason for the decrease exists. Too much credit has been given to tougher policing and harsher prison sentences and too little to the deeper institutional forces that played a far greater role in what happened. The most important factor was the extraordinary economic boom in the United States in the last decade of the twentieth century. This caused unemployment to drop and pulled people into the labor force who would otherwise have never gotten the opportunity. However, poverty is still endemic in the United States and concentrated in the cities. Two different worlds exist in regard to predatory violence, the world of U.S. minority poor and the world of everyone else. Racial differences in violent death are so large that they parallel the influence of gender and of age.

Chapter Five at a Glance

- Differentiation and domination are basic features of human relationships.
- Humans live in stratified societies in a stratified world; some positions are ranked higher than other positions and rewarded with greater amounts of privilege, power, and prestige.
- A degree of social stratification is both necessary and beneficial; differential distribution of scarce resources motivates people to do their best and rewards them for their contributions.

- Social inequality can easily become a problem when groups of people use their possession of privilege, power, and prestige to increase their control even more of these valuable resources.
- Relationships between societies around the world are becoming more extensive, and the increase in interdependence means that inequality is a global phenomenon.
- Modernization theory explains a society's position in the global pecking order, along with its degree of social development, in terms of that society's institutional structure, technological sophistication, and cultural values and norms.
- World-system theory explains a society's position in the global pecking order, along with its degree of social development, in terms of its relationship to other societies, especially its position as either exploited or exploiting.
- U.S. society is divided into the primary labor market, which contains most of the good jobs, and the secondary labor market, which contains most of the bad jobs.
- Social mobility is extensive in an open society like the United States as lone individuals, occupations, groups, or communities shift positions.
- Social inequality in a society—especially if it becomes extensive and persistent—has a destructive impact on the fabric of life in a society.
- Humans construct categories of gender, race, and ethnicity along which they divide themselves, producing social differentiation and stratification.
- Some individuals experience upward social mobility because they are on a glass escalator, while others stay near the bottom because they hit a glass ceiling (or are on a mommy track).
- Difference and domination lead to the construction of social deviance, in which people break the rules that other people have created.
- Secure and orderly communities are difficult to maintain in an economic system that condemns some people to misery and degradation while visibly enriching others.
- Violence may be either interpersonal or structural, but both forms are more likely in a highly stratified society.
- Crime and deviance are likely to become permanent features of a social landscape when certain troubling conditions become the object of concern of the iron quadrangle, a constellation of (1) experts, (2) the government, (3) political activists, and (4) media representatives. These four sectors mutually reinforce each other's interest in finding new crimes and acts of deviance to worry about and in creating moral panics.
- A crisis in institutions and a loss of legitimacy, especially among disadvantaged minority communities in the United States, is an important factor that produces increases in rates of crime and deviance.

Glossary

achieved status   a position that an individual occupies voluntarily and that is possible to change (e.g., occupation)

ascribed status a position that an individual occupies that is practically impossible to change (e.g., race or sex)

closed societies   characterized by little or no social mobility

collective efficacy   a sense of potency and purpose that gives community members the confidence to work together to combat violent crime in their neighborhoods; people can stop crime—at least up to a point—by forming cohesive, interdependent neighborhoods

conflict theory   it views stratification as a generally unfair distribution of scarce resources that is created by the privileged and powerful in order to benefit themselves (and their descendants)

discrimination   an action based on arbitrary criteria like sex or race that interferes with the ability of members of some group or category to compete fairly and fully with others

doubly dissimilar encounters   interactions between people who differ not only in regard to some nominal category like sex, race, or occupation but also in regard to scarce resources like money, property, or power

ethnicity   a socially created category of humans that considers its members to be and act alike because of a shared ancestry or cultural heritage

gender   characteristics that members of a society use to identify masculinity and femininity; the psychological and social attributes of maleness and femaleness

gendered society   a society in which social rewards are distributed unequally based on gender

glass ceiling   an invisible but still fixed barrier that exists to keep certain people (or certain *kinds* of people) from moving up too far in the stratification system of an organization or society

glass escalator   a career track that quietly and effectively moves certain people

(or certain *kinds* of people) rapidly up the job ladder or organizational hierarchy

horizontal or geographical mobility   movement from one position to another with no corresponding change in one's possession of social rewards of privilege, power, or prestige

human capital   an explanation for upward or downward mobility exclusively in terms of an individual's attributes and abilities

ideology   beliefs or statements that benefit one group more than others and help to justify and reproduce systems of stratification or inequality

interpersonal violence   an individual (or individuals) intentionally kills, maims, rapes, or in some way harms another individual (or individuals)

intergenerational social mobility   social movement of individuals as compared to previous generations, especially to their parents

intragenerational social mobility   social movement in an individual's life as compared to the movement of his or her peers

iron quadrangle   a constellation of (1) experts, (2) the government, (3) political activists, and (4) media representatives that, taken together, mutually reinforce each other's interest in finding new crimes and acts of deviance to worry about

modernization theory   it explains the level of development in a country by characteristics of that country like level of technology and cultural and psychological characteristics of its members

mommy track   a career track that allows women to manage family responsibilities and the demands of young children while they accept lower rewards and different kinds of job responsibilities and opportunities

moral panic   artificially created wave of concern over public issues; characterized by a pervasive sense of dread, coupled with a strong feeling of righteousness and the determination to do something, often of a punitive nature, to make things right

multinational corporation a company that operates in two or more countries at the same time

offensible space an area in which police have a heavy presence and are constantly on the alert to the possibility of deviance and crime

open societies characterized a great deal of vertical social mobility

power the social reward received by occupants of some social position that allows them to get what they want despite opposition from others

prejudice an attitude of dislike or contempt for members of some group

prestige the social reward of high status or respect

primary labor market those jobs that are characterized by high pay, pleasant working conditions, chances for advancement, job security, and unionization

privilege the social reward of income, wealth, or property

race a socially created category of humans based on the premise that its members are all alike because of inherited physical characteristics like skin color, profile of the nose, hair texture, or shape of the eyes

racism enduring systems of prejudice and discrimination based on race; the belief that one race is innately inferior (or superior) to all other races

secondary labor market those jobs that are characterized by low pay, poor working conditions, rapid turnover, and no unionization

shared monopoly four or fewer firms control 50 percent or more of a market

social deviance a departure from a norm that produces social reactions designed to stop the rule breaking

social mobility an individual's move-ment from one social position to another; fluctuations in the relative standings of entire groups or categories

social rewards privilege (money or property), power, and prestige

social stratification a hierarchical arrangement of positions in which positions at the top receive greater social rewards than those at the bottom

status consistency individuals are high (or low) on all three dimensions of inequality (privilege, power, and prestige)

stereotyping a cultural image of an entire category, race, ethnicity, sex, or gender that is negative and inaccurate

structural-functional theory a view that depicts stratification as necessary and beneficial, ensuring that the most important positions will be occupied by the most talented and dedicated individuals

structural mobility upward or downward movement that is produced by changes in the number of available positions at the top and/or bottom

structural violence injury or death to individuals because they lack opportunities or necessary resources, produced principally by the injustices of that society's system of stratification

vertical mobility movement from one position to another with a corresponding change in one's possession of social rewards of privilege, power, or prestige

wilding an individual (or individuals) hurts or even kills another (or others) because he or she thinks it is fun and exciting; use of violence to relieve a pervasive sense of boredom and restlessness

world-system theory a view of global inequality that focuses on the exploitative process by which some countries have amassed great wealth and power at the expense of other countries

References

Adams, Annemarie and Peta Tancred. 2000. *"Designing Women": Gender and the Architectural Profession.* Toronto: University of Toronto Press.

Alderson, Arthur and Francois Nielsen. 1999. "Income Inequality, Development, and Dependence: A Reconsideration." *American Sociological Review* 64:606–31.

Ashenfelter, Orley and Cecilia Rouse. 2000. "Schooling, Intelligence, and Income in America." Pp. 89–117 in *Meritocracy and Economic Inequality*, edited by Kenneth Arrow, Samuel Bowles, and Steven Durlauf. Princeton, NJ: Princeton University Press.

Baker, Wayne, Robert Faulkner, and Gene Fisher. 1998. "Hazards of the Market: The Continuity and Dissolution of Interorganizational Market Relationships." *American Sociological Review* 63:147–77.

Bales, Kevin. 1999. *Disposable People: New Slavery in the Global Economy.* Berkeley: University of California Press.

Bean, Frank and Stephanie Bell-Rose, editors. 1999. *Immigration and Opportunity: Race, Ethnicity, and Employment.* New York: Russell Sage Foundation.

Beattie, John. 1995. "Crime and Inequality in Eighteenth-Century London." Pp. 116–39 in *Crime and Inequality*, edited by John Hagan and Ruth Peterson. Stanford, CA: Stanford University Press.

Becker, Howard. 1963. *Outsiders: Studies in the Sociology of Deviance.* New York: Free Press.

Best, Joel. 1999. *Random Violence: How We Talk about New Crimes and New Victims.* Berkeley: University of California Press.

Blau, Judith and Peter Blau. 1982. "The Cost of Inequality: Metropolitan Structure and Violent Crime." *American Sociological Review* 47:114–29.

Blau, Peter and Otis Dudley Duncan. 1967. *The American Occupational Structure.* New York: Wiley.

Bluestone, Barry and Bennett Harrison. 2000. *Growing Prosperity: The Battle for Growth with Equity in the Twenty-First Century.* Boston: Houghton Mifflin.

Blumstein, Alfred and Joel Wallman, editors. 2000. *The Crime Drop in America.* New York: Cambridge University Press.

Bowles, Samuel and Herbert Gintis. 2000. "Does Schooling Raise Earnings by Making People Smarter?" Pp. 118–36 in *Meritocracy and Economic Inequality*, edited by Kenneth Arrow, Samuel Bowles, and Steven Durlauf. Princeton, NJ: Princeton University Press.

Box, Steven. 1983. *Power, Crime, and Mystification.* London: Tavistock.

Bradshaw, York and Michael Wallace. 1996. *Global Inequalities.* Thousand Oaks, CA: Pine Forge.

Braun, Denny. 1997. *The Rich Get Richer: The Rise of Income Inequality in the United States and the World*, 2nd edition. Chicago, IL: Nelson-Hall.

Brownstein, Henry. 2000. *The Social Reality of Violence and Violent Crime.* Boston: Allyn and Bacon.

Budig, Michelle and Paula England. 2001. "The Wage Penalty for Motherhood." *American Sociological Review* 66:204–25.

Burns, Ronald and Charles Crawford. 1999. "School Shootings, the Media, and Public Fear: Ingredients for a Moral Panic." *Crime, Law & Social Change* 32:147–68.

Burstein, Paul and Marie Bricher. 1997. "Problem Definition and Public Policy: Congressional Committees Confront Work, Family, and Gender, 1945–1990." *Social Forces* 76:135–68.

Cerulo, Karen. 1998. *Deciphering Violence: The Cognitive Structure of Right and Wrong.* New York: Routledge.

Chambliss, William. 2000. *Power, Politics, and Crime.* Boulder, CO: Westview Press.

Chasin, Barbara. 1997. *Inequality and Violence in the United States.* Atlantic Highlands, NJ: Humanities Press.

Cohen, Stanley. 1972. *Folk Devils and Moral Panics: The Creation of the Mods and Rockers*. London: MacGibbon and Kee.

Coleman, James William. 2002. *The Criminal Elite: Understanding White-Collar Crime*, 5th edition. New York: Worth.

Collins, Chuck and Felice Yeskel with United for a Fair Economy. 2000. *Economic Apartheid in America: A Primer on Economic Inequality and Insecurity*. New York: The New Press.

Correll, Shelley. 2001. "Gender and the Career Choice Process: The Role of Biased Self-Assessments." *American Journal of Sociology* 106:1691–730.

Cotter, David, Joan Hermsen, and Reeve Vanneman. 1999. "Systems of Gender, Race, and Class Inequality: Multilevel Analyses." *Social Forces* 72:433–60.

Cowie, Jefferson. 1999. *Capital Moves: RCA's Seventy-Year Quest for Cheap Labor*. Ithaca, NY: Cornell University Press.

Cox, Carole. 2000. "Why Grandchildren Are Going to and Staying at Grandmother's House and What Happens When They Get There." Pp. 3–19 in *To Grandmother's House We Go and Stay: Perspectives on Custodial Grandparents*, edited by Carole Cox. New York: Springer.

Crompton, Rosemary, editor. 1999. *Restructuring Gender Relations and Employment: The Decline of the Male Breadwinner*. New York: Oxford University Press.

Crompton, Rosemary and John Scott. 2000. "Introduction: The State of Class Analysis." Pp. 1–15 in *Renewing Class Analysis*, edited by Rosemary Crompton, Fiona Devine, Mike Savage, and John Scott. Oxford, UK: Blackwell.

Currie, Elliott. 1985. *Confronting Crime: An American Challenge*. New York: Pantheon.

———. 1989. "Confronting Crime: Looking Toward the Twenty-First Century." *Justice Quarterly* 6:5–25.

———. 1998a. *Crime and Punishment in America*. New York: Metropolitan Books, Henry Holt and Company.

———. 1998b. "Race, Violence, & Justice since Kerner." Pp. 95–115 in *Locked in the Poorhouse: Cities, Race, and Poverty in the United States*, edited by Fred Harris

and Lynn Curtis. Lanham, MD: Rowman and Littlefield.

———. 1999. "Reflections on Crime and Criminology at the Millennium." *Western Criminology Review* 2(1). [Online]. Available: http://wcr.sonoma.edu/v2n1/currie.html.

Danziger, Sheldon and Deborah Reed. 2000. "Winners and Losers: The Era of Inequality Continues." *Foresight* 7:1–4.

Davis, Kingsley and Wilbert Moore. 1945. "Some Principles of Stratification." *American Sociological Review* 10:242–49.

DeLeon-Granados, William. 1999. *Travels Through Crime and Place: Community Building as Crime Control*. Boston: Northeastern University Press.

Derber, Charles. 2002. *The Wilding of America: Greed, Violence and the New American Dream*, 2nd edition. New York: Worth.

Doremus, Paul, William Kelley, Louis Pauly, and Simon Reich. 1998. *The Myth of the Global Corporation*. Princeton, NJ: Princeton University Press.

Feagin, Joe. 2001. "Social Justice and Sociology: Agendas for the Twenty-First Century." *American Sociological Review* 66:1–20.

Fox, James Alan and Jack Levin. 2001. *The Will to Kill: Making Sense of Senseless Murder*. Boston: Allyn and Bacon.

Gest, Ted. *Crime and Politics: Big Government's Erratic Campaign for Law and Order*. New York: Oxford University Press.

Giarrusso, Roseann, Marril Silverstein, and Vern Bengston. 2001. "How the Grandparent Role Is Changing." Pp. 253–61 in *Seeing Ourselves*, 5th edition, edited by John Macionis and Nijole Benokraitis. Upper Saddle River, NJ: Prentice-Hall.

Gilligan, James. 1996. *Violence: Reflections on a National Epidemic*. New York: Vintage.

Gilroy, Paul. 2000. *Against Race: Imagining Political Culture Beyond the Color Line*. Cambridge, MA: Belknap Press of Harvard University Press.

Goesling, Brian. 2001. "Changing Income Inequalities within and between Nations: New Evidence." *American Sociological Review* 66:745–61.

Goffman, Erving. 1963. *Stigma: Notes on the Management of Spoiled Identity.* Englewood Cliffs, NJ: Prentice-Hall.

Goode, Erich and Nachman Ben-Yehuda. 1994. *Moral Panics: The Social Construction of Deviance.* Oxford, UK: Blackwell.

Gould, Roger. 1999. "Collective Violence and Group Solidarity: Evidence from a Feuding Society." *American Sociological Review* 64:356–80.

Grimes, Michael and Joan Morris. 1997. *Caught in the Middle: Contradictions in the Lives of Sociologists from Working-Class Backgrounds.* Westport, CT: Praeger.

Grodsky, Eric and Devah Pager. 2001. "The Structure of Disadvantage: Individual and Occupational Determinants of the Black-White Wage Gap." *American Sociological Review* 66:542–67.

Gusfield, Joseph. 1981. *The Culture of Public Problems.* Chicago, IL: University of Chicago Press.

Gustafsson, Björn and Mats Johansson. 1999. "In Search of Smoking Guns: What Makes Income Inequality Vary over Time in Different Countries?" *American Sociological Review* 64:585–605.

Hacker, Andrew. 1997. *Money: Who Has How Much and Why.* New York: Scribners.

Hagan, John. 1994. *Crime and Disrepute.* Thousand Oaks, CA: Pine Forge.

Hagan, John and Holly Foster. 2001. "Youth Violence and the End of Adolescence." *American Sociological Review* 66:874–99.

Hagan, John and Ruth Peterson. 1995. "Criminal Inequality in America: *Patterns and Consequences.*" Pp. 14–36 in *Crime and Inequality,* edited by John Hagan and Ruth Peterson. Stanford, CA: Stanford University Press.

Harris, Fred. 1998. "The Kerner Report Thirty Years Later." Pp. 7–19 in *Locked in the Poorhouse: Cities, Race, and Poverty in the United States,* edited by Fred Harris and Lynn Curtis. Lanham, MD: Rowman and Littlefield.

Harris, Fred and Lynn Curtis, editors. 1998. "Introduction." Pp. 1–5 in *Locked in the Poorhouse: Cities, Race, and Poverty in the United States,* edited by Fred Harris and

Lynn Curtis. Lanham, MD: Rowman and Littlefield.

Hauser, Robert, John Warren, Min-Hsiung Huang, and Wendy Carter. 2000. "Occupational Status, Education, and Social Mobility in the Meritocracy." Pp. 179–229 in *Meritocracy and Economic Inequality,* edited by Kenneth Arrow, Samuel Bowles, and Steven Durlauf. Princeton, NJ: Princeton University Press.

Herrnstein, Richard and Charles Murray. 1994. *The Bell Curve: Intelligence and Class Structure in American Life.* New York: Free Press.

Hilgartner, Stephen and Charles Bosk. 1988. "The Rise and Fall of Social Problems: A Public Arena Model." *American Journal of Sociology* 94:53–78.

Hodson, Randy and Robert Kaufman. 1982. "Economic Dualism: A Critical Review." *American Sociological Review* 47:727–39.

Hurst, Charles. 1995. *Social Inequality,* 2nd edition. Boston: Allyn and Bacon.

Jackson, Robert Max. 1998. *Destined for Equality: The Inevitable Rise of Women's Status.* Cambridge, MA: Harvard University Press.

Jasso, Guillermina. 2001. "Studying Status: An Integrated Framework." *American Sociological Review* 66:96–124.

Jenkins, J. Craig and Stephen Scanlan. 2001. "Food Security in Less Developed Countries, 1970–1990." *American Sociological Review* 66:718–44.

Jenkins, Philip. 1998. *Moral Panic: Changing Concepts of the Child Molester in Modern American.* New Have, CT: Yale University Press.

Johnson, Jacqueline, Sharon Rush, and Joe Feagin. 2000. "Doing Anti-Racism: Toward an Egalitarian American Society." *Contemporary Sociology* 29:95–110.

Keister, Lisa. 2000. *Wealth in America: Trends in Wealth Inequality.* New York: Cambridge University Press.

Kimmel, Michael. 2000. *The Gendered Society.* New York: Oxford University Press.

Knapp, Peter, Jane Kronick, William Marks, and Miriam Vosburgh. 1997. *The Assault on Equality.* Westport, CT: Praeger.

Koggel, Christine. 1998. *Perspectives on Equality: Constructing a Relational Theory.* Lanham, MD: Rowman & Littlefield.

Kogut, Bruce and Gordon Walker. 2001. "The Small World of Germany and the Durability of National Networks." *American Sociological Review* 66:317–35.

Korenman, Sanders and Christopher Winship. 2000. Pp. 137–78 in *Meritocracy and Economic Inequality*, edited by Kenneth Arrow, Samuel Bowles, and Steven Durlauf. Princeton, NJ: Princeton University Press.

LaFree, Gary. 1998. *Losing Legitimacy: Street Crime and the Decline of Social Institutions in America.* Boulder, CO: Westview.

Lenski, Gerhard. 1954. "Status Crystallization: A Nonvertical Dimension of Social Status." *American Sociological Review* 19:405–13.

Levin, Jack and James Alan Fox. 2001. *Dead Lines: Essays in Murder and Mayhem.* Boston: Allyn and Bacon.

Levine, Felice and Katherine Rosich. 1996. *Social Causes of Violence: Crafting a Science Agenda.* Washington, DC: American Sociological Association.

Lipset, Seymour Martin and Reinhard Bendix. 1959. *Social Mobility in Industrial Society.* Berkeley, CA: University of California Press.

Lorber, Judith. 2000. "Guarding the Gates: The Micropolitics of Gender." Pp. 270–94 in *The Gendered Society Reader*, edited by Michael Kimmel with Amy Aronson. New York: Oxford University Press.

Lucas, Samuel. 2001. "Effectively Maintained Inequality: Education Transitions, Track Mobility, and Social Background Effects." *American Journal of Sociology* 106:1642–90.

Mare, Robert and Meei-Shenn Tzeng. 1987. *Father's Ages and the Social Stratification of Sons.* CDE Working Paper 87–36. University of Wisconsin-Madison: Center for Demography and Ecology.

———. 1989. "Fathers' Ages and the Social Stratification of Sons." *American Journal of Sociology* 95:108–31.

Marshall, Gordon. 1997. *Repositioning Class: Social Inequality in Industrial Societies.* Thousand Oaks, CA: Sage.

Mauer, Marc. 1999. *Race to Incarcerate.* New York: New Press.

McCall, Leslie. 2000. "Gender and the New Inequality: Explaining the College/Non-College Wage Gap." *American Sociological Review* 65:234–55.

McCammon, Holly, Karen Campbell, Ellen Granberg, and Christine Mowery. 2001. "How Movements Win: Gendered Opportunity Structures and U.S. Women's Suffrage Movements, 1866 to 1919." *American Sociological Review* 66:49–70.

Memmi, Albert. 2000. *Racism*, translated by Steve Martinot. Minneapolis, MN: University of Minnesota Press.

The Milton S. Eisenhower Foundation. 1999. *To Establish Justice, to Insure Domestic Tranquility: A Thirty Year Update of The National Commission on the Causes and Prevention of Violence.* Washington, DC: Author.

Nelson, Robert and William Bridges. 1999. *Legalizing Gender Equality: Courts, Markets, and Unequal Pay for Women in America.* New York: Cambridge University Press.

Petersen, William. 1997. *Ethnicity Counts.* New Brunswick, NJ: Transaction Publishers.

Prechel, Harland. 2000. *Big Business and the State: Historical Transitions and Corporate Transformation, 1880s–1990s.* Albany: State University of New York Press.

Reiman, Jeffrey. 2001. *The Rich Get Richer and the Poor Get Prison: Ideology, Class, and Criminal Justice*, 6th edition. Boston: Allyn and Bacon.

Ridgeway, Cecilia, Elizabeth Heger Boyle, Kathy Kuipers, and Dawn Robinson. 1998. "How Do Status Beliefs Develop? The Role of Resources and Interactional Experience." *American Sociological Review* 63:331–50.

Ridgeway, Cecilia and Shelley Correll. 2000. "Limiting Inequality through Interaction: The End(s) of Gender." *Contemporary Sociology* 29:110–20.

Rodriguez, Clara. 2000. *Changing Race: Latinos, the Census, and the History of Ethnicity in the United States.* New York: New York University Press.

Rogers, Jackie Krasas. 2000. *Temps: The*

Many Faces of the Changing Workplace. Ithaca, NY: Cornell University Press.

Ross, Catherine, John Mirowsky, and Shana Pribesh. 2001. "Powerlessness and the Amplification of Threat: Neighborhood Disadvantage, Disorder, and Mistrust." *American Sociological Review* 66:568–91.

Rubin, Gayle. 1975. "The Traffic in Women: Notes on the 'Political Economy' of Sex." Pp. 157–210 in *Toward an Anthropology of Women*, edited by Rayna Reiter. New York: Monthly Review Press.

Salzman, Philip Carl. 1999. "Is Inequality Universal?" *Current Anthropology* 40:31–44.

Sampson, Robert and Stephen Raudenbush. 1999. "Systematic Social Observation of Public Spaces: A New Look at Disorder in Urban Neighborhoods." *American Journal of Sociology* 105:603–51.

Schur, Edwin. 1969. *Our Criminal Society.* Englewood Cliffs, NJ: Prentice-Hall.

Schwarz, John. 1997. *Illusions of Opportunity: The American Dream in Question.* New York: Norton.

Sewell, William, Archibald Haller, and George Ohlendorf. 1970. "The Educational and Early Occupational Status Attainment Process: Replication and Revision." *American Sociological Review* 35:1014–27.

Shelden, Randall. 2001. *Controlling the Dangerous Classes: A Critical Introduction to the History of Criminal Justice.* Boston: Allyn and Bacon.

Shirk, Martha, Neil Bennett, and J. Lawrence Aber. 1999. *Lives on the Line: American Families and the Struggle to Make Ends Meet.* Boulder, CO: Westview Press.

Sorokin, Pitirim. 1959. *Social and Cultural Mobility.* New York: Free Press.

Stark, Rodney. 2001. *Sociology: Internet Edition*, 8th edition. Belmont, CA: Wadsworth.

Starr, Amory. 2000. *Naming the Enemy: Anti-Corporate Movements Confront Globalization.* New York: St. Martin's Press.

Stier, Haya, Noah Lewin-Epstein, and Michael Braun. 2001. "Welfare Regimes, Family Supportive Policies, and Women's Employment along the Life-Course." *American Journal of Sociology* 106:1731–60.

Thompson, Kenneth. 1998. *Moral Panics.* New York: Routledge.

Thomson, Esme Fuller, Meredith Minkler, and Diane Driver. 2000. "A Profile of Grandparents Raising Grandchildren in the United States." Pp. 21–33 in *To Grandmother's House We Go and Stay: Perspectives on Custodial Grandparents*, edited by Carole Cox. New York: Springer.

Tilly, Charles. 1998. *Durable Inequality.* Berkeley: University of California Press.

Tropman, John. 1998. *Does America Hate the Poor? The Other American Dilemma.* Westport, CT: Praeger.

U.S. Census Bureau. 1999. Current Population Reports, P60-206. *Money Income in the United States: 1998.* Washington, DC: USGPO.

Walker, Samuel. 2001. *Sense and Nonsense about Crime and Drugs*, 5th edition. Belmont, CA: Wadsworth.

Wallerstein, Immanuel. 1974. *The Modern World System.* New York: Academic Press.

Webster, Jr., Murray and Stuart Hysom. 1998. "Creating Status Characteristics." *American Sociological Review* 63:351–78.

Weinberg, Daniel. 1996. "A Brief Look at Postwar U.S. Income Inequality." *Current Population Reports* P60-191:1–4.

Weiss, Linda. 1998. *The Myth of the Powerless State.* Ithaca, NY: Cornell University Press.

West, Candace and Don Zimmerman. 2000. "Doing Gender." Pp. 131–49 in *The Gendered Society Reader*, edited by Michael Kimmel with Amy Aronson. New York: Oxford University Press.

Williams, Christine. 2000. "The Glass Escalator: Hidden Advantages for Men in the 'Female' Professions." Pp. 294–310 in *The Gendered Society Reader*, edited by Michael Kimmel with Amy Aronson. New York: Oxford University Press.

The Private Realm

On September 19, 1991, just around high noon, two hikers (Helmut and Erika Simon) came upon a body that was partially encased in a glacier in Austria's Ötztal Alps, near the Italian border. The only part of the body that was visible was its face-down torso. The head was hairless, as were the shoulders and upper back. The skin was brown, and the body was shriveled. The find was unusual but not without precedent. The Alpine glaciers had been melting, and the summer of 1991 had produced some extreme thawing. Five other bodies had already been discovered in the glaciers of Austria, and the Simons assumed that what they had found was simply one more victim of a recent accident. However, things were not as they seemed, and the Simons and the rest of the world were in for a very big surprise.

The corpse in the ice—a male—had been there much longer than anyone originally thought or could even imagine; it was certainly *not* a victim of a recent accident. Nine sets of radiocarbon datings were eventually completed on the body. They agreed closely enough to be confident that the date of the man's death was 3300 B.C.E. (Before Christian Era), making the corpse found in the ice over 5,000 years old! While he has an official name of Hauslabjoch Man (Fowler 2000:70), he is usually referred to by his nickname of Iceman or Ötzi (Fowler 2000:58). He went on display in the South Tyrol Museum of Archaeology on March 28, 1998, and more than 250,000 visitors have passed by the special chamber built for him and wondered about his life, his times, and his death.

Who was this man and what was he doing so high in the Alps on the day he died? Why was he exposing himself to such danger? Maybe he was a hunter (he carried a bow and arrows with him). Maybe he was a prospector; prehistoric people were searching for ore deposits at the time he lived (Fowler 2000:42). He might have been a herder who spent the summer months up in the mountains, watching over his goats or sheep (Fowler 2000:111). Maybe Ötzi was visiting a lady friend in a neighboring valley (Fowler 2000:42). Maybe he was an outlaw, and he was forced to leave his camp with little time to gather weapons, food, or protective gear (Adler, Mueller, and Laufer 2001:61). Perhaps Ötzi's village was the target of a bloody massacre during which he was wounded, but he was able to get to the high country where he died (Fowler 2000:188–94). An arrowhead was embedded in his back.

This astounding tale of the Iceman took an even more bizarre turn. The rumor started that his scrotum contained viable sperm, and a number of Austrian women tried to get permission to be inseminated artificially so they could have Ötzi's baby (Taylor 1996:3). Even gay men staked out a claim on the Iceman. A Viennese gay magazine (*Lambda Nachrichten*) claimed that sperm were found in Ötzi's rectum, proving beyond dispute that he was the first known passive homosexual man (Taylor 1996:15). In actuality, no sperm were found in Ötzi's rectum because the rectum itself has never been discovered; it was destroyed during an early attempt to extract the body from the ice by unskilled excavators (Taylor 1996:15).

In death, the Iceman has many tales to tell; it was hardly less true when he was alive. What kind of man was he? Was he married? Did he have children or grandchildren? Was he conservative? Did he worry about how others—perhaps members of his family—would get along without him after he died? What would he think about his celebrity status all these years later? So many questions with so few answers! One thing is certain. It is always risky to put together an individual's story by looking only at what he or she owns or his or her physical characteristics. An individual's inner experience—thoughts, feelings, remembrances—is a crucial part of him or her (and therefore of *understanding* him or her), and inner experience cannot be isolated from social relationships. What makes each of us "tick" are the relationships to others that each of us has and how these connections mold and shape us. The public and the private, the wider society and personal experience, interpenetrate each other in countless ways. Interpersonal relationships influence powerfully our individual perceptions, thoughts, feelings, and remembrances. Changing relationships always produce changes in our inner experiences, and these inner experiences, in turn, continually affect our relationships to others.

Public and Private Interconnections

The industrialization and urbanization of U.S. life encouraged a separation of family life and the world of work. Two separate, and in certain ways mutually exclusive, spheres developed, the public and the private. The public sphere became the site of competition, self-interest, and an unemotional approach to the world (Oliker 1998:23). The private sphere became the site of emotionality, generosity, and spiritual/moral goodness. When in public, it was acceptable to be ruthless and calculating, but things were supposed to be different at home. The private sphere existed as a haven in a heartless world, and men and women were expected to develop relationships with one another that were characterized by love and caring. "Companionate ideals, holding that husbands and wives should be intimate best friends, replaced older marriage ideals that emphasized patriarchal authority and wifely deference" (Oliker 1998:25). While women may have become more economically dependent on men, men became more emotionally dependent on women (Oliker 1998:26). Marriage came to be defined more and more as the legitimate site for total commitment and as *the* relationship within which self-disclosure and personal fulfillment could be achieved (Giddens 1992).

One of the significant social changes in the United States has been the emergence of the **dual-earner family,** in which both partners must work at a paid job (Newman 2002:209–11). The dual-earner family is particularly susceptible to what Hochschild (1997) calls a **time bind,** in which the demands of work and the demands of home are difficult to reconcile. More and more, a home is really not a place to relax and unwind from a hard day at the office. The home is just one more workplace, a workplace where one is neither paid in tangible rewards nor recognized or appreciated for all the contributions one makes to the house and its operation. Individuals may return home after a day at work to change children's diapers, do laundry, fix meals, drive the family shuttle bus, answer the phone, cut the grass, wash the cars, balance the checkbook, and help children with their homework, all without receiving much gratitude. Home is no longer a haven in a heartless world, and work is no longer simply an alienating job. Work is a place to escape *to* rather than escape from, a place where troubles at home can be discussed with sympathetic or even caring others.

> In this new model of family and work life, a tired parent flees a world of unre-solved quarrels and unwashed laundry for the reliable orderliness, harmony, and managed cheer of work. The emotional magnets beneath home and work-place are in the process of being reversed (Hochschild 1997:44).

As stresses and demands of home become increasingly difficult to manage, work becomes the principal site of identity, interaction, and inspiration. Sim-ply, for many people, home has become work and work has become home.

We all perform **emotion work** in which we manage our hearts and our emotional displays for the benefit of others, some of whom we care about and whom we want to feel a particular way (Hochschild 1983). We may try our darnedest to produce the kind of feeling that we think we should have (and that the situation demands), while suppressing uncalled for or unwanted feel-ings. Guests at a boring party may show more excitement than they actually feel out of consideration for the host and/or hostess, and mourners at a funeral may act more depressed than they actually feel out of respect for the deceased (Hochschild 1983:18). It is also true, however, that emotion work is a central part of the marketplace and a commodity that can be bought and sold, used to achieve other objectives that are high on the corporate agenda (Hochschild 1983:14). More and more, whatever native capacity we have to manage our emotional expression is being engineered and harnessed by organizations to accomplish their objectives (Hochschild 1983:20). **Feeling rules** transform private emotions into the products of exchange and manipulation (Hochschild 1983:20). We know—or at least suspect—that the early morning follow-up call of concern from the dentist's office is part of the show and service, some-thing that every patient receives right along with the bill.

The family is often considered a "relief zone" away from the emotional demands of work, a place where one is free to be one's self. It may indeed be a refuge from the emotion work of the workplace, but it quietly imposes emo-tional obligations of its own. The more intimate the relationship, the greater the demand for emotion work, even though individuals may be unaware of all the emotion work that they actually do (Hochschild 1983:68–9). Moments of inappropriate feeling or recurring interpersonal conflicts may often be the re-sult of misunderstandings about exactly what emotion is required and how much of it is owed to family members. A husband, for example, may privately feel that he should receive more thanks for his work around the house than he gets from his wife, even though he is stingy with the gratitude that he gives her for all that she does (Hochschild 1983:78–9). The commercialization of feelings in public territories may spill over into our more private relationships, and we may manipulate our emotions to get what we want from other family members (Hochschild 1983:160–1).

The Friendship Trip

Friendships are an important part of what makes us human, and friendships, of course, are important social relationships. Friendships can help individuals manage the stresses and strains of the wider society, just as they can sometimes make life in the wider society more difficult (Allan and Adams 1998:188–9). A fight with a friend or the termination of an important relationship can have enduring effects on the thoughts and feelings of the individuals involved. In some cases, the memories linger on and on, and details of the relationship are played out mentally again and again. Friendships may be as important now as they have ever been, and friends are fulfilling the functions that once were filled entirely by family members (Pahl 2000). However, the expectations and meanings of friendship have changed. Friendships are enmeshed in a cultural complex of self-interest and personal introspection (Oliker 1998:20–1).

Our choice of friends and decisions about how close to get to them may be more thoroughly under our control than at any other time in history (Allan 1998:84). Nonetheless, friendships are still shaped by the constraints of time, place, and the intricacies of interaction (Adams and Allan 1998:11–2). That special someone might never have come into your life if you had not gone on that blind date; if you had enrolled in a different college, your friendships would have been different from what they are now. A summer romance is different from a long-term relationship at college, and arranged marriages may lack the elements found among those marriages that are more voluntary. As the social context changes, so will the relationships that are dependent upon it (Adams and Allan 1998:5–10).

Children's friendships are directly influenced by the nature of their parents' relationships to them, to each other, and to people outside the family. Marital discord and divorce in a home weaken children's emotional ties to their quarreling parents and produce psychological problems in the children that can persist into adulthood (Amato and Sobolewski 2001:910–4).

> . . . children from families in which parents have insecure attachment styles, discordant marital relations, enmeshed parent-child relations, and/or no adult friendships are less likely to participate in friendships (Doyle and Markiewicz 1996:122).

A child's first relationships are almost always with adults, but relationships with other children become more commonplace as a child gets older (Hartup 1996:216–7; Howes 1996:69). Friends exert a mutual influence on each other, and they seem to get more alike the more they are together (Newcomb and Bagwell 1996:305). This is true whether the change is negative (e.g., delinquency, smoking, drinking, disinterest in school) or positive (e.g., holding jobs, success at school, plans to attend college). Friendship networks mark social boundaries in a world of change, and these informal ties are an important way to establish and sustain personal identities (Allan and Adams 1998:193; Laursen 1996).

Some individuals invest a great deal of time in forming relationships in formal organizations and community settings. These people go to church meetings, belong to civic organizations and clubs, work on community projects, and follow politics. These are the *machers* or movers and shakers of public life (Putnam 2000:93–4). Other people have very active social lives, but their involvement is more spontaneous and flexible, less public than private. These individuals go to (or host) dinner parties, play cards with friends, talk to people on the phone, e-mail, spend time in bars and restaurants, visit relatives, and send greeting cards. They are the *schmoozers* (Putnam 2000:94). While it is certainly possible for an individual to be connected *both* formally and informally—*machers* can be *schmoozers* and vice versa—many people are active in only one of these two spheres, and many people are active in neither (Putnam 2000:94).

Individuals in the United States are connected to other people, formally and/or informally, and we have a fairly high level of voluntary association membership (Schofer and Fourcade-Gourinchas 2001). However, we do seem to be more loosely connected nowadays than we once were, and we are connecting less and less (Putnam 2000:98; Vela-McConnell 1999; Wuthnow 1998). Visiting friends or entertaining them in our homes is going the way of other endangered species, and the speed of the decline in this social activity in the recent past has been extraordinary (Putnam 2000:100). We do not break bread with family members as often as we once did, either. The number of family members who still eat an evening meal together has been decreasing, and all forms of family togetherness have become less common (e.g., family vacations, watching television together, attending church together, sitting around talking together), suggesting either a loss of, or a change in, family connections and friendships (Putnam 2000:101).

> We spend less time in conversation over meals, we exchange visits less often, we engage less often in leisure activities that encourage casual social interaction, we spend more time watching (admittedly, some of it in the presence of others) and less time doing. We know our neighbors less well, and we see old friends less often (Putnam 2000:115).

Putnam notes that even when we bowl—and more of us are bowling than ever before—we tend to do it alone or with a loose network of others rather than with an organized team. *League* bowling is becoming a thing of the past (Putnam 2000:112–3). (For an analysis of Putnam's claims about changing relationships, see Edwards and Foley 2001; Etzioni 2001; Wilson 2001.) One major exception remains in this move toward a weakening of social ties. When it comes to joining religious associations or churches, we in the United

States rank exceptionally high in our level of participation (Curtis, Baer, and Grabb 2001).

The Social Organization of Inner Experience

Social Lenses and Selective Perception

How we perceive things reflects how things are perceived by others and how others think things should and should not be perceived (Zerubavel 1997:23). What we see, smell, hear, taste, and touch is filtered through social lenses that make it possible for us to differentiate and respond to some things, while ignoring many other things (Zerubavel 1997:24). Perception is dependent on two basic processes: (1) **lumping** and (2) **splitting** (Zerubavel 1991:21). People, objects, situations, and experiences that are believed to be alike in some way must be lumped together into a single perceptual cluster, and then this cluster must be split from other clusters. Red roses, yellow daisies, and pink tulips are all lumped together in the cluster called "flowers," even though they are of different sizes, colors, and shapes, just as St. Bernards and Chihuahuas are both called dogs, even though they look different in many ways. Splitting occurs when dogs are separated from flowers, and animals and flowers are split from billiard balls, teacups, and knitting needles. It is easy to miss the arbitrary and conventional nature of lumping and splitting, especially if we had no hand in the construction of these perceptual clusters in the first place. These distinctions seem to be natural facts that we can neither ignore nor wish away (Zerubavel 1991:32). In actuality, however, they could be unmade just as easily as they were made (Zerubavel 1991:74).

While some of our perceiving is completely idiosyncratic, on the one hand, or a reflection of what we are as humans, on the other, the bulk of our perceiving reflects our social positions and social relationships. Socialization is in large part a process of learning a particular family's, community's, or society's distinctive systems of perception and classification, that is, the preferred methods of lumping and splitting (Zerubavel 1991:77). These lenses tell us what to attend to and what to ignore and overlook.

> The proverbial Martian cannot see the mental partitions separating Catholics from Protestants, classical from popular music, or the funny from the crude. Like the contours of constellations, we "see" such fine lines only when we learn that we should expect them there. As real as they may feel to us, boundaries are mere figments of our minds. Only the socialized can "see" them. To all cultural outsiders they are totally invisible (Zerubavel 1991:80).

Put cheese on a pizza and it is a cheese pizza. Then add pepperoni and it becomes a pepperoni pizza. A sprinkling of basil and oregano, however, does not turn that pizza into a basil and oregano snack, even though it would be perfectly correct to see things that way. The "one-drop rule" that was once used in the U.S. South to determine an individual's race shows that perception and categorization really are selective (Zerubavel 1991:56–7). When this "rule" was used, one single drop of "black blood" was sufficient for an individual to be seen and categorized as entirely black; you were not considered totally and undeniably white if you were defined as having any "black blood" at all running in your veins. (Of course, it is not the "color" of an individual's blood that determines his or her race anyway.) The one-drop rule is simply one example of what is called a **hypodescent rule,** in which people who are declared to be racially mixed are placed into the category that is most devalued or subordinate (Davis 1991).

It is true that certain qualities of stimuli may make it more likely that they will be perceived and responded to by living creatures (Howard 1995:94). Even fish will cue on conspicuous physical structures—a sunken log, a physical break between a sandy bottom and a weed line, a sudden drop—as they move to and from shore in search of food. At the human level, however, these processes of attending and disattending to even conspicuous stimuli cannot be isolated from the social context, nor can they be isolated from the social experiences we have had or expect *to* have (i.e., our expectations about future events influence what we attend to in the present). If everyone had blue skin, your blueness would not be conspicuous; and if everyone had one big eye in the middle of the forehead, then your one big eye would not stand out in a crowd, either. While a few universal or natural laws of perception and attention do exist because we are human beings (and not frogs or lions), for the most part, our experience of perception and attention is best viewed as a fluid, dynamic, socially constructed process. "It is our social environment that normally determines what we attend to but then ignore. In helping set the horizons of our attention and concern, it is often society that defines what we consider relevant" (Zerubavel 1997:42).

Mindscapes and Social Cognition

Not only is what enters our consciousness through perception and attention irreducibly social, so is the process of thinking and knowing. **Social cognition** refers to the content of knowledge, knowledge creation and affirmation, and the transmission of knowledge from one group to another (Howard 1995:91). We are members of one or more **thought communities** or **cognitive subcultures,** each with its own cognitive traditions and customary ways of thinking and perceiving, that have a crucial impact on what each of us knows and how each of us thinks (Zerubavel 1997:9–12). Experiences in our thought communities provide each of us with a **mindscape,** a socially constructed cognitive system that each of us uses for viewing the world and the people in it (Zerubavel 1997:8). We *think* about and *know* the world as sons, daughters, clamdiggers, circus clowns, Southern Baptists, atheists, magicians, surfers, conservatives, liberals, fundamentalists, knife collectors, or as members of some other thought community.

> . . . we think not only as individuals and as human beings, but also as social beings, products of particular social environments that affect as well as constrain the way we cognitively interact with the world (Zerubavel 1997:6).

Different thought communities can and do carve up the world differently, and our participation in specific thought communities produces differences in how we think and what we know. U.S. residents, unlike the ancient Romans, would not find it particularly attractive to witness the execution of real-life convicts on stage during a theatrical performance (Zerubavel 1997:61).

You are what you eat? Maybe, but it is more correct to say that what you eat reflects what you are—at least in terms of group membership and social relationships. Good to eat means good to *think* to eat, and what you think is good to eat is not something that you figure out all by yourself. What people *like* to eat and what they think *other* people should like to eat reflect differences in the cognitive subcultures or thought communities to which people belong.

> . . . when we notice that many Americans find the idea of eating snails revolting, we should recognize that what we are seeing is more than just a random collection of individuals with some peculiar phobia that somehow happens to be shared by so many of their compatriots yet, for some odd reason, by only a few French (Zerubavel 1997:5).

Bedouin tribes of northern Africa consider sheep eyes to be a real treat to eat, and they would be most insulted if a visitor refused to eat and enjoy sheep eyes, too. While most people in the United States place raw fish low on their list of things to eat, the Japanese consider it a delicacy. Hindus will not beef, and Jews will not eat pork. Chinese, however, *will* eat snakes because they like the taste and think eating them will produce a special strength and power. The potato was rejected as a food at one time in Europe—it grew from a tuber rather than from a seed—but by the eighteenth century the potato prejudice had disappeared, and potatoes were a popular food (Farb and Armelagos 1980:64). Westerners will generally refuse to eat insects like grasshoppers or locusts (even though they are a good source of protein and nutrients like vitamin A) but will eat—and enjoy—other invertebrates like lobsters, crabs, shrimp, clams, oysters, and mussels (while avoiding squid). Eating likes and dislikes are a product of many things (Harris 1985; Harris 1987:82), it is true, but certainly the influence of cognitive subcultures must be at the top of the list.

The central claim of the sociology of cognition is that we think as social beings and not simply as human beings. How we think, then, is neither naturally nor logically inevitable. In fact, it is often utterly *conventional* (Zerubavel

1997:9). What we know and understand is closely related to what other people know and understand.

> It is the process of *cognitive socialization* that allows us to enter the social, intersubjective world. Becoming social implies learning not only how to act but also how to think in a social manner. As we become socialized and learn to see the world through the mental lenses of particular thought communities, we come to assign to objects the same meaning that they have for others around us, to both ignore and remember the same things that they do, and to laugh at the same things that they find funny (Zerubavel 1997:15).

Symbolic communication is the principal way that an individual's thoughts and perceptions are transformed into something more objective or public and the principal way that thoughts are received from others to transform one's own cognitive landscape. Interaction with others produces the kind of intellectual stimulation that can form new synapses and pathways in the brain, release new chemicals, and actually create and re-create the physical structures that are involved in the thinking process (Carper 2000:33).

In most societies, an extensive **cognitive division of labor** exists in which different parts of accumulated knowledge are the province of separate groups and individuals. I may learn my morals from my father, how to throw a football from a coach at school, how to shoot pocket billiards from a close friend, and how to wash a car from my mother. The more extensive the culture and the greater its cognitive demands, the less likely that any one person could possess all the accumulated knowledge of the group. While most people know enough to break a window on a car to get at the keys they locked inside, most people do not know how to locksmith a new key or how to use a jimmy to unlock a door to get the keys safely without damage to the vehicle. Likewise, not everyone knows how to deal aces from the bottom of a deck of cards, to skydive, to reupholster a chair, or to replace a water pump on an automobile.

The Emotional Self

A crucial part of human inner experience is **emotion, affection, sentiment,** or **mood.** These words are often used interchangeably to refer to feelings we have in regard to people, objects, situations, and experiences (Smith-Lovin 1995:118–9). Because emotions can and do operate without being consciously identified—they may explode from us—they seem to be more mysterious, unruly, and idiosyncratic than other parts of inner experience (Katz 1999). We are not always able to put what we are feeling into words (Baszanger 1998). This sense that emotionality is asocial and unmanageable is even more likely because emotional experiences usually involve physical responses like changes in breathing, a reaction in the pit of the stomach, changes in skin temperature, elevated blood pressure, rapid heart beat, and glandular changes (Turner 2000). Nonetheless, our emotional experiences are still heavily influenced by our relationships to others and by sociocultural processes.

> A bodily feeling or sensation may be experienced as "internal" but the way in which we interpret it as evidence of an "emotion" is always already a product of acculturation into a particular society (Lupton 1998:167).

Every human experience is emotional at some level (Turner 2000). However, no human experience can be only emotional, and no emotional experience can be purely physiological (Lindesmith, Strauss, and Denzin 1999:132). In the absence of symbolic and cognitive abilities and capacities, what we would normally call an emotion would be nothing more than a wordless sensation or a raw physiological response. Emotions do have a strong foundation in neuro-physiological processes—some people are depressed by rain without fully understanding their despondency—but emotions are still flexible and responsive to cultural norms and values, as well as to the behavior of others (Elster 1999:205; Stinchcombe and Heimer 2000:313). Thought and emotion are not opposed processes as much as they are distinguishable parts of one continuous process (Barbalet 1998:45).

Doing Emotions. While we locate emotions inside of us, the truth is that it is more accurate to say that an individual is part of an emotional experience. Emotions are unfolding and constantly developing interactive events, not things that we have or do not have (Lupton 1998:1–2). Imagine how different your emotions will be if your incredibly annoying secretary slams a door in your face as opposed to the same door being slammed by the wind, by a custodian who is leaving your office, or by a child who is playing with it. The stimulus is the same, that is, a loud noise, but the emotional reactions are not. Extreme anger may result from the secretary's act but not from the slam caused by the wind, the custodian, or the child. What triggers an emotion, how it is expressed (and when and why) and *how* it is supposed to be expressed (or not expressed)—even what qualifies as an emotional response in the first place—are all powerfully influenced by social factors (Brody 1999:19). The labeling, interpretation, and assessment of feelings is a central part of what the emotion is and how it unfolds over time (Frijda 1998:271).

Emotions go through their own brand of fads and fashions. Sensitivity and overt emotional displays may be "in" during some periods, but "out" at others (Lupton 1998:95). In France, during the 1700s, public displays of weeping and sorrow were quite acceptable for both men and women so long as they did not become excessive; these emotional displays were viewed as evidence of a highly developed and admirable sensibility (Lupton 1998:82–3). New emotional disorders are identified all the time, and what qualifies as a healthy or unhealthy emotion is subject to change. In the contemporary United States, emotional expression is now seen as important for members of both sexes, and men and women are both encouraged to get in touch with their feelings and to display emotional sensitivity (Lupton 1998:113). Individuals, especially males, can now be afflicted with *alexithymia,* a medical diagnosis that makes the inability to feel or to express emotions itself a disease (Kimmel 2000:233). The man who is too unemotional is now viewed as a callous and sterile individual, someone in danger of losing himself and injuring his psychic health (Lupton 1998:113). Certain emotions are considered to be appropriate for certain people in certain situations but wholly inappropriate for other people in different social situations (Smith-Lovin 1995:126).

The Emotion Triad.   Human emotions—and emotional experiences—have a **triadic nature** (Lindesmith, Strauss, and Denzin 1999:130–1). First, a stimulus or situation must be defined or interpreted in some way. ("What is that rattling sound behind that tree?") Second, some internal response to the definition of the situation occurs, involving both symbolic/cognitive elements and physiological responses. (An individual feels faint and experiences a sinking feeling in the stomach, along with the self-directed command to "get moving" because the rattling is coming from a poisonous snake.) Third, some external and customary response occurs through word and/or deed that serves to show observers that some inner emotional experience is happening. (An individual runs frantically away from the reptile.) An individual may, of course, inhibit the outward expression of an emotion and display it at a later time. All human emotions have a symbolic component, and all emotions are interpreted by the self at some level of awareness (Lindesmith, Strauss, and Denzin 1999:135).

Emotion scripts exist. These are shared understandings about what should be found or what should occur in an emotional response. An emotion script involves knowledge of exactly what type of emotion is called for in response to some stimulus (e.g., "I don't know whether to be angry or not at what you did"), followed by knowledge of how the particular emotional response should unfold. For example, the emotion script called "anger" starts when an individual receives an actual or imagined personal insult, decides that anger is the correct emotion, and follows it up with physiological responses (flushed skin and clenched jaw) and behavioral responses like verbally putting down the insulting individual; it concludes with some assessment of what happened and why (Smith-Lovin 1995:127). Children start mastering these emotion scripts as they start mastering other parts of the social heritage, somewhere around the age of 2 (Smith-Lovin 1995:127). While it is possible for children to be agitated and express emotional outbursts early in life, these displays lack crucial elements of a more mature emotional response. Secondary or higher-level emotions like embarrassment or empathy are not possible until children develop a capacity for self-consciousness (Lewis, Sullivan, Stanger, and Weiss 1998).

Reflected Emotion. Emotions unfold along a process that we will call **reflected emotion.** We imagine how we feel in light of how we should feel from the standpoint of others, we evaluate our feelings and the directions that they could go, and then we have feelings about our feelings. Humans can and do produce emotional reactions when faced with the expectations and responses—imagined and real—of others (Clark 1997). Our generalized feeling of excitement might easily be crystallized into a specific emotion by the reactions of others, our reactions to their reactions, and our subsequent reactions to our own reactions. We might then reflect back upon the whole emotional experience. Who among us has not had the experience of being accused by someone of being in a bad mood and finding that, sure enough, the individual was right? The accusation by another individual channeled our feelings in a direction that they would not have gone in the absence of the accusation.

Emotions we feel may reflect exactly what features of a relationship we choose to focus on, the good or the bad. The same person, the same relationship, or the same event almost always produces a range of emotions in an individual like love, hate, anger, disappointment, and so on. It is impossible to experience all these different feelings at once. What happens is that from moment to moment we focus on different features of a situation (Hochschild 1983:224), or we reevaluate or recategorize what we are feeling in different or new ways. The emotions that move us to the heights of love and affection can also lead to a bad choice of partners, to abusive behavior toward those whom we love (or profess to), to stalking behavior toward another individual, or to the murder of a spouse (Buss 2000a:55). Jealousy, for example, may come from strong feelings of love and affection, but it can easily destroy even the best and most harmonious of relationships (Buss 2000b:27–30). **Compound emotions** are serial perceptions, and they are a direct result of exactly what we choose to focus on, think about, or remember as the mind's eye moves from one point to another in our emotional relationships to others (Hochschild 1983:224). Emotions tie us to some people, just as they keep us separated from some other people (Lawler and Yoon 1998:889–91; Margolis 1998:133–8).

Certain objects and places are special to us precisely because they can create certain moods and feelings or turn a bad mood into a good one. With some of our cherished items, it is easy for anyone to understand their emotional significance: awards, high school yearbooks, photographs, diplomas, and the like. However, other items may be every bit as central to our emotional lives but more individualized and difficult for others to identify as the emotional objects that they are: those earrings given to us by a long-gone lover, the pen we received as a graduation gift, the gold watch given to us when we retired, the candle given to us by a close friend so many years ago. If we can invest deep feelings in our possessions, we can do the same thing with spaces and places. Oceans, lakes, rivers, mountains, deserts, the countryside—all of these may evoke particular emotions in those who visit them.

Things That Go Bump in the Night.   Even so basic and primary an emotion as fear cannot be divorced from our relationships to others. The fears of our youth are different from the fears of our adulthood or old age. Humans can become terrified at the prospect of developing cancer, losing a job, or being deserted by a loved one (Tomkins 1998:210). At one time, a principal fear is staying home the night of the big dance, while at some other time, the principal fear is that one will be unable to provide enough security for one's family or take care of one's ailing parents. More females than males report that they are afraid to walk alone at night (Maguire and Pastore 1999:118), and it is probably the near-poor who worry most about the specter of poverty.

Societies contain **cultures of fear,** socially created and socially sustained ideas about threats to our collective and individual well-being. These cultures of fear change over time, and they may give us a distorted sense of exactly what we should fear. With so many potential things to be afraid of, and with so many new fears being discovered, invented, and publicized all the time, it is certain that some of our fears—maybe most of them—are unfounded or irrational (Shermer 1997). Immense money and power fall to those individuals and groups that are able to play on our insecurities and convince us that they can save us from what frightens us (Glassner 1999:xxviii). Scares that have a powerful sponsorship and receive a great deal of media attention are the ones most likely to be convincing to the widest audience.

> A scare can continue long after its rightful expiration date so long as it has two things going for it: it has to tap into current cultural anxieties, and it has to have media-savvy advocates behind it (Glassner 1999:177).

Things that today seem ordinary, commonplace, or business as usual would undoubtedly have been frightening or even traumatizing to past generations (Glassner 1999:5). The growth of "shock television" and the "tabloid press" has encouraged the presentation and reporting of stories that are sensational enough to attract large audiences (Jenkins 1994:31). The social construction of fear and of frightening people is principally a matter of who can pin the label on whom.

Much like a door-to-door salesperson who makes a big sale by getting a foot in the door, once a fear is created and institutionalized, it can be used to create other scares. An ambiguous event is linked or mapped with some other event that is already widely defined as scary or frightening (Jenkins 1994:7). This **mapping** of one fear with another guarantees that attention will be paid to a new issue, and linking an old fear with a new one raises the danger threshold of the lesser activity (Jenkins 1994:7). If the use of pornography can be linked with serial murder, it makes pornography look even more danger-ous and frightening than it is. Anything that can be linked with serial murder, because predatory violence is high in terms of its fright value, will automati-cally seem more frightening. This process of mapping, then, will offer rich re-wards to those groups that are able to accomplish it (Jenkins 1994).

Levels of fear in a society cannot be separated from the statistical descrip-tions of frightening events, and statistical descriptions cannot be separated from political and moral struggles.

> People use statistics to support particular points of view, and it is naive simply to accept numbers as accurate, without examining who is using them and why (Best 2001:13).

The fear of some particular social problem almost always can be traced to the efforts of problem promoters like reporters, private organizations, activists, ex-perts, and government officials (Best 2001:16). These problem promoters ei-ther create their own definition of a problem or use an existing one that capitalizes on whatever collective anxieties exist. They may draw even greater attention to some problem by supplying a numeric estimate of its size (Best 1987). All statistics, even good and reliable ones, are created by people, and all statistics, even good and reliable ones, reflect the interests and decisions of the people and organizations that create them (Best 2001:160–1).

Some statistical descriptions are bad from the get-go; they are wrong—dead wrong—and should be discarded as soon as possible. For example, in the 1980s, it was authoritatively claimed that 4,000 to 5,000 people were killed *every* year by serial killers (Jenkins 1994:22), when the actual number was closer to 200 to 300 (Jenkins 1994:28). Other statistical descriptions, however, deteriorate with the passage of time, especially as they are mangled in the transmission from one reporter to another. This makes them into **mutant statistics** (Best 2001:62). Sometimes, the mutated statistic is better and more valid than the original, but not usually (Best 2001:63–5). The Children's De-fense Fund (an advocacy agency for children's rights) reported in 1994 that the number of U.S. children killed with guns had doubled since 1950. That means, for example, that if one child were killed with a firearm in 1950, then two children were killed this way forty-four years later in 1994. However, the original report of the Children's Defense Fund mutated until it was garbled beyond recognition. A professional journal claimed that *every year* since 1950 the number of U.S. children gunned down had doubled, an assertion that gives a vastly different picture of the number of gunned-down children. If one child were killed in 1950 by a gun, then two children were killed that way in 1951; four children in 1952; eight in 1953; and so on. By 1994, over 35 trillion children would have been gunned down (Best 2001:1–3), a number far larger than the number of humans who have *ever* lived on earth. (Incidentally, the FBI [1995:18] actually reported that 1,512 individuals under age 18 were murdered with firearms in 1994.) Even good statistics can get butchered with the passage of time, sometimes inadvertently, but sometimes through deliberate manipulation.

Collective Recollections and Individual Memories

Over thirty years ago I was in an audience, watching a magic show presented by a local magic club. One of the performers was on the faculty at Purdue University, a person I knew and admired. He had not gotten far into his act when he stumbled and fell to the stage. The curtain closed and one of his assistants, a young female, entered through the curtains and asked for the help of a physician. None was present, and we in the audience waited. Another performer entered through the curtains, stood at center stage, and did a trick with large cards. When the trick was finished, the show was called to an end, and I made my way to my dorm room. I learned later what had happened. The fallen performer had experienced a heart attack while on stage and died during the performance. He had a weak heart, and he had gotten so nervous during his performance that it was more than his heart could take. The memory of his fall to the stage is as vivid today as it was the day it happened. I even remember what trick he was doing. It is certain that my memories of this event—my thoughts and feelings about it—are a direct reflection of my experiences in the groups to which I belonged at the time, as well as the experiences that I have had since. My memories are certainly different from those of people who had a different relationship with him, such as his wife or other members of his family.

Collective Remembrances.   Because groups and social relationships influence our thoughts and our emotions, they also influence how and what we remember (Howard 1995:95). The past finds its way into the present as a socially constructed reality that impacts all those who share in the terrain of a **remembrance environment.**

> . . . we can identify a relatively unexplored intellectual terrain made up of various "remembrance environments" lying somewhere between the strictly personal and the absolutely universal. These environments (which include, for example, the family, the workplace, the profession, the fan club, the ethnic group, the religious community, and the nation) are all larger than the individual yet at the same time considerably smaller than the entire human race (Zerubavel 1997:81).

Most of our important memories are memories of things that happened with, around, or because of others: first dates, marriages, divorces, birthdays, vacations, important books we've read, the death of a loved one, favorite movies, a summer romance, our child's birth, and the like. It is equally true that much of what we remember is shared with other people, and these relationships constitute the lens through which memories are constructed, recalled, and renewed. Magicians are most likely to remember the life, times, and death of Harry Houdini; baseball fans are most likely to remember the life and death of Mickey Mantle; and rock and roll fans are most likely to remember the birthday and death of Buddy Holly. Certain memories and recollections are found among Latin Americans, anthropologists, or astronauts and nobody else. Members of a group may work out among themselves exactly what happened (and why), and these social constructions are what pass into the collective memory. These memories—distorted or not—may become harder and firmer with the passage of time.

Groups are characterized by a **memory division of labor** in which different parts of collective memory are allocated to different people (Wegner 1987:189–99). For example, mom may remember most of the details of that trip to Canada the year Christy graduated from high school, while dad may remember the trip to Graceland to buy Elvis Presley memorabilia the year Jennifer went off to college. Just as a university, city, or state may have its "official historian," so do most groups. Some people are better rememberers and noted for their abilities to recall events and report them without bias or error to everyone else. Brownmiller (1984:215–6) claimed that females are the ones who are taught from birth to be keepers of the heart and keepers of the sentimental memory. They are the ones expected to remember the emotional connections by sending the thank-you notes, making the long-distance calls, and buying the presents for the holidays. Brownmiller's claims may be less true nowadays than they were when she wrote them—men also buy gifts and write notes of appreciation—but it is beyond dispute that differences in age, gender, personality, culture, and so on will produce differences in how memory is organized, who remembers what, and how memories are expressed (Pillemer 1998:177–212). This fits what we all know to be true. If we are interested in the history of a state, city, town, community, university, family, or relationship, some people are more informed and better to consult than others. They have been around longer, have had more varied experiences, remember better, or are more willing to discuss what things were like in the good old days.

Every collectivity—nation, community, corporation, family—has things that it wishes to remember and other things that it wishes to forget (or that new members are expected to ignore). Many battles are fought over how we should remember the past, who should be given central roles in it, where a given history should start and end, when particular events should be remembered and celebrated, and whose version of history is the most "correct" or best one. Group memories are almost always contested memories, and they are continually constructed, deconstructed, and reconstructed (Irwin-Zarecka 1994; Zerubavel 1997:12). Native Americans will look at their history and the history of the United States in a way that is very different from how whites will (Rosenzweig and Thelen 1998:164–70), and women may have a different sense of history than men may have. A disgruntled employee has a different sense of the work group's history than do other members who are relatively content. Remembering is regulated by many **rules of remembrance** that tell us all what we should remember and what we should forget (Zerubavel 1997:84).

While historical events themselves happened at some past time and are unchanging, the representations and memories of them are not. Many World War II veterans can no longer remember the difference between what actually happened to them and what Hollywood movies about the war showed. Cultural memories embodied in film images have replaced the personal memories of those people who were actually there (Sturkin 1997:6). This is also true for Vietnam veterans. They claim that they can no longer remember whether their memories came from their own direct experiences, Hollywood movies, or documentary photographs (Sturkin 1997:20).

> For, unlike photographs or film images, memories do not remain static through time—they are reshaped and reconfigured, they fade and are scripted. Though an image may fix an event temporally, the meaning of that image is constantly subject to contextual shifts (Sturkin 1997:21).

Every image remembered is some other image forgotten (Sturkin 1997:20). The struggle over what should be included in our collective memories is more than a struggle over what really happened; it is also a struggle over *who* will get to decide. The power to control memory is bound up with the power to control the representations of history.

We are what we remember (Lembcke 1998). What we remember, however, is not necessarily the way we were. Our memories and our narratives about past events are biased and distorted and influenced by the passage of time. Some of what we think happened in our society, or even to us personally, did not (or at least not exactly the way we remember). Collective memories of the Vietnam War, for example, often contain an image of returning veterans being harassed and abused by protesters against the war. Central to this recollection is the image of protesters spitting upon the returning soldiers. Did this spitting actually occur?

Some incivilities existed between returning veterans and anti-war activists (Lembcke 1998:67–8). With hundreds of thousands of war veterans and millions of war opponents, how could it be otherwise? The country was divided over what was happening in Vietnam, and these were days of rage. However, the dominant feature of the relationships between veterans and protesters was amicability. War protesters, after all, were protesting the war, and not the warriors who were forced to fight and die in it. Protesters were against sending soldiers *to* Vietnam, not bringing them home again (Lembcke 1998:145). No concrete or corroborating evidence of spitting exists—no pictures, no police reports of arrests of spitters, no news reports—suggesting strongly that spitting on veterans did not happen (Lembcke 1998:73–4). The only material representation of a returning veteran being spit upon by protesters appeared in a *GI Joe* comic book in the mid-1980s (Lembcke 1998:141). No doubt exists, however, that as the years passed, a large number of people came to believe that Vietnam veterans were spat upon by hippies and radicals and badly treated by members of the anti-war movement (Lembcke 1998:127).

Flashbulb Events and Personal Memories.   Public happenings of a shocking or consequential nature (e.g., a presidential assassination) are important memory pegs. They galvanize our own personal memories and make it more likely that we will each remember what we were doing when we heard the news of the event, saw the actual event on television, or witnessed it in person. These **flashbulb memories** have a vitality and vividness that make them an enduring part of both our lives and our personal reflections on our lives (Brown and Kulik 1977:74). The memory is not only of the shocking event itself, but principally of the circumstances of one's own life when one learned of the tragedy. Any American who had reached the age of reason in 1963 still has a flashbulb memory of the assassination of John F. Kennedy in Dallas, Texas. I can still remember mine. I was a junior in high school, and the principal announced over the intercom that the president had been shot. Our disbelief that this could be happening quickly turned to shock, and rumors started to fly. In one, a black man had done the shooting; in another, the vice president had also been killed. I remember being in English class, waiting for some news. One of the students started sobbing, I assumed over the shooting. I remember being surprised because she always seemed so quiet and in total control all the time. Other things were happening that I noticed and probably remembered for a while. I do remember the feelings of sadness and loss that I and the people around me experienced on that day.

Old flashbulb memories are often dislodged by new ones. Most people in the United States—and many people in other countries—now share another flashbulb memory. It will be hard for anyone to forget what he or she was doing on the morning of September 11, 2001, when the United States came under attack by terrorists. The twin towers of the World Trade Center in New York were destroyed, as was a section of the Pentagon. While terrorism was no stranger to Americans, the attack of September 11 came closer to home and with far more devastating results. About 3,000 people died in the attack on the World Trade Center, more than died during the attack on Pearl Harbor, along with an enormous loss of property. Others died in the attack on the Pentagon and in the crashes of the planes used by the terrorists. Still more people died—police, firefighters, medical personnel, clerics—as they rendered aid to victims of the initial attacks.

All of us have private memories of where we were and what we were doing when we heard the news, saw the event in person or on television, or read about it. (I was walking to class when a student told me what had happened, and I thought she was surely mistaken.) Many vivid memories linger from September 11 and those days that followed—firefighters raising the U.S. flag at the wreckage, perhaps, or police officers hanging their heads in sorrow—but one of the strongest must be the image of jetliners hitting the twin towers of the World Trade Center as people on the ground watched in horror and disbelief. The events of September 11, 2001, will be a powerful flashbulb memory in the years ahead, and it is unlikely that we will ever forget the terrorist attacks or what we were doing when we learned of them.

While unexpected events that involve prominent individuals or momentous public events can easily produce flashbulb memories, private shocks can, too, like the death of a loved one, a friend's suicide, the loss of a job, or an automobile accident (Brown and Kulik 1977:75). Flashbulb events are quickly printed into our memories (Brown and Kulik 1977:84–7); it is not until later that a personal narrative will be constructed to describe one's feelings and thoughts, a narrative that will be reorganized and embellished through subsequent tellings and retellings (Pillemer 1998:98–9). Traumatic events in the life of an individual—rapes, molestations, or being present on the Titanic the day it sank—and their memory can abruptly and permanently alter the entire fabric of one's existence (Pillemer 1998:31).

Mistaken Memories and False Beliefs.   Not all memories are correct reflections of things that actually happened, and false beliefs are easy enough to concoct (Boudon 1994). Paranormal beliefs in things like unidentified flying objects or fortune telling are created and contested all the time (Goode 2000). In the late 1980s, some individuals in the United States claimed that they had been tortured and brutalized by members of satanic cults, and they reported recurring memories of the abuse they endured. The acts inflicted upon them, if true, would make even the strong at heart shudder. The list almost always included accounts of forced blood drinking, ritual sex acts, pornography, murder, and cannibalism. Some women even claimed that they had been used as "breeders," that is, women who were forced to reproduce so that children would be available to be sacrificed in satanic rituals (Jenkins and Maier-Katkin 1991:127). Curiously, claims of abuse and of repressed memories of it were often accepted on the flimsiest of evidence. In fact, the more preposterous the claim, the more likely it was to be believed (Jenkins and Maier-Katkin 1991:131). Even children's memories of abuse were accepted as factual (Nathan 1991:84–8).

Even though some minimal agreement exists in stories of satanic abuse, even greater disagreement exists. Children need a great deal of help from adult interviewers in order for them to come anywhere close to constructing an integrated view of satanic abuse, and teenagers' memories are oddly inconsistent, perhaps remembering details about what was done to them but offering few specifics about who, what, where, or when the abuse took place (La Fontaine 1998). Many reasons exist for individuals to fabricate tales of satanic abuse and to remember themselves as victims of it—psychological problems, desire for attention, suggestibility—even though no abuse occurred (Jenkins and Maier-Katkin 1991:142). Latter accounts of satanic abuse may simply be derivatives of early accounts and memories, which themselves are suspect at many levels.

The Manufacture of Memory. It seems likely that all of us have clear memories of events, some momentous and some minor, that did not actually occur. Past events may be misremembered, and sizable distortions do sometimes occur. For example, individuals are susceptible to the **originological fallacy.** When people think about their past, they give a great deal of emphasis and causal significance to events that were actually of minor importance in forming them (Pillemer 1998:85–6). They may also forget or suppress events that were very important in their lives. We may remember an insult from a friend as being far more important than it actually was at the time, or we may forget a cruel statement from a close family member that left a permanent scar. When distortions in memory do occur, it is almost always the details that are confused, not central events (Pillemer 1998:59). A person who is mugged may have difficulty remembering exactly where it happened and all the characteristics of the criminal and details of the crime, but the survivor will have no trouble remembering that it was a mugging and not, say, a rape. Not only do we have memories of events, we have memories of our feelings about those events—something like **emotional memory** (Pillemer 1998:99). We may not only remember the general appearance of our "first love," we can also remember the intensity of the feelings this relationship aroused in us. While memories fade with the passage of time, the most durable ones are the ones associated with intense emotional experiences (Schmidt and Winters 2002:53).

The **dual memory model** divides memory experiences into an **imagistic memory** (implicit or nonconscious), on the one hand, and a **narrative memory** (verbal, purposeful, conscious, explicit), on the other (Pillemer 1998:100). Imagistic memory is more primitive and develops first. The dog that returns to the buried bone or the bird that returns to the site of hidden seeds has some imagistic memory that need not even be conscious. Imagistic memory represents people, objects, and events in the *brain's* eye, and these images can persist over time, even at an unconscious level. Narrative memory evolves along with the development of symbols; words exist for describing images and perceptions. Symbolization crystallizes these images, moving them from the level of perception to the level of cognition and conscious awareness. These subjective memories then can be shared with others in the telling and retelling. Later they may be written down and passed on to future generations (Bogen and Lynch 1996). The first line of response, then, in memory construction is imagistic: Events must be seen, heard, tasted, touched, or smelled. The second part of memory construction is reached when the recalled images are turned into a coherent, storylike, verbal memory narrative that can be shared with others (Pillemer 1998:52–3).

The average age of the earliest memory reported by individuals is between 3 and 4 years of age. It is almost impossible for a child to remember even flashbulb or traumatic events like an assassination of a world leader, a death in the family, a birth of a sibling, or a marriage of a close relative if the events happened during the child's first two or three years of life. The absence of language, the restricted sense of self, and the immature cognitive abilities mean that it is hard to recall personal events and even harder to discuss them with others (Pillemer 1998:20). Traumatic events that occur early in life can still influence children's development, however, coming out in personality changes, play, dreams, or fears (Pillemer 1998:101).

The transition from imagistic memory to a more conscious narrative is not only dependent on maturation and the development of language. It also depends on the nature of the interactions between parents (or other caregivers) and children about relevant happenings in the child's early development (Pillemer 1998:115). Adults directly and indirectly show the child what is acceptable memory content, as well as the value of having and sharing memorable moments (Pillemer 1998:118). Distinctive strategies for representing and sharing personal event memories are *co-constructed* during parent-child interactions. Parents differ in the ways that they engage in memory talk with young children and in the value that they place on children's recall of personal events (Pillemer 1998:21). The young come to remember things that other people have helped them to remember, partly through descriptions and narratives, and partly through the use of physical artifacts like photos from family albums, videotapes of important or memorable events (the child's birth, perhaps, first birthday party, or first haircut), and possessions belonging to the child that were given as presents or souvenirs. Eventually, a child develops an autobiographical memory; he or she possesses a repository of personal event memories *and* the verbal abilities to share them with others (Pillemer 1998:129).

Family gatherings and reunions, trips to historic sites, visits to museums, movies and books, old photographs, and the like are the core of the process of recalling and reminiscing about a past that connects people to their own history. Our personal construction of the past pays only scant attention to the kinds of history we learned in history classes, because this information is too data oriented and boring to be of much use to us (Rosenzweig and Thelan 1998:109–13). The family group is crucial for bringing the past into the present. Reflections upon past experiences and discussions among family members are the glue that helps to sustain the family as a social unit even when family members are physically apart. Even people who have died can still be a part of the family history, especially when the family history is taught to children who did not know their ancestors directly. Revisiting the past creates a sense of cohesion that comes from sharing a sense of history and purpose with others (Rosenzweig and Thelan 1998:50). In the final analysis, it may be more than the search for identity that encourages us to reflect on our pasts. The desire for immortality also encourages us to do what we can to make sure our past memories live on in the memories of our descendants (Rosenzweig and Thelan 1998:60–1).

Conclusions

A sociology of the private realm reminds us that we perceive, think, feel, and remember not simply as individuals or human beings but as members of social environments. Social lenses exist that make it possible for us to lump certain people, objects, situations, and experiences together into one perceptual cluster and split this cluster off from other perceptual clusters. In this process of interacting with the world and the people in it, we do it as members of one or more thought communities or cognitive subcultures. These communities or subcultures help us to develop mindscapes that allow us to think about the world in ways that our societies and groups expect us to think about the world. Our emotional selves are also powerfully influenced by relationships to others and by the historical, social, political, and economic contexts within which emotions are created and expressed. We also remember as members of particular remembrance communities that tell us what to remember and what to forget.

Chapter Six at a Glance

- Our relationships to others are of paramount importance in the creation of our inner experiences, which, in turn, impact our relationships to others.
- The interconnections between the public world and the more private world of family and friends produce a time bind in which the demands of one sphere are difficult to reconcile with the demands of the other.
- While individuals may form friendships, both in public and in private, many of us spend less time in making these connections than we once did. We even tend to bowl alone nowadays.
- Individuals experience cognitive socialization, during which they develop mindscapes, which serve as frames or lenses for perceiving and knowing in ways considered appropriate and inappropriate for members of the society.
- Emotional experiences are socially constructed—even primary emotions like fear—and an individual's emotional self cannot be separated from his or her social relationships and social experiences.
- Emotions are flexible and responsive to cultural norms and values, as well as to the behavior of others. Emotions must be interpreted and defined before they will have their full range of effects.

- Because groups and social relationships influence our thoughts and our emotions, they also influence how and what we remember.
- Every collectivity—society, community, corporation, family—has things that it wishes to remember and things that it wishes to forget. Battles are fought over how we should remember the past, who should be given central roles in it, where a given history should start and end, when particular events should be remembered and celebrated, and whose version of history is the most correct.
- Group memories are almost always contested memories, and they are continually constructed, deconstructed, and reconstructed.
- Flashbulb memories are remembrances people have as they think back to the point of some shocking event like an assassination of a political figure or a terrorist attack.
- The initial phase of memory is an imagistic one during which happenings are recorded perceptually in our memory banks. This is followed by a narrative phase during which memory is verbally recorded and symbolically organized.

Glossary

cognitive division of labor   the members of some groups know things that members of other groups do not know

compound emotions   an emotional experience that involves more than one emotion; an emotional experience characterized by the existence of many feelings

culture of fear   shared understandings about what is—or should be—most frightening in a particular place and time

dual-earner family   a family unit were both partners work outside the home for pay

dual memory model   memory experiences involve both an imagistic experience (perceptual and nonverbal) and a narrative experience (conscious and verbal)

emotion (or affection, sentiment, or mood)   the experiencing of feelings in regard to people, objects, experiences, or situations

emotion scripts   shared understandings about what should occur in an emotional experience

emotion work   emotions that are presented for the benefit of others and consistent with shared understandings about what the situation demands

emotional memory   a memory of past feelings

feeling rules   shared understandings about just what emotions—and to what degree—are appropriate in a given situation

flashbulb memories   shocking or consequential events that focus individuals sufficiently for them to be able to remember, sometimes for years, what they were doing when the event occurred

hypodescent rule   people who are defined as racially mixed are placed into the category that is most devalued or subordinate

imagistic memory   a remembrance of some past event as a nonverbal image or imagination of what happened

lumping   perceptual sensations are placed together into a single category or cluster, for example, a rose and a petunia are both perceived to be flowers

machers individuals who are active in formal organizations and community settings like at church meetings, civic organizations, community projects, or political organizations

mapping linking together troubling events, a process that raises the danger threshold of the lesser activity

memory division of labor different groups—and different individuals in those groups—have a specialized knowledge of the past that other groups and individuals lack

mindscape a socially constructed cognitive system that each of us uses for viewing the world and the people in it

mutant statistics statistical descriptions of troubling events that deteriorate with the passage of time as they are mangled in the transmission from one reporter to another

narrative memory the verbal/symbolic organization of imagistic memory, allowing memories of events to be crystallized, embellished, and shared with others in tellings and retellings

originological fallacy the belief that a particular event in one's life was more important than it really was

reflected emotion an emotional response produced by an imagination of how we think others think we should feel and some personal evaluation of the unfolding emotional experience

remembrance environments distinctive collectivities that share and maintain—and ultimately transmit to others—remembrances of past events important in the history of the particular group

rules of remembrance shared understandings about how and what to remember, understandings that become particularly relevant when teaching the history of the group to the young

schmoozers individuals who are socially active in a more private way by hosting (or going to) dinner parties, playing cards with friends, talking on the phone, or visiting relatives

social cognition the content of knowledge, knowledge creation and affirmation, and the transmission of knowledge from one group to another

splitting a cluster of perceptions is separated from other perceptual clusters, for example, dogs are separated from cats

thought communities or **cognitive subcultures** customary ways of thinking and knowing that groups have incorporated into their subculture

time bind an individual's difficulty to reconcile the demands of work with the demands of home

triadic nature of emotion an emotional experience involves a definition of a stimulus, an inner feeling, and an outer response

References

Adams, Rebecca and Graham Allan. 1998. "Contextualising Friendship." Pp. 1–17 in *Placing Friendship in Context*, edited by Rebecca Adams and Graham Allan. Cambridge, UK: Cambridge University Press.

Adler, Freda, Gerhard Mueller, and William Laufer. 2001. *Criminology*, 4th edition. New York: McGraw-Hill.

Allan, Graham. 1998. "Friendship and the Private Sphere." Pp. 71–91 in *Placing Friendship in Context*, edited by Rebecca Adams and Graham Allan. Cambridge, UK: Cambridge University Press.

Allan, Graham and Rebecca Adams. 1998. "Reflections on Context." Pp. 183–94 in *Placing Friendship in Context*, edited by Rebecca Adams and Graham Allan. Cambridge, UK: Cambridge University Press.

Amato, Paul and Juliana Sobolewski. 2001. "The Effects of Divorce and Marital Discord on Adult Children's Psychological Well-Being." *American Sociological Review* 66:900–21.

Barbalet, J. M. 1998. *Emotion, Social Theory, and Social Structure: A Macrosociological Approach.* Cambridge, UK: Cambridge University Press.

Baszanger, Isabelle. 1998. *Inventing Pain Medicine: From the Laboratory to the Clinic.* New Brunswick, NJ: Rutgers University Press.

Best, Joel. 1987. "Rhetoric in Claimsmaking: Constructing the Missing Children Problem." *Social Problems* 34:101–21.

———. 2001. *Damned Lies and Statistics: Untangling Numbers from the Media, Politicians, and Activists.* Berkeley: University of California Press.

Bogen, David and Michael Lynch. 1996. *The Spectacle of History: Speech, Text, and Memory at the Iran-Contra Hearings.* Durham, NC: Duke University Press.

Boudon, Raymond. 1994. *The Art of Self-Persuasion: The Social Explanation of False Beliefs*, translated by Malcolm Slater. Cambridge, UK: Polity Press.

Brody, Leslie. 1999. *Gender, Emotion, and the Family.* Cambridge, MA: Harvard University Press.

Brown, Roger and James Kulik. 1977. "Flashbulb Memories." *Cognition* 5:73–99.

Brownmiller, Susan. 1984. *Femininity.* New York: Linden Press/Simon & Schuster.

Buss, David. 2000a. "Prescription for Passion." *Psychology Today* 32:54–61.

———. 2000b. *The Dangerous Passion: Why Jealousy Is as Necessary as Love and Sex.* New York: The Free Press.

Carper, Jean. 2000. *Your Miracle Brain.* New York: HarperCollins.

Clark, Candace. 1997. *Misery and Company: Sympathy in Everyday Life.* Chicago, IL: University of Chicago Press.

Curtis, James, Douglas Baer, and Edward Grabb. 2001. "Nations of Joiners: Explaining Voluntary Association Membership in Democratic Societies." *American Sociological Review* 66:783–805.

Davis, F. J. 1991. *Who Is Black?* University Park: Pennsylvania State University Press.

Doyle, Anna Beth and Dorothy Markiewicz. 1996. "Parents' Interpersonal Relationships and Children's Friendships." Pp. 115–36 in *The Company They Keep: Friendship in Childhood and Adolescence*, edited by William Bukowski, Andrew Newcomb, and Willard Hartup. Cambridge, UK: Cambridge University Press.

Edwards, Bob and Michael Foley. 2001. "Much Ado about Social Capital." *Contemporary Sociology* 30:227–30.

Elster, Jon. 1999. *Strong Feelings: Emotion, Addiction, and Human Behavior.* Cambridge, MA: MIT Press.

Etzioni, Amitai. 2001. "Is Bowling Together Sociologically Lite?" *Contemporary Sociology* 30:223–4.

Farb, Peter and George Armelagos. 1980. *Consuming Passions: The Anthropology of Eating.* Boston: Houghton Mifflin

Federal Bureau of Investigation (FBI). 1995. *Crime in the United States 1994.* Washington, DC: USGPO.

Fowler, Brenda. 2000. *Iceman: Uncovering the Life and Times of a Prehistoric Man Found in an Alpine Glacier.* New York: Random House.

Frijda, N. H. 1998. "The Laws of Emotion." Pp. 270–87 in *Human Emotions: A Reader*, edited by Jennifer Jenkins, Keith Oatley, and Nancy Stein. Malden, MA: Blackwell.

Giddens, Anthony. 1992. *The Transformation of Intimacy: Sexuality, Love and Eroticism in Modern Societies.* Stanford, CA: Stanford University Press.

Glassner, Barry. 1999. *The Culture of Fear: Why Americans Are Afraid of the Wrong Things.* New York: Basic Books.

Goode, Erich. 2000. *Paranormal Beliefs: A Sociological Introduction.* Prospect Heights, IL: Waveland Press.

Harris, Marvin. 1985. *Good to Eat: Riddles of Food and Culture.* New York: Simon & Schuster.

———. 1987. "Foodways: Historical Overview and Theoretical Prolegomenon." Pp. 57–90 in *Food and Evolution: Toward a Theory of Human Food Habits*, edited by Marvin Harris and Eric Ross. Philadelphia, PA: Temple University Press.

Hartup, Willard. 1996. "Cooperation, Close Relationships, and Cognitive Development." Pp. 213–37 in *The Company They Keep: Friendship in Childhood and Adolescence*, edited by William Bukowski, Andrew Newcomb, and Willard Hartup. Cambridge, UK: Cambridge University Press.

Hochschild, Arlie Russell. 1983. *The Managed Heart: Commercialization of Human Feeling*. Berkeley: University of California Press.

———. 1997. *The Time Bind: When Work Becomes Home and Home Becomes Work*. New York: Henry Holt and Company.

Howard, Judith. 1995. "Social Cognition." Pp. 90–117 in *Sociological Perspectives on Social Psychology*, edited by Karen Cook, Gary Alan Fine, and James House. Boston: Allyn and Bacon.

Howes, Carollee. 1996. "The Earliest Friendships." Pp. 66–86 in *The Company They Keep: Friendship in Childhood and Adolescence*, edited by William Bukowski, Andrew Newcomb, and Willard Hartup. Cambridge, UK: Cambridge University Press.

Irwin-Zarecka, Iwona. 1994. *Frames of Remembering: The Dynamics of Collective Memory*. New Brunswick, NJ: Transaction.

Jenkins, Philip. 1994. *Using Murder: The Social Construction of Serial Homicide*. New York: Aldine de Gruyter.

Jenkins, Philip and Daniel Maier-Katkin. 1991. "Occult Survivors: The Making of a Myth." Pp. 127–144 in *The Satanism Scare*, edited by James Richardson, Joel Best, and David Bromley. New York: Aldine de Gruyter.

Katz, Jack. 1999. *How Emotions Work*. Chicago, IL: University of Chicago Press.

Kimmel, Michael. 2000. *The Gendered Society*. New York: Oxford University Press.

La Fontaine, J. S. 1998. *Speak of the Devil: Tales of Satanic Abuse in Contemporary England*. Cambridge, UK: Cambridge University Press.

Laursen, Brett. 1996. "Closeness and Conflict in Adolescent Peer Relationships: Interdependence with Friends and Romantic Partners." Pp. 186–210 in *The Company They Keep: Friendship in Childhood and Adolescence*, edited by William Bukowski, Andrew Newcomb, and Willard Hartup. Cambridge, UK: Cambridge University Press.

Lawler, Edward and Jeongkoo Yoon. 1998. "Network Structure and Emotions in Exchange Relations." *American Sociological Review* 63:871–94.

Lembcke, Jerry. 1998. *The Spitting Image: Myth, Memory, and the Legacy of Vietnam*. New York: New York University Press.

Lewis, M., M. W. Sullivan, C. Stanger, and M. Weiss. 1998. "Self Development and Self-conscious Emotions." Pp. 158–167 in *Human Emotions: A Reader*, edited by Jennifer Jenkins, Keith Oatley, and Nancy Stein. Malden, MA: Blackwell.

Lindesmith, Alfred, Anselm Strauss, and Norman Denzin. 1999. *Social Psychology*, 8th edition. Thousand Oaks, CA: Sage.

Lupton, Deborah. 1998. *The Emotional Self: A Sociocultural Exploration*. London: Sage.

Maguire, Kathleen and Ann Pastore. 1999. *Sourcebook of Criminal Justice Statistics 1998*. Washington, DC: USGPO.

Margolis, Diane Rothbard. 1998. *The Fabric of Self: A Theory of Ethics and Emotions*. New Haven, CT: Yale University Press.

Nathan, Debbie. 1991. "Satanism and Child Molestation: Constructing the Ritual Abuse Scare." Pp. 75–94 in *The Satanism Scare*, edited by James Richardson, Joel Best, and David Bromley. New York: Aldine de Gruyter.

Newcomb, Andrew and Catherine Bagwell. 1996. "The Developmental Significance of Children's Friendship Relations." Pp. 289–321 in *The Company They Keep: Friendship in Childhood and Adolescence*, edited by William Bukowski, Andrew Newcomb, and Willard Hartup. Cambridge, UK: Cambridge University Press.

Newman, David. 2002. *Sociology: Exploring the Architecture of Everyday Life*, 4th edition. Thousand Oaks, CA: Pine Forge.

Oliker, Stacey. 1998. "The Modernisation of Friendship: Individualism, Intimacy, and Gender in the Nineteenth Century." Pp. 18–42 in *Placing Friendship in*

Context, edited by Rebecca Adams and Graham Allan. Cambridge, UK: Cambridge University Press.

Pahl, Ray. 2000. *On Friendship*. Malden, MA: Polity Press.

Pillemer, David. 1998. *Momentous Events, Vivid Memories*. Cambridge, MA: Harvard University Press.

Putnam, Robert. 2000. *Bowling Alone: The Collapse and Revival of American Community*. New York: Simon & Schuster.

Rosenzweig, Roy and David Thelen. 1998. *The Presence of the Past: Popular Uses of History in American Life*. New York: Columbia University Press

Schmidt, Brad and Jeffrey Winters. 2002. "Fear Not." *Psychology Today* 35:46–54.

Schofer, Evan and Marion Fourcade-Gourinchas. 2001. "The Structural Contexts of Civic Engagement: Voluntary Association Membership in Comparative Perspective." *American Sociological Review* 66:806–28.

Shermer, Michael. 1997. *Why People Believe Weird Things: Pseudoscience, Superstition, and Other Confusions of Our Time*. New York: W. H. Freeman

Smith-Lovin, Lynn. 1995. "The Sociology of Affect and Emotion." Pp. 118–48 in *Sociological Perspectives on Social Psychology*, edited by Karen Cook, Gary Alan Fine, and James House. Boston: Allyn and Bacon.

Stinchcombe, Arthur and Carol Heimer. 2000. "Retooling for the Next Century: Sober Methods for Studying the Subconscious." *Contemporary Sociology* 29:309–19.

Sturkin, Marita. 1997. *Tangled Memories: The Vietnam War, the AIDS Epidemic, and the Politics of Remembering*. Berkeley: University of California Press.

Taylor, Timothy. 1996. *The Prehistory of Sex: Four Million Years of Human Sexual Culture*. New York: Bantam.

Tomkins, S. S. 1998. "Script Theory: Differential Magnification of Affects." Pp. 209–18 in *Human Emotions: A Reader*, edited by Jennifer Jenkins, Keith Oatley, and Nancy Stein. Malden, MA: Blackwell.

Turner, Jonathan. 2000. *On the Origins of Human Emotions: A Sociological Inquiry into the Evolution of Human Affect*. Stanford, CA: Stanford University Press.

Vela-McConnell, James. 1999. *Who Is My Neighbor? Social Affinity in a Modern World*. Albany: State University of New York Press.

Wegner, Daniel. 1987. "Transactive Memory: A Contemporary Analysis of the Group Mind." Pp. 185–208 in *Theories of Group Behavior*, edited by Brian Mullen and George Goethals. New York: Springer-Verlag.

Wilson, John. 2001. "Dr. Putnam's Social Lubricant." *Contemporary Sociology* 30:225–7.

Wuthnow, Robert. 1998. *Loose Connections: Joining Together in America's Fragmented Communities*. Cambridge, MA: Harvard University Press.

Zerubavel, Eviatar. 1991. *The Fine Line: Making Distinctions in Everyday Life*. New York: Free Press.

———. 1997. *Social Mindscapes: An Invitation to Cognitive Sociology*. Cambridge, MA: Harvard University Press.

Changing Relationships
Are the Only Constant

Over 100 years ago, in 1893, the American Press Association (APA), a ready-print syndicate based in New York City, commissioned seventy-four distinguished Americans to prepare short essays about how they thought things would look in the United States 100 years in the future (in 1993). These forecasters were asked to offer predictions about the nature of religion, the state of corporations, the structure of society and government, styles of dress, levels of

173

crime, and even the future of temperance legislation. The APA ran these accounts in newspapers across the country on May 1, 1893, as a way of publicizing the World's Columbian Exposition in Chicago and the Exposition's twin themes of the inevitability of progress and the power of technology.

The panel of forecasters included capitalists like George Westinghouse, attorneys like William Jennings Bryan, and an assortment of journalists, politicians, and writers. In general, the forecasters believed that 100 years down the road technology would solve all of society's problems and human nature would continue to improve (Walter 1992:23). Their predictions—most of them at any rate—were not only wrong, they were incredibly wrong. They are a sober reminder of how drastically things change—and how quickly. John Habberton, editor and author, predicted that insurance companies would disappear (house fires would not occur because brick, stone, or iron houses would replace wood ones), and chemical stimulants would no longer be used (because of proper cooking techniques and better living conditions). He believed that all marriages would be happy because the law would put to death men and women unfit for matrimony (Walter 1992:154–156). The journalist Junius Henri Browne believed the law would become so simple that the number of attorneys would be reduced. He also believed that criminals would be less severely punished and that there would be far fewer of them because improvements in general education would lessen crime (Walter 1992:182–183). Most of the forecasters believed inequality would be reduced as more of society's resources were shared by more people.

Some of the forecasters bubbled over with optimism. The Indiana-born poet Joaquin Miller believed people would be handsomer, healthier, happier, and better, if only given a chance to be good (Walter 1992:149). The journalist Edgar Watson Howe confidently predicted the evolution of greater simplicity and honesty as high-pressure living conditions disappeared (Walter 1992:158). John James Ingalls, attorney and U.S. senator, was certain that the railway and the steamship would go the way of the stagecoach. What would replace them? Citizens would simply call for their dirigible balloons. He did correctly predict that electricity would become a dominant energy source and that light metals would be used to construct aerial cars that would travel in the skies (Walter 1992:143–4). None of the forecasters predicted automobiles or computers, and very few imagined either the changes that were to come in social institutions or the impact of the Industrial Revolution. The reason most of the predictions were wrong is that these forecasters were unable to anticipate how dialectical change was to become, with one change producing many other changes and then itself being transformed in the process.

The inability to anticipate correctly future changes is not only found among journalists and politicians. At the end of the nineteenth century, most physical scientists around the world were confident that the physical universe had been correctly described and that most of the questions about it had been satisfactorily answered. No big, new discoveries were likely to be made. These hard-core, no-nonsense empiricists would have been astounded at what lay ahead in the twentieth century.

> If you were to say to a physicist in 1899 that in 1999, a hundred years later, moving images would be transmitted into homes all over the world from satellites in the sky; that bombs of unimaginable power would threaten the species; that antibiotics would abolish infectious disease but that disease would fight back; that women would have the vote, and pills to control reproduction; that millions of people would take to the air every hour in aircraft capable of taking off and landing without human touch; that you could cross the Atlantic at two thousand miles an hour; that humankind would travel to the moon, and then lose interest; that microscopes would be able to see individual atoms; that people would carry telephones weighing a few ounces, and speak anywhere in the world without wires; or that most of these miracles depended on devices the size of a postage stamp, which utilized a new theory called quantum mechanics—if you said all this, the physicist would almost certainly pronounce you mad (Crichton 1999:vii–viii).

It is not simply that what is now taken for granted was once considered improbable; it is that what is now taken for granted was considered impossible in terms of what was known about natural laws. Even if a forecaster had been able to predict the development of the airplane or automobile, he or she would still be very surprised at the scope of its use in today's world. What seems impossible today—not only in technology but in social institutions and interpersonal relationships—may very well be old-hat and taken for granted at some future time. Change is the only constant, and it is impossible to understand ourselves without understanding changes in our societies and social relationships.

Community and Society

Sentiments and Social Organization

Ferdinand Tönnies's (1855–1936) major work, published in 1887, was titled *Gemeinschaft und Gesellschaft*. His objective was to identify scientific concepts that would allow him to make sense of social change and historical development, as well as to compare different societies at different stages of sociocultural evolution. He believed that humans were social by nature, but they would only fulfill their destiny by living and acting together in collectivities like families and neighborhoods, even while they could form relationships by agreement to achieve certain goals (Heberle 1957:xi–xii; Loomis and McKinney 1957:9). One type of society—called *Gemeinschaft*—is characterized by a preponderance of relationships based on **natural will (*Wesenwille*)**. A second type of society—called *Gesellschaft*—is characterized by a preponderance of relationships based on **rational will (*Kürwille*)** (Tönnies 1957:103–25). While

Tönnies did describe the prevailing "will" in a society as the principal way to categorize its type, it is actually more correct to say that relationships are his basic datum; better to talk about natural or rational *relationships*.

Societies, groups, or relationships that are "natural" have a special look and feel to them. Everyone knows and cares about everyone else, and a high degree of peace, order, harmony, and tranquility exists. Individuals trust others to contribute to the common good because they themselves are trusted to do the same. A great deal of unity exists in an individual's life as he or she moves from status to status in the home, at work, or in the community. As individuals grow old, they know what will happen. What they did as children with their parents is what they will do with their own children. Because of the unity in one's life, a great deal of certainty and predictability exist. When you die, you know who will bury you, care for your family, and take care of family matters. If you get sick, you know who will take care of you until you get well. If your barn burns to the ground, you know who will be there to help you build a new one. Members of the society are strongly committed to each other; while they may not share the same bloodline, they may still feel as if they are all members of the same family. In other words, the dedication that exists is to the whole collectivity, not just one's blood relatives. Much of this unity and commitment may be possible because of the widespread sharing of aims, norms, and values, which produces a great deal of homogeneity. *Gemeinschaft* societies are characterized by unity, commitment, and cohesion.

When rational will prevails, human relationships are far more pragmatic and based more completely on self-interest. Individuals look out principally for themselves, and every relationship is judged in terms of how it contributes to one's personal interests and satisfactions. Societies that are based on these more rational and pragmatic relationships are characterized by a great deal of complexity, impersonality, conflict, and heterogeneity. In *Gesellschaft* societies, social change is rapid and social structure is complex, characterized by a multitude of institutions and conflict and competition between them. Because so many institutions exist, the family may find that its traditional functions evaporate as institutions like the state and the capitalist economy become influential forces in people's lives. The unity of earlier times evaporates, and what cohesion exists is primarily due to rational considerations of costs and benefits in some system of generalized exchange. Rather than being evaluated on the basis of ascribed status characteristics or personal qualities of the self, individuals in a *Gesellschaft* society are viewed in terms of what they do and, more important, in terms of what opportunities they offer for other people to get what they want (Tönnies 1957:182). *Gesellschaft* societies are characterized by competition, self-interest, and heterogeneity.

In a *Gemeinschaft* society, a patron may buy gasoline at Pete's Garage regardless of the price; Pete is a good guy and has been selling gas for a long time in the neighborhood. In a *Gesellschaft* society, however, what matters most is the price of gasoline. People still like Pete as a person but if a new station opens up with better prices, that is where most motorists will go for their fuel. Tönnies's work compared the original primitive communities of *Gemeinschaft* social organization with the modern industrial *Gesellschaft* form of social organization. He, like Marx, used an economic interpretation of historical change. The growth and diffusion of trade relationships oriented toward profit and based on the existence of money would transform the *Gemeinschaft* nature of a society so that it became more *Gesellschaft*—capitalistic and rationalistic—in form (Loomis and McKinney 1957:2–3).

Division of Labor and Social Solidarity

Some societies are characterized by a form of organization or integration called **mechanical solidarity** (Durkheim 1933:70–110). This is found in less complex societies, and it is an organization characterized by individual sameness or similarity. Most of the people, most of the time, are doing the same things; as a result, they are very much alike in personalities, temperaments, and interests and a high degree of homogeneity exists. The solidarity found in societies with a mechanical solidarity comes from an overwhelming sense of shared destiny found among all its members (Durkheim 1933:109).

As societies change over time, they develop a different kind of organization called **organic solidarity** (Durkheim 1933:111–32). This is based on the existence of individual differences—not similarities—but individual differences that are actually solidifying and integrating for the society (Durkheim 1933:131). Different people perform different tasks, so an extensive **division of labor** and a high degree of heterogeneity exist, but the task that each individual performs contributes directly to maintaining a society and in achieving its objectives. While individuals have less in common in organic solidarity than in mechanical solidarity, they still have a strong commitment to perform those tasks that fall to them. This produces a high degree of **functional interdependence** in which the performance of one task is dependent on the performance of other tasks for its successful completion. Carpenters will be unable to build a good house without the work of electricians, and vice versa.

Turtles and Social Change

The Miskito Indians of Nicaragua were propelled by sociocultural changes beyond their control and understanding away from being a *Gemeinschaft* society, based on unity, cohesion, and commitment—and a strong sense of communal conscience and a homogeneous division of labor—to a *Gesellschaft* society, characterized by self-interest and competition. The Miskito raised bananas, plantain, and a few other crops, and they hunted a few animals, principally the green turtle (Farb and Armelagos 1980). Not only was the green turtle an important source of food for them, it was the foundation of a system of mutual obligation. Meat from green turtles was shared freely by members of the community, and this cemented social bonds and reinforced feelings of loyalty and trust. Men hunted and fished, and women grew and cultivated the crops. The green turtle kept the entire society afloat, and no one resource was overused and in danger of extinction.

Trading companies became interested in the Miskito once they learned of their ability to find and catch green turtles. Turtle meat was in big demand at restaurants far distant from the eastern coast of Nicaragua to be used as turtle steak, as was calipee (the gelatinous material that is found under both the top and bottom shells of a turtle) to be used to make turtle soup. The arrival of foreign capital transformed the Miskito. Catching turtles to sell to outsiders was a far different enterprise from catching turtles for personal and community use. This limited resource, priceless for the Miskito's way of life, had become a commodity that was being caught almost entirely for economic reasons (Nietschmann 1995:229). The Miskito were pressured to catch as many turtles as they could, but very little of their catch was being used by them for food or as gifts to family and friends.

The commercialization of the green turtle had severe repercussions for Miskito's social relationships and cultural traditions. The Indians had to go farther and farther to find the turtles that were becoming harder and harder to find. They worked harder and longer to catch and sell turtles to get money that they needed to buy food at stores established by the trading companies. The Indians were more undernourished and less healthy—and the quality of their lives was poorer—than they were before the companies started buying the turtle meat. With commercialization came an erosion of communal life. The turtle hunters were forced to look out for their own interests to the neglect of practically everything else. Turtle meat that once would have been given freely to kin or to friends was kept and sold (Nietschmann 1995:230). Suspicion of others and an unwillingness to embark upon any joint venture or cooperative pursuit became commonplace.

The traditional subsistence activities of the Miskito (hunting, fishing, gathering, and growing) were replaced by a market economy based almost exclusively on catching turtles. In this setting, change creates more change, most of it highly destructive of custom and community. More and more of the Miskito had to get involved in hunting for a rapidly disappearing resource. Debts increased as Miskito had to buy not only food but also nets and other fishing equipment. This made it even less likely that the average Miskito turtle hunter would show a profit (Nietschmann 1995:233). The Miskito were forced to work more and more for less and less and the quality of their lives was ruined in the process (Farb and Armelagos 1980:71). They lost their independence, their harmony with nature, and their solidarity with one another. In fact, they lost much of what had made their lives worth living: community integration, shared rituals, companionship, and a sense of group purpose. Feelings of mutual suspicion and antagonistic social relationships flourished.

Shifting Societies:
The Nature of Sociocultural Change

While social relationships are not infinitely flexible and technology cannot make everything possible—social inertia and stubborn resistance to change are central features of social life—people acting together do have a great deal of power to change themselves as they change their relationships. Sometimes, **sociocultural change**—the alteration in systems of shared knowledge, institutional structures, and interpersonal relationships—is temporary and short-lived. Sociologists use the term **collective action** to describe the transitory and relatively unregulated forms of collective behavior like riots, fads, crazes, and rumors. At other times, sociocultural change is more organized and has enduring effects on the society, group, or world order of which it is a part (Snow and Oliver 1995:571–2). In this situation it is called a **social movement** to emphasize its organization and permanence.

Sociocultural change may take place through either **reform** (a social movement that produces gradual and ongoing changes in a society) or **revolution** (a social movement that produces dramatic and sweeping changes in a society, often intended to overthrow an entire governmental apparatus). Deliberate change can do more harm than good in a society if it produces sweeping changes for which people are unprepared. We must learn from the past and allow institutions room to grow and develop. Those institutions that develop through trial and error of dozens of generations may work better than those that have been consciously changed through deliberate action (Chirot 1994:127).

The First Technological Revolution

An eventful sociocultural change in human development was humans' transformation from being food hunters, gatherers, and fishers to being food producers, a transformation in subsistence activities known as the **first technological revolution** (Perry and Perry 1993:253). **Hunting and gathering** is a risky and difficult way to live (Diamond 1999:109–13). Wild foods are not in limitless supply, and it is easy for humans to deplete the available food; most wild plants and animals are not edible, especially without some kind of preparation, or even deadly to eat. Periods of feast are almost always followed by periods of famine for hunters and gatherers, and the most pressing problem for them is to find enough food to survive on a day-to-day basis. When humans learned how to produce food, however, it gave them a greater degree of certainty and dependability in regard to their food supply than they had ever before had, while it made it possible for them to produce and store a surplus of food. The shift from total reliance on whatever wild foods were available to almost total reliance on domesticated foods took a long time, even where it happened rather quickly (Diamond 1999:106). In some places food production never started—people continued to hunt and to gather—and in other places it only started when people migrated there with their knowledge and abilities to produce food (Diamond 1999:104); it began in the Americas around 3500 B.C. (Diamond 1999:96).

Those people who could produce food would find themselves encouraged to produce more and more of it. The production of a surplus of food and increases in population size encouraged the development of a more sedentary lifestyle, far less dependent on roaming in search of food. This new way of subsisting would then stimulate more population growth and a search for ways to store personal possessions, food surpluses, and other paraphernalia that no longer had to be carried. This created further pressures to produce more food in more efficient ways to nourish and sustain members of the society. The denser populations—and the advantages that came from more advanced forms of social organization—made it possible for food producers to conquer, displace, or absorb hunting-and-food-gathering societies across the planet. Hunters and food gatherers either adopted food production themselves or they were quickly bowled over by larger, stronger, and more ruthless populations (Diamond 1999:109–13).

Horticulturalists and Herders

The technological innovations of **horticultural society** involve new ways of doing things and new ways of understanding how things should be done. Horticulturalists were able to grow their own food, and they made and used both digging sticks and hoes. These are simple tools, to be sure, but in their own way, quite profound. A digging stick may be little more than a straight stick from which all the limbs, twigs, and leaves have been removed. The stick is thrust into the ground, moved around until a hole exists, and a seed is placed in it and covered with dirt. The hoe, primarily to clear the area around the seed plants and keep the weeds down, completed the horticulturalists' list of farming tools. No longer did farmers have to spend the work day on their knees or crouching, pulling out weeds that might overwhelm young plants. Horticulturalists adopted a **slash-and-burn cultivation strategy**. This involved burning—so it was dependent on the invention of fire—of standing shrubs, trees, and other vegetation. Burning produced a layer of ash that was an excellent place to plant and grow crops. However, the nutrients in the soil were exhausted after only a few years, and horticulturalists had to search for new lands to cultivate.

Parts of the earth, of course, are unsuitable for farming. They lack sufficient rain (less than twenty-five inches per year makes growing of plants for human consumption risky), suitable land (too mountainous), or a long enough growing season. Even if terrain and climate were favorable for farming, people still might have lacked the knowledge and technology to culti-vate the land (the digging stick and hoe were insufficient to do much farming in tougher soils). In these places, people lived in something other than a horti-cultural society. Survival strategies evolved that were more dependent on the availability of domesticated animals like goats, sheep, and cattle than on farm-ing. These animals are attractive as domesticates for many reasons, not the least of which is the fact that they are herd animals—and so easier to control (control a few and you control the many)—and they neither compete with humans for food nor try to eat humans as food (Diamond 1999:168–74). This type of society—called **herding or pastoral society**—has some important differences from horticultural society.

Pastoralists, because they are tied to their flocks more than to their land, are nomadic. They live in terrain with few geographical barriers, so they can move in search of suitable grazing lands for their herds. Communities tend to be smaller in size than those of horticultural societies, resources are less abun-dant, people are less prosperous, and large and dense settlements are nonex-istent (Lenski, Nolan, and Lenski 1995:227). Because livestock—the type and the number—is the measure of one's worth and influence, pastoralists con-tinually try to expand the size of their herds, and they must protect their live-stock against those who would steal or destroy them. Much raiding and warfare occur because a good way to increase your holdings is to steal some or all of it from someone else. Having a large family is an asset because it is easier to protect what one has if more people are around to help with the job. Pastoralists tend to be patriarchal and male-dominated, and inequality be-tween the sexes is conspicuous.

Pastoralists have knowledge of what livestock is good for and how it can be used to enhance human comforts. Because of their physiology (a multi-chambered stomach), these herd animals can eat food that is not fit for human consumption and transform it into items of great value for humans: meat, blood, milk, hides (for clothing or for shelters), tallow, fleece, and bones (to be used as ornaments or as weapons). Pastoralists also possess knowledge of what kinds of food and environmental conditions are best for livestock, knowledge of how livestock reproduce, and knowledge of selective breeding. While sur-pluses are less likely in pastoral society than in horticultural society—meat is more perishable and usually consumed more quickly—some surplus does exist, some inequality is tied to the surplus, and some trading exists between pastoralists and people from other societies. Pastoralists quickly learned the advantages of riding animals like horses, camels, or mules. It gave them geo-graphical mobility and military superiority in wars with their less mobile neighbors who farmed the land. Herding groups attacked farming societies throughout Europe and China, and they were often successful in conquering these more sedentary people.

The spread of the skills and knowledge of food production from one re-gion to another was a crucial factor in sociocultural change around the world.

People in one region transmitted their knowledge and technology of how to grow and herd—or the crops and livestock themselves—to other regions (Diamond 1999:176–7). Physical areas that were located east or west of each other—and so were at the same general latitude—shared very similar seasonal and climatic conditions (Diamond 1999:176–82). Movements in the northern or southern direction changed latitudes, which usually produced dramatic changes in climate and growing conditions. This geographical fact meant that food (plants and animals) and technologies of food production could spread more easily east or west than north or south. What was true for livestock and crops, was also true for other things. Those societies that exchanged food and technologies of food production were more likely to exchange items like wheels, writing skills, alphabets, metal-making abilities, and the technology of beer and wine production (Diamond 1999:190).

Pressures for change may come either from inside or outside a particular society, and cultural change may be the result of a large number of haphazard or unconnected occurrences (Lieberson 2001). One type of sociocultural change is called **cultural innovation.** It exists when an individual or group creates and externalizes a new piece of cultural knowledge that is then learned and used by other members of the society. For example, the invention of the cotton gin by Catherine Littlefield Greene (widow of a Revolutionary War soldier General Nathaniel Greene) and its building and patenting by Eli Whitney transformed the U.S. cotton industry. It became possible through the use of the machine to clean as much cotton in a day as fifty people could clean by hand. A second important type of sociocultural change is called **cultural diffusion.** It exists when cultural knowledge is transmitted from one place to another. Spaghetti has been part of Italian cooking for centuries, a food that in all likelihood was brought to the country either by Arabs or by Indians (Patrick 1982:644) and not by Marco Polo on his way back from China as is commonly thought (Davidson 1999:232). However, this pasta dish is now popular throughout the world. When it comes to technological inventions and political institutions, most societies receive more from other societies than they themselves invent (Diamond 1999:406). This is why diffusion, migration of peoples, and barriers to migration play such an important role in sociocultural change in any society.

Cultural diffusion exists in two forms. In one form, called **blueprint copying,** an invention or custom can be directly seen or observed as it is copied in a new place. Having a wheel exported from another country in front of me when I build my own wheel is an example of blueprint copying. Another form of cultural diffusion is called **idea diffusion.** This exists when all an inventor has received is an idea or suggestion (Diamond 1999:224–5). If I hear that somebody in an adjacent town has invented a round object that can be attached to a wagon to make it easier to pull food, then this is an example of idea diffusion. Most things will be easier to create with a blueprint than with only an idea as a guide, and some things will be very difficult to create without a blueprint. A wheel is easier to make with only foreknowledge of the object than is gunpowder.

Agrarian Society

Agrarian societies were responsible for many inventions or cultural innovations; however, the plow is the one that had the greatest impact on further sociocultural change (Lenski, Nolan, and Lenski 1995:175). It made it possible for members of this type of society to grow an abundance of food for human consumption. Early plows were made of wood, and they were pulled by humans. However, plows eventually came to be made of metal, and they were pulled by animals like oxen or castrated bulls. The use of the plow, instead of a hoe or digging stick, coupled with the use of animal power rather than human power, had immediate and important effects on the entire course of human development. Far more land could be cultivated, and the soil could be turned over more thoroughly and effectively, getting nutrients to the surface that would have been beyond any human using a hoe or even beyond the roots of most plants to reach.

Many cleavages characterized agrarian society—between urban and rural, between the literate and illiterate, between the governed and the governors—but the most important and most problematic was between the relatively small number of exceptionally prosperous elites and everyone else. Increases in the division of labor are found as agrarian societies mature, principally because of increases in the surplus of food and other valuable resources. Elites fought one another and jockeyed for a better position (Lachmann 2000), while peasants fought each other to obtain more and better land for themselves and their families (Lenski, Nolan, and Lenski 1995:205). Elites appropriated as much as they could of what the labors of peasants had produced, caught, or gathered. A system of stark inequalities existed along with an exquisitely unfair system of exploitation that made it possible for elites to live in the lap of luxury while everyone else crawled for crumbs. This system was surprisingly stable because the individuals who were in the best position to change the way things would be done—elites—were the ones who benefited most from not changing things much at all.

While necessity certainly can be the mother of invention, more often some catastrophe is the precipitating event. Plagues and wars have regularly changed the course of human history by producing political breakdowns and economic collapses. In fact, wars and disease often go hand in hand, and it is not hard to understand why. A surplus of food and a more extensive division of labor mean that most people in a society are freed from the demands of food production. The surplus can be used to feed and maintain—and make possible the existence of—kings and queens, bureaucrats, soldiers, priests (who offer divine interpretations and justifications for wars and for disease), artisans (who can craft metal into swords, guns, and other weapons of war), and scribes (to record the history of the society, of its wars, and of its plagues) (Diamond 1999:90). Strong pressures develop for growth and expansion. In the beginning, it is easy to find good land inside the boundaries of a society, and new technologies are invented to farm the land more effectively. Crops grow quickly with minimal investment of time and work. However, as greater and greater demands are placed on available soils, what once worked no longer does.

For a while, the invention of new and effective technologies produced enough food from the available land to satisfy the increasing human demand. The **agricultural revolution** (improved knowledge of growing food) entailed the adoption of a **three-field system.** Four fields were used for growing food but one always lay fallow or uncultivated; one year in four a given field was allowed to rest. By rotating the field that was uncultivated, it made it possible for its soil to be replenished. Eventually, the field rotation system became unnecessary. First the Dutch and then the British learned that they could use clover as a crop to revitalize soils (it added nitrogen to the land) and to serve as an excellent food source for grazing animals. A field no longer had to lay fallow, meaning more lands could be used for food production (Chirot 1994:42). These innovations helped, to be sure, but only for a while. Agrarian societies had to come up with better ways to feed a growing population.

New soils had to be found that would produce enough food to sustain population growth, particularly the growing numbers of people who were no longer directly involved in food-producing activities (e.g., scribes, priests, metallurgists). When the natural cycles of poor weather conditions and natural parasites are added to the equation, it is easy to see that crop yields from the existing acreage might never be large enough. To make matters worse, elites usually placed more and more demands on peasants at that point where peasants had the least to give. These factors worked together to cause extreme tensions inside a society and the motivation to expand into other lands. Anytime warriors went into an adjoining area, they carried their weapons and their diseases with them to populations that had neither protection against the weapons of the invading armies nor immunity to their germs. These forces of conquest and domination transformed societies, states, and social relationships in profound ways (Diamond 1999:85–92).

State Power

The invention of the state about 5000 years ago was an important social invention that determined how societies would be organized and directed (Chirot 1994:11). Two important statuses existed in the early states. One was the shaman, soothsayer, or mediator. This individual was skilled at interpreting signs, telling the future, and, most important, resolving disputes over how much people's labor was worth and who would earn what. The second status was the war leader. This individual was skilled at waging war or resolving disputes with people *outside* the boundaries of a society (Chirot 1994:15). Having people who could resolve disputes or wage war was functional for a society. However, the increasing power and influence of mediators and warriors did have a price, sometimes a dear one. It made it easier for them to institutionalize policies and procedures to benefit themselves and to deprive others of their own independence and much of what they had accumulated. Nonetheless, people learned to accept, or even depend on, the power and authority of their mediators and warriors (Chirot 1994:17).

The change from prestate to state society was not an easy transition. Leaders almost always engaged in acts of brutality and violence, much of it excessive and unnecessary, to show that they were people to be feared and followed. It required impressive shows of force to get the masses to work longer and harder, and then to give much of what they had earned to elites through taxes; to fight or die for the newly formed state; and to accept levels of inequality that were previously unknown. The more successful nation-states started expanding into areas outside of their borders in order to find more people to tax and more people to abduct to serve as slaves. Sometimes, all that was needed for a successful crusade was control of the army. At other times, however, civil wars erupted and what was needed was support from religious and family institutions, a convincing ideology, and levels of prosperity that were high enough that most people in the land thought that they benefited along with their leaders, even while clear examples existed that they did not (Midlarsky 1999).

From savage beginnings, characterized by brutal exploitation of the powerless by the powerful, came things of value: great civilizations, high cultures, art and literature, innovative technologies, influential philosophies, powerful religions, science, entertainment, music, and institutional forms that still have parallels in contemporary societies throughout the world. Institutional forms went through their own process of natural selection. Some of them were brought to a society by outsiders and caught on; others resulted from planned changes and lasted because they worked; still others just seemed to evolve and become popular. Sociocultural change is rarely smooth, being characterized by periods of quick, dramatic change followed by long periods of relative stability (Giugni, McAdam, and Tilly 1999).

Modern Times

Unless forms of agriculture exist that are capable of sustaining rapidly growing and dense populations—something requiring both a suitable climate and advanced farming technologies—then **capitalism** (an economic system based on private profit) will probably not develop (Harris 1999:172–3). England was the first society to become an **industrial society**—in the 1700s—to the point that more than half of its income came from activities based on machines that were powered by energy sources other than humans and/or animals. The

Industrial Revolution was a continuous process of change (and resistance to change) with certain important pulses that substantially changed social relationships and set the foundation for further changes (Lenski, Nolan, and Lenski 1995:248–60). Initially, new tools and machines like the spinning wheel or loom were invented to make human labor power more efficient. In time, tools and machines were invented that depended upon inanimate sources of power such as steam or coal. The invention of the steam engine by James Watt was applied to a multitude of tasks, from jobs in the textile industry to the powering of locomotives. Goods and people were eventually ferried by steamships, as well as by locomotives, as knowledge of the potential of steam propulsion increased and as iron and steel were available for building ships that once would have been made out of wood and moved by a paddle wheel.

Tools and machines were invented that were propelled by sources of power like natural gas, electricity, petroleum, or nuclear energy (Lenski, Nolan, and Lenski 1995:248). The internal combustion engine was invented, as well as machines that could generate electricity in large enough quantities to meet the needs of a growing public. The automobile industry grew in size and influence, and it stimulated the development of other industries like steel, rubber, iron, glass, petroleum, road construction, and all the businesses and amusements that rely on tourist trade. The communications industry, especially because of the telephone, became a potent force in sociocultural change, and advances in airline technology, plastics, electronics, computers, and nuclear power accelerated during the late stages of industrialization. As a society becomes more thoroughly mechanized, machines run and control other machines. New materials are invented and synthesized, and they often replace old standards like steel or iron. It is no accident that plastics have found their way into more and more items because of their relative cost, strength, and versatility. As energy costs continue to rise, modern nations search for power in some of the oldest energy sources: solar energy and the power of the wind.

Society grew to maturity in western Europe, even though other societies had become more advanced earlier (e.g., China or parts of the Middle East). What distinguished western Europe was its uninterrupted or continuous growth (Hopcroft 1999). Rainfall was more constant and evenly distributed throughout the area, and it was less likely for western Europeans to experience cycles of feast and famine. The sources of wealth and mobility changed. It became less important who you or, more important, who your parents were. What became most important was your ability to calculate, to take advantage of opportunities, to think freely, and to follow the money.

> Western European societies became rich and powerful because they allowed their intellectuals greater freedom to explore new ideas, because towns were more independent, and because commercial rationality became a more important part of social life than elsewhere (Chirot 1994:108).

Better food-growing abilities, better transportation systems for getting the food to market, and better ability to control some of the diseases afflicting humankind made it possible for dramatic growth of the populations of western Europe. After about 1000 A.D., western Europe experienced a period of continuous growth in population, trade, agriculture, and cultural refinements.

Western Europe had a unique constellation of social and political factors. It had a language that allowed a shared experience and outlook among its residents—and the possibility for communication—and it was also a place divided into cities, kingdoms, and principalities. The absence of a politically unified center allowed these autonomous regions to compete with one another, which encouraged the growth of self-governance and the capitalist spirit.

> A larger area or population means more potential inventors, more competing societies, more innovations available to adopt—and more pressure to adopt and retain innovations, because societies failing to do so will tend to be eliminated by competing societies (Diamond 1999:407).

The joint operation of a capitalist economic system and a democratic political system, coupled with a cultural system that encouraged rationality, individualism, and curiosity, offered the greatest opportunity for innovation and rapid social change.

Self-interest and greed—the accumulation of resources beyond any sense of need or fairness—came to be viewed as a valuable mechanism for improving society itself. Free enterprise and the **capitalistic imperative**—the legitimation or even glorification of unrestrained accumulation—encouraged or even demanded an outlook that was innovative, creative, and opportunistic. Boundless accumulation was celebrated as being the best for everyone. Improved economic performance in a society seemed to benefit both the buyer and the seller, and economic success gradually replaced other kinds of successes: in war, in physical strength, in moral excellence, in family devotion, and in spiritual reverence. The pursuit of profit for its own sake became defined as morally proper, even while detractors did insist that capitalism undercut a sense of communal solidarity, disrupted the status quo, and made equality practically impossible to achieve.

The social changes that started and caught on in western Europe have now been carried throughout the world, and the industrial way of life is changing societies across the planet in fundamental ways. With industrialization comes changes in population (it increases in size, at least for a time), the growth of cities and urbanization (at least until people grow tired of overcrowded, polluted, dangerous cities and move to the suburbs), the growth of bureaucracies and a more formal organization of life, the growth in the number and complexity of social institutions, and the substitution of the impersonal ties of the market for kinship ties and other primary relationships.

Other institutions—families, schools, religions, governments—change along with economic changes. Families become smaller and more mobile to have any chance of being able to benefit from changing economic opportunities; schools teach skills and values appropriate for life in an industrial society like punctuality, self-control, literacy, ambition, self-reliance, a willingness to compete, and the value of hard work; religious organizations profess the importance of humility, morality, and devotion to kin and country; and so on. No place in an industrializing society is safe from the transformation that occurs in institutional structures and social relationships. The capitalistic imperative was an idea whose time had come, and the pressures of the market were too strong and the promise of great riches and individual success were too seductive to be resisted for long.

One major reason for the success of western Europe is that Europeans were able to conquer or destroy other peoples because of Europeans' possession of steel tools and manufactured products, their guns and weapons, armored body suits for protection, horses to ride, maritime technology and ships, bureaucratic political organization, writing and literacy, and, importantly, the nasty germs that they carried with them to lands where the resident populations had no immunity whatsoever (Diamond 1999:23). "Smallpox, measles, influenza, typhus, bubonic plague, and other infectious diseases endemic in Europe played a decisive role in European conquests, by decimating many peoples on other continents" (Diamond 1999:77).

Sociocultural change is directly affected by subsistence activities and food production, which, as we have seen, are strongly influenced by environmental conditions. Those people who remain at the level of hunters and food-gathers—who can only find food, not produce it—have the deck stacked against them when it comes to world conquest.

> . . . food production was indirectly a prerequisite for the development of guns, germs, and steel. Hence geographic variation in whether, or when, the peoples of different continents became farmers and herders explains to a large extent their subsequent contrasting fates (Diamond 1999:86).

Food producers have larger and healthier populations than hunters and gatherers because they cultivate and eat safe and nutritious foods (Diamond 1999:88). A well-fed, large population is just the beginning of the advantages enjoyed by the more advanced food producers, however.

Because hunting-gathering societies have little or no surpluses of food, most of the people in a society are involved in food-gathering activities. Men will hunt; women and children will gather. Even if these individuals could accumulate a surplus, they really have no place to store it anyway. The food would quickly rot and be either inedible or toxic. A surplus of food, however, stored for long periods of time, is essential if a society is to have the kind of people who can wage wars successfully. No bureaucrats, soldiers, politicians, chiefs, kings, metallurgists or other artisans, priests, scribes, or physicians means, for all practical purposes, that the people will live in a society where the number of internal conflicts is low, technology is simple, and little or no interest exists to wage war to dominate other peoples in order to amass more wealth and power (Diamond 1999:55–7).

Those societies that produced food first had a distinct advantage and put them on the fast track to guns, germs, and steel (Diamond 1999:103).

> Farmers tend to breathe out nastier germs, to own better weapons and armor, to own more-powerful technology in general, and to live under centralized governments with literate elites better able to wage wars of conquest (Diamond 1999:195).

The availability of horses, camels, or other large animals that could be used as pack animals or as mounts increased the geographic mobility of food-producing people, which helped them even more to conquer other populations. However, these animals had a more important effect. They were the source of many of the infectious diseases that now plague humans. These animal-derived afflictions had the power to kill members of those societies who had had no opportunity to develop an immunity to the germs that caused them (Diamond 1999:92). A larger number of animals had been domesticated in Eurasia than in the Americas, and most of the Eurasian animals were sources of disease-carrying germs. Only the turkey, guinea pig, Muscovy duck, the dog, and the llama/alpaca had been domesticated in the Americas, most not an important source of disease (Diamond 1999:212–3). Far more Native Americans died from Eurasian germs than died in battle from European swords and guns (Diamond 1999:210). Clearly, members of food-producing societies had distinct advantages when it came to world conquest because they exhaled deadlier germs, had better weapons, possessed more highly developed technology, were better organized, and were highly motivated to wage wars against other populations.

Sociocultural Change in the United States

Changes in U.S. society are impressive and at times even a little frightening. An increase has occurred in the number of flexible, temporary relationships, based on self-interest and immediate pleasure (Rubin 1996:4), and conflicts seem to be all around us. Some of our problems in living exist in part because some parts of a society change faster than other parts. Introducing a new technology into a society and getting it adopted and used is difficult (McLaughlin, Rosen, Skinner, and Webster 1999). It can produce a **cultural lag** as the more sluggish parts try to catch up with the parts that changed first (Ogburn 1932;

Ogburn 1964). The cultural lag may seem to be abnormal or undesirable when it is just an inevitable correlate of a society on the move.

The Economic Institution

The **economic institution** is the social institution that organizes human relationships that are responsible for finding or producing the goods and/or services that are necessary for human survival and for distributing these goods and services to other members of the group. Labor-capital relationships in the United States evolved that were based on a tacit understanding: If workers worked hard and well, without complaint, then they could expect job security, monetary gain, and stable employment (Rubin 1996:37). This stable accord between workers and their employers was undermined when opportunities arose that made it possible for employers to increase profits without worrying overmuch about the wants or needs of U.S. workers (McCall 2001:524). Unions were weakened and destroyed; temporary or part-time workers were hired in place of full-time workers; mechanized systems of production made it possible to lay off or fire workers; and employers moved their plants and businesses to places where workers were crawling all over one another to get jobs no matter what they were paid or what they were asked to do.

The economy has entered a stage of **postindustrialism** and U.S. society is now a **postindustrial society.** The principal economic activity during the stage of postindustrial development is the provision of services to a consuming public. Employees are encouraged to be creative, and they are rewarded for it. The boundaries between different organizations are more open, and mobility is possible within organizations, as well as from one organization to another (Hage and Powers 1992). Dentists, elementary school teachers, mechanics, and bank presidents (as well as prostitutes and professional killers) all make a living from supplying services to others for some kind of payment.

The flexibility of the postindustrial world allows businesses to respond quickly to changing demands no matter what they are and no matter where they occur. If Asians want food that tastes like what they are accustomed to, the McDonald's corporation can quickly supply their needs in McDonald's restaurants in the Far East. If General Motors learns that drivers want a car with a larger trunk, changes can be made in computer software to adjust machinery to make the modifications in trunk design. In a postindustrial world, production becomes far more flexible, and what is of greatest importance is not what is made as much as how it is packaged and delivered. The information explosion, where huge financial transactions can be accomplished with computers in the blink of an eye, has contributed to this flexibility.

In the early days of industrialization, workers were intentionally **deskilled** by their bosses. Work was reduced to its lowest common denominator so that anyone could do the work of practically anyone else. Even unskilled, poorly paid, unmotivated workers could do what they were asked to do. De-skilling maximized the control of workers (anyone can be replaced at a moment's notice with little difficulty), while it eliminated the need to pay enough money to attract highly skilled and highly motivated workers. In a postindustrial society, things are different. A good job is one that offers a chance for advancement, a handsome income, and an opportunity to learn and grow (Rubin 1996:63). Workers in the transformed economy have greater discretion, more opportunities, and frequent encouragement to become active participants in the production process (Rubin 1996:73–4). Even service work can provide opportunities for self-fulfillment (Frenkel, Korczynski, Shire, and Tam 1999).

The Political Institution

The **political institution** is the social institution that organizes human relationships oriented toward the possession and use of legitimate power (and efforts to keep it or to get more of it). Rapidly changing economies are associated with rapid changes in other parts of a society. Prior to World War II and the Great Depression, the U.S. government had little impact on the day-to-day lives of ordinary citizens, even while it was actively involved in the market and the affairs of corporations and other businesses. By the end of the Second World War, however, the U.S. government had changed its role substantially.

> The restructured role entailed a set of policies, institutions, and budgets targeting a wide range of the citizenry, previously relatively ignored. What emerged were systematic government attempts to secure the well-being of even the most disadvantaged citizens of society (Rubin 1996:116).

In order to provide the kind of assistance that citizens came to expect from an active government—clean environments, crime-free communities, social services for people in need (the poor, the unemployed, the sick, the elderly, the homeless, the young), quality schools, protection from external enemies—required a huge outlay of funds. However, the U.S. government found it increasingly difficult to maintain the interventionist role that it had carved out for itself, especially in the rapidly changing global economy. A huge and growing gap developed between what the government needed in order to do what citizens and businesses expected of it and the funds that were actually available for the job (O'Connor 1973). The U.S. government entered a period of transition in which it became more distracted and less involved in the day-to-day affairs of ordinary citizens (Rubin 1996:126–46).

Individuals in the United States lost confidence in the capacity of their government to help them in their time of need. In the vacuum left behind, they were forced to rely more heavily on market forces and the economic system. However, this may have been a mistake. The deterioration of the basic accord between workers and their employers meant that businesses in the United States were far less willing to provide high enough wages and other benefits to really help members of the U.S. work force and their dependents. Workers were fragmented, easy to control, and, most important, easy to ignore. The power of the federal government to aid and to assist the needy has been diminished by massive budget cuts, deregulation of private industry, and the privatization of government functions. As government support dwindles and the power of the economic system grows, it hurts all those who cannot or will not embrace the market (e.g., children, the aged, the poor, the unemployed, and the unemployable). To these individuals, the market offers only an illusion of opportunity (Blau 1999).

Parallel Changes: Families, Religions, Schools

Changes in the economic and political institutions are correlated with changes in other U.S. institutions: family, religion, and education.

> When major corporations raise prices, relocate plants, or lay off large numbers of employees, the impact is wrought upon families, schools, and churches; alternatively, however, the typical family, school, or congregation does not affect such a corporation in any significant way (Blasi 1998:110).

The **family institution** is the social institution that organizes human relationships oriented toward the birthing and raising of children; members of a family unit are related by blood, marriage, or adoption. At the end of the 1800s in the United States, most families lived on farms and were producing units. While families did buy a few of the things that they needed, most of what they used was made by them. Aunt Martha might have made great bread but grew lousy corn. Therefore, her nephew would exchange some of the corn that he grew for some of her bread. This system of barter or exchange was particularly effective because the family was more extended than it is today, and family members felt responsible for one another (Rubin 1996:92).

The modern family is more of a consuming unit than it is a producing unit, and contemporary families buy more and more of what they need on the open market. If family members have become more consumption oriented, then relationships between husbands and wives and between parents and children have become based less on authority and discipline and more on companionship and emotional support (Rubin 1996:93). The levels of freedom and emotional encouragement that are now given to children would have been unthinkable to parents of previous generations (Zelizer 1994). Mothers and fathers and their offspring have formed their own **nuclear family,** apart from the influence of other family members, and members of the nuclear family unit now feel more obligated than they once did to support, encourage, correct, control, and guide each other (Weiss 2000).

In a rapidly changing world, people often search for some kind of stability and security, even if little exists. As a response to rapid sociocultural change, some individuals search for comfort and security in tradition and what appear to be absolute truths (Yang and Ebaugh 2001:280–1). The **religious institution** is the social institution that organizes human relationships that are oriented toward spirituality and other sacred matters and supplies answers to questions about death and the possibilities of an afterlife. Within U.S. religious institutions, despite the secular movement of our society, a discernible trend exists toward **fundamentalism** and spirituality. Fundamentalists embrace an other-worldly stance toward the temptations of this world and resist many of the institutional forces for social change. Another response to change is the desire to take advantage of it. The **educational institution** is the social institution that organizes human relationships toward the teaching and learning of important or even essential knowledge like facts, basic skills, values, and norms. The educational institution is viewed as distinctly capable of providing us with the kinds of knowledge, skills, and capacities that will prepare us for success in an ever-changing world.

Iron Cages, Fast Food, and Disenchantment

Max Weber clearly understood the potential for bureaucracies to become so routinized, rational, and impersonal that they would develop into **iron cages** that would be as imprisoning and stultifying as they would be efficient. He believed the inexorable movement toward efficiency and rationality in western societies would generate increased levels of alienation, decreased levels of meaning, and a pervasive sense of disenchantment (Bendix 1962:458). As more and more areas of social life become bureaucratized, individuals become less and less important as they are reduced to cogs in large, impersonal, social machines (Hughes, Martin, and Sharrock 1995:120–2). While Weber held out hope that some inspirational or **charismatic leader** would come forth who could bring a sense of excitement and enchantment to a depersonalized world, he was not very optimistic. Modern society, he thought, would probably evolve into a dictatorship of bureaucrats and technical experts (Bendix 1962:459), and routinization and rationality would be permanent features of social life.

The charge that bureaucratization produces iron cages has been repackaged for contemporary audiences by George Ritzer. For him, an inexorable social process is what he calls the **McDonaldization of society** in which norms and values of more and more sectors of U.S. society—education, work, health care, leisure activities—are resembling more and more what goes on in the fast-food industry (Ritzer 2000:1–2). To the extent that McDonaldized institutions, organizations, and relationships predominate, to that extent the creativity and flexibility of a postindustrial society are severely jeopardized.

The four cornerstones that support the golden arches of McDonaldized social life are (1) efficiency, (2) calculability, (3) predictability, and (4) control.

Efficiency exists when methods and procedures produce the optimum method for getting from one point to another (Ritzer 2000:12). People who act efficiently follow rules to accomplish a clearly defined task without disrupting the flow of human activity (e.g., cooking and selling a burger to someone who will eat it quickly and without complaint). Efficiency exists when we can buy our eyeglasses in under an hour or find enough cash registers at the supermarket that we do not have to wait much time at all. *Calculability* is really about the clarity of the value of goods and services. Consumers must come to believe—and be able to calculate—that they have received something of value at a quick rate of speed. Sellers try to convince consumers that providing a lot of something in record time is what makes it good (Ritzer 2000:12). "Upsizing" your Happy Meal seems to make it even happier. *Predictability* assures consumers that the items they buy and the services they receive will always meet the standards that they have come to expect (Ritzer 2000:14). A bucket of the Colonel's fried chicken in Kentucky is identical to the same item in California, Florida, or Kansas. What is more, the setting, personnel, and general operating procedures are similar no matter where you go. The final element is *control*, both of employees and of customers (Ritzer 2000:14). This control comes from the construction of physical layouts that encourage people to take care of their business quickly and then leave. Surprisingly, the one element that Ritzer left out in his analysis of McDonaldization was *profitability*, the foundation for all the rest.

Efficiency, calculability, predictability, and control can have advantages for consumers, and the existence of these can make positive changes in organizations, institutions, and societies. Consumers know what they are getting even if what they are getting is not exactly what they would like or need, and McDonaldized goods and services do offer them a comfort and security. Consumers are being served in a familiar environment (even if they are in a strange city), by people who look familiar and act in familiar ways. However, McDonaldization (like rationalization and bureaucratization) is a double-edged sword. For every advantage that comes from an efficient, calculable, predictable, and controlled way of doing things, a disadvantage is not far behind. Rational systems are only rational in a very limited sense, and they almost always create irrationalities, dehumanizing conditions, and environmental destruction. What sense does it make to force people to do the same job over and over again, sometimes for years and years, to make them efficient while they are dehumanized and alienated in the process? We should always ask efficient, calculable, predictable, and controlled for whom and to what end? We may find that the irrationalities and contradictions of life in a McDonaldized society are its most salient features.

A wholly predictable cultural theme in a McDonaldized society is the belief that the rationality, routinization, and monotony of everyday life can be overcome by buying and consuming more and more. Much like the addict who takes more and more of that forbidden substance in the search for the ultimate thrill, so do consumers in the United States try to purchase more and more enchantment and fun. **Cathedrals of consumption** are continually transforming themselves to look more fun, frivolous, and enchanting, while they continue to be based even more and more on efficiency, control, and profitability (Ritzer 1999:x). This facade of fun and frivolity seduces and soothes the unwary shopper, even while it encourages frenzied consumption. We consume more than we ever did, often alone, purchasing a wide range of goods and services in one place, with other people, many of whom are strangers to us (Ritzer 1999:x). Shopping has become a bona fide social activity, and the places where shopping takes place have become distinctive social worlds with their own economies, cultures, police forces, media centers, recreational activities, restaurants, movies, parking garages, and child-care centers. Consumption is a driving force, and it becomes practically impossible to escape from the cultural imperative to shop and buy (Ritzer 1999:x–xi). The reason the cathedrals of consumption are successful—shopping malls, restaurants, bookstores, supermarkets, car dealerships—is that they appear to offer not only something of value to consumers but in a special and fun setting.

Genuine pleasures are hard to find in a social setting that is efficient, predictable, and tightly managed. A night out, a day at the races, or a vacation at Disney World seems to offer the prospect of fun and excitement, and sometimes an outing does deliver. However, it does so partly because it is something different—a departure from the ordinary and mundane—but mostly because the *belief* that some experiences are supposed to be fun is itself a hook that keeps people coming back for more and more.

Fun in the United States is both alienating and liberating (Deegan 1998b:77). The rituals associated with fun reinforce and reflect social inequalities—they remind us of the contrast between fun lives and all else—even while they create the appearance that we are escaping from the inequality and drudgery of our lives in these happy places and fun experiences (Deegan 1998a:5). In order to be able to participate in the **fun culture,** individuals must have the ability and/or willingness to lay out the cash to buy the fun times. From the hundreds and hundreds of dollars a trip to an amusement park may cost, to the price of admission to a rock concert or professional athletic event, or even to the cost of a prepared dish to take to the church social, some people will be better able to "enjoy the show" than others. In a curious twist, it may be the high price of something that makes it seem more attractive and enjoyable. That string of *faux* (false or phony) pearls—even though it looks exactly like the genuine article—is not pleasurable to receive or to give. What fun is it to go on the cheap?

My Society, My Relationships, My Self

Sociocultural factors have a direct and powerful impact on all parts of our individual experience—how we think, how we feel, how we act, and how we look. It is no surprise, then, that sociocultural *changes* are responsible for both the changes that we ourselves go through in our own lives and the way we understand those changes.

Appearance Norms

New priorities in regard to appearance emerge as technologies change (Sullivan 2001), as other parts of culture and society change, and as appearance entrepreneurs (e.g., Calvin Klein or Helena Rubinstein) usher in new standards of beauty (Husain 1998:6). It would be mistaken, however, to assume that any one standard of beauty is universal.

> In the 1850s [United States], for instance, the dominance of the frail, thin, and pale model of beauty prompted fashionable women to cultivate the palest possible complexions and sometimes to go so far as to paint their faces white. Yet at the same time voluptuousness was coming to be considered beautiful, and so fashionable women padded their bosoms. Finally, some circles were beginning to regard an aspect of independence and even athleticism as attractive. Therefore white-faced women with padded bosoms were likely to stride the streets in a manner that combined femininity with sensuality and yet contained more than a hint of assertiveness (Banner 1983:4–5).

Women confront mixed messages in regard to appearance, and women who are battling to be beautiful may shift from style to style in rapid succession as they discover that a particular fashion did not make it possible for them to be all that they wanted to be. The pressures on women to be forever young and healthy—and to look that way—are enormous (Jackson 1992:213).

> The irrational dislike that sometimes overtakes a mature woman when she sees a vision of loveliness many years her junior is based on a realistic understanding that this is her competitor in a contest whose outcome has been preordained. There is little solace in the knowledge that the new Snow White's season will also be brief (Brownmiller 1984:166).

Older women who still want to be considered physically attractive are almost required to defy their age through strict attention to all facets of personal appearance (Banner 1983:225). Their passport to beauty comes from spending the time and effort to diet and to exercise so that they can look younger and healthier than other women their age.

The term generally used to describe a pleasing appearance in a male throughout the nineteenth century in the United States was "manly." Several models of masculinity existed, however, and these competed for ascendancy well into the twentieth century.

> Before the Civil War, the prevailing model of masculinity was a youthful one, characterized by a clean-shaven face and a slim figure. The Civil War encouraged the appearance of the full-bearded portly man—the representative of a

middle-aged conservative business civilization—although youthful variations existed throughout the post–Civil War years. By late century, however, the youthful type issued a striking challenge, as the vogue of athletics became preeminent and the beard went out of fashion (Banner 1983:240).

The growing popularity of sports, especially the competitive, contact variety, was important in changing the standards of male appearance to a more rugged, muscular ideal as immigrants to the United States—German, Irish, and English—brought their love of sports (e.g., boxing) with them (Banner 1983:229–32). While the rotund male physique never was as admired as was the muscular male physique, for several decades after the Civil War he did hold his own (Banner 1983:232). Large girth became a way for a man to show outwardly his prosperity and maturity; he might even have grown a full beard to show onlookers that he was successful.

With globalization and the aggressive marketing of a uniform body image as the best one, the definitions of desirable and worthy are becoming increasingly narrow (Baird 1998:9). Advertising encourages females of all ages to determine their worth and attractiveness by how thin they are (Stephens, Hill, and Hanson 1994:137). The diffusion of ideals of appearance from one society to another (or from one subculture to another)—most apparent with cosmetics and clothes—can nudge people from very different parts of the world in the direction of greater uniformity in regard to body, face, hair, voice, and general temperament. A beautiful appearance comes to be defined as a product that is within reach of anyone who is willing to expend the effort. When one standard of appearance is fiercely promoted as the only worthy one, this pits individuals who want to stay in the "face race" against one another in a strange form of survival of the physically fittest (Brownmiller 1984:50). This may give rise to a situation in which the world's beautiful people are expected to look very much alike in all respects except skin color.

If you want to be taken seriously, you have to dress like a person who should be taken seriously. Fashion in clothing reflects identity, class, and gender, but individual choice is always affected by both technology (what can be produced) and those fashion moguls who make and supply clothing (Crane 2000). Prior to the 1800s, men and women dressed remarkably alike, at least in the upper class. Over three centuries ago in Europe, prosperous and powerful men who wanted to look fashionable wore wigs, powder on their faces, beauty marks, stockings, velvet robes, furs, and high heels (Miller and Costello 2001:593). Members of both sexes wore a great deal of lace, perfume, and brightly colored silks. It was not until the impact of capitalism, industrialization, and the isolation of the private world from the public that men stopped their flamboyant style of dressing and adopted a far more studied and somber look, at least when they were in public (Finkelstein 1998:55). Black clothing and a large, black, uncomfortable stovepipe hat—the standard male dress of the nineteenth century—was associated with punctuality and dependability in financial dealings (Banner 1983:235). Things have been more difficult for women. The fashion industry has been able to create a degree of insecurity among them by regularly refurbishing ideal fashion styles: working woman, family woman, liberated woman, companion woman, domestic woman, sports woman, or educated woman (Finkelstein 1998:64).

The Civilizing Process

The Middle Ages in Europe was a dangerous time, and threats to health and well-being were around practically every corner (e.g., war, disease, hunger). The struggle for existence was an ever-present force, and magic and superstition were sometimes the only protections to which people could turn. The precariousness of life encouraged a search for immediate gratification, and feelings of helplessness and despair were commonplace. Little attention was given to the future, and emotional states were spontaneous and expressed openly and directly, with little concern for their influence on others.

> Few regulations existed to encourage people to engage in self-restraint in relation to sensual pleasures and emotional expression, and as a result, impulses tended to be followed without thought for the need to control or moderate them (Lupton 1998:72).

The body was considered permeable and porous, which meant that personal boundaries were viewed differently from how they are viewed today. The exchange of body fluids between one human and another—as might come from drinking from the same cup or eating the same meal from the same plate—was a way to establish closeness and intimacy. According to a Welsh custom from the sixteenth and seventeenth centuries, a young man proved his love for a woman by urinating on her dress (Lupton 1998:74).

Behaviors that would today only be tolerated among the youngest of children were commonplace among adults, and prohibitions in regard to natural functions were far fewer in number than they are today (Elias 2000:114–20). In medieval society, individuals regularly blew their noses directly into their hands, even if they were eating (although they were not supposed to blow into the hand holding the food) (Elias 2000:126). Peasants were permitted to wipe their noses on their coats or hats, and sausage makers were permitted to wipe their noses on their arms or elbows (Elias 2000:49). While the use of the hands for cleaning the nose never really did disappear entirely, this practice did eventually get defined as vulgar and common (Elias 2000:126).

Changes occurring in early modern European states during the sixteenth, seventeenth, and eighteenth centuries were crucial in transformation of the self into something that was more controlled and contained. Humans became more compartmentalized and privatized, separate and separable from one another, as the number of regulations grew concerning the proper way to comport one's self and to handle body wastes. Humans were expected to regulate their emotions, actions, body, bodily secretions, and thoughts. The demise of the feudal order and the emergence of industrial society fostered a new concern with proper public behavior. The true measure of an individual was his or her ability to remain unruffled, even in the face of great stress, and to be able to control behavior, facial expressions, physical gestures, and emotional displays (Elias 2000:60–172). With the arrival of the nineteenth century, the things that were once viewed as fun and good sport (e.g., public torture of humans and animals; public executions) no longer were (Lupton 1998:77).

The Industrial Revolution encouraged even further the development of self-control and a more closed body. As the size of the population increased and people were more isolated from one another, face-to-face observation and censure ceased to have much regulatory power. This situation demanded even higher levels of self-control, deferred gratification, and long-term planning (Elias 2000:379–80). Individuals were expected to monitor and control their own bodies on a continual basis (Mellor and Shilling 1997:44). As the modern body was closed off from others, it became more receptive to the influence of personal inspiration, and an inner-directed approach to the world and social relationships developed. While cognition continued to be important in human affairs, sensuality and passion also became important elements (Mellor and Shilling 1997:53).

Changing Relationships, Changing Selves

One of the most important offerings from any society is the menu of selves that exist for individuals to take up and present to others. Certain selves will fit some places, times, and relationships better than others, and certain people will embrace certain selves more thoroughly than they do other selves. Changes occur all the time in the menu of selves and in what is required from any particular self. These selves have their own dynamic, along with their own built-in identity, morality, and script for interaction. Self is an ever-changing process of self-reflection and self-presentation, and we humans are infinitely inventive about who we are (Margolis 1998:5–6).

A pivotal self, no stranger to most Westerners, is the **exchanger self.** This self emerged in the sixteenth century (Margolis 1998:15), but it did not reach ascendancy until the eighteenth century (Margolis 1998:5). The corner-stone of this self is an individualistic, self-centered, rational approach to social relationships and everyday life. The exchanger calculates and manipulates in order to make the best deal he or she can in terms of whatever is of greatest value in the market of the place and time. Emotional control, willingness to take advantage of others, and the preparedness to do whatever is required in order to advance socially and profit materially are the central identity pegs of the successful exchanger. John D. Rockefeller, the architect of the first and greatest monopoly in the United States, had the elements of the exchanger self down pat.

> He [Rockefeller] was a soft-spoken, unsmiling man, somewhat sandy of complexion. Between high cheekbones were blue eyes that could blaze, though few, even in his family, were permitted to see this. His mouth was a thin slit. On rare occasions, especially when he brought off a big business deal, his face lit up, and he clapped his hands and was even seen to dance a little jig. He feared only God and thought of nothing but his business. His was the temper of a military chieftain, combining audacity with thoroughness and shrewd judgment. He seemed to take account of no one's feelings in his plans. He flew in the face not only of human liberties but of deep-rooted custom and common law. What he worked for was done in profound secrecy, but with unceasing will (Solberg 1976:31).

In pure market exchange, social obligations and personal feelings are distractions, and they are kept out of human relationships as much as possible. People must be ready to move, and move quickly—socially and geographically—if they are to take advantage of rapidly changing economic opportunities.

Every society, even one founded on exchange, will have the **obligated self.** The obligated self gains its existence from a web of relationships that is characterized by a high degree of mutual obligation and mutual concern; self-sacrifice and loyalty are the main ingredients of the obligated self. The obligated self does not stand alone, and it is part of a larger and more important whole (Margolis 1998:48). Honor and duty, shared commitments, emotions like love and affection, altruism, and the willingness to do one's duty no matter what and no matter how long it takes—without concern for one's own well-being—are what differentiate the obligated from the exchanger self. Systems of mutual obligation exist because the marketplace and its morality of exchange for profit cannot provide the moral grounding and emotional experiences that are necessary for human survival (Margolis 1998:83). When the battle cry is profit or perish, grow or die, and when the only morality is the morality of exchange—when acquisition is its own reward—then individuals are ships without rudders. Eat or be eaten is hardly a sound way to run a human society.

The **cosmic self** concerns itself with human connections, feelings, and spiritual transcendence (Margolis 1998:87). For the cosmic self, the search for meaning and self-exploration are what matter. Ultimately, the cosmic self works toward the development of a feeling of love for all things in the circle of life (Margolis 1998:98). The cosmic self finds something higher by greater degrees of self-exploration and introspection. The cosmic self, along with the obligated self, appears in practically all societies. This is because each society must have an institutionalized way to guarantee that no matter what the level of material rewards, some individuals will be caring toward others and concerned with spiritual matters (Margolis 1998:107).

Self is a process of acting and reacting, and even a committed exchanger may find himself or herself lapsing into moments of spirituality (even Rockefeller feared God) or obligation. Ebenezer Scrooge, one of the enduring characters from Dickens's *A Christmas Carol*, fits the image of an exchanger as well as anyone. By the end of the story, however, he is not the man he was. New features of self surfaced: He wanted to help Tiny Tim (obligated self), he certainly had acquired a sense of his own mortality, and he wanted to be thought of well by others (cosmic self). Societies offer both opportunities and encouragements for the expression of certain kinds of selves rather than others, but the larger and more complex a society becomes, the greater the likelihood that many different selves will be available. Different selves may coexist or even compete in the lives of individuals as they construct their relationships with others.

Conclusions

This chapter discussed social shifts from the simple to the complex in terms of the nature of social organization. Change is all around us and is, in fact, the only real constant. Social transformations alter everything about humans—their societies, their institutions, their groups, their relationships, and, ultimately, individual lives and views of self. Change is dialectical, and every change sows the seeds of its own destruction or transformation.

We are free, or at least freer than we once were, to move in and out of relationships—marriages, family networks, jobs, schools, religions, friendships. Greater freedom and more flexible relationships increase the potential for fragmentation, alienation, and isolation of self (Pescosolido and Rubin 2000:64). Because social support is not guaranteed, individuals who either cannot or will not take the initiative to establish connections with others may find that they lack a primary group with primary relationships to support them in their times of need and distress. They will also lack group-based understandings and definitions to help them make sense of their lives and times.

The relationship between social changes and social selves is a reciprocal one. Not only do selves reflect and respond to broad currents of sociocultural change, personal experiences and collective actions can have powerful impacts on sociocultural events. It is possible for local communities to resist and often times challenge the dominance of powerful organizations and even market forces themselves. Global events do influence what happens in local communities, but people in these communities can and do resist, challenge, and transform global processes (Finn 1998:242). One thing is certain: People working together have the potential to change the world (Easterbrook 2001:214).

Chapter Seven at a Glance

- Sociocultural change—alterations in shared knowledge, social institutions, and social relationships—is constant and ongoing.

- Societies and social relationships shift from *Gemeinschaft*—with its feelings of unity, cohesion, and commitment—to *Gesellschaft*, where self-interest and individualism dominate.
- Some societies are characterized by mechanical solidarity, where the division of labor is slight and based principally on age or sex, to organic solidarity, where the division of labor is extensive and people are divided in many ways.
- The first technological revolution happened when humans learned to produce food instead of hunting and gathering it.
- Human societies take a variety of forms based on how food is found and/or produced and how social institutions and social relationships evolve. Hunting and food gathering was followed by other societal forms like horticultural, pastoral or herding, agrarian, industrial, and postindustrial.
- The evolution of a capitalist economic system and a democratic political system, coupled with a cultural system that encouraged rationality, individualism, and curiosity, offered the greatest opportunity for innovation and rapid social change.
- Much of the change in an area is a result of cultural diffusion (transmission of information from some other region) instead of cultural innovation (invention of an idea locally).
- Societies that developed steel and weapons first had a distinct advantage in world conquest because their armies carried nastier germs and more deadly diseases with them wherever they went.
- U.S. institutions—families, businesses, governments, schools, religions—influence one another in a multitude of ways, even though some cultural lag exists in which the more sluggish parts of the institutional structure must adapt to the more quickly changing parts.
- U.S. society has been partly McDonaldized and the principles of efficiency, calculability, predictability, control, and profitability have pervaded more and more sectors of social life.
- The pressures in U.S. society to consume are enormous, and cathedrals of consumption have evolved to make it easier (but more expensive) to shop until you drop.
- Appearance norms change along with other changes in a society, and individuals may feel pressured to change how they look and their clothing styles on a continual basis.
- As societies have experienced a general civilizing process, the view of proper and improper has changed and so has what is considered mannerly.
- Societies offer a menu of selves to individuals for them to take up and present to others, and certain selves will fit some places, times, and relationships better than others.
- Core offerings on a society's menu of selves include the exchanger self (which encourages a self-centered approach to the world), the obligated

self (which encourages concern for others and a commitment to help them whenever possible), and the cosmic self (which encourages a concern with matters of spirituality, human connections, and emotional expression).

- Sociocultural change is the only constant, and people acting together create and change cultural forms, social institutions, and social relationships.

Glossary

agrarian society a society that uses its knowledge and technology to cultivate large areas of land with animals pulling plows to produce a surplus of food

agricultural revolution new and efficient technologies make it possible to grow an abundance of crops

blueprint copying an invention or custom is seen directly and then copied

capitalism an economic system in which the technologies for producing goods and services are owned privately, as are the profits

capitalistic imperative the glorification of unrestrained accumulation for private use

cathedrals of consumption places like shopping malls or amusement parks that are structured in ways to encourage consumers to purchase an excess of goods or to pay for more services than they need

charismatic leader an individual who influences others through some special or exceptional quality

collective action transitory and relatively unregulated forms of collective behavior like riots, fads, crazes, and rumors

cosmic self concerned with human connections, feelings, and spiritual transcendence; the search for meaning and the development of the capacity for personal introspection are what matter

cultural diffusion the spread of a piece of cultural knowledge from one society or group to some other society or group

cultural innovation the invention or discovery of a new piece of cultural knowledge (e.g., technology) inside the boundaries of a society

cultural lag some parts of culture change faster than other parts, which generates pressures for sociocultural change throughout a society

de-skilled jobs that once required a great deal of training, skill, and motivation are transformed into jobs that can be done by practically anyone, even someone with minimal abilities and little motivation

division of labor the existence of many separate tasks and activities for members of a society to perform, such as being a police officer, firefighter, student, or teacher

economic institution the social institution that organizes human relationships that are responsible for finding or producing the goods and/or services that are necessary for human survival and for distributing these goods and services to other members of the society

educational institution the social institution that organizes human relationships toward the teaching and learning of the important or even essential knowledge of the society

exchanger self characterized by emotional control, greed, and a willingness to take advantage of others in order to advance socially and profit materially

family institution the social institution that organizes human relationships oriented toward the birthing and raising of children; members of a family unit are related by blood, marriage, or adoption

first technological revolution the stage in sociocultural evolution when humans became food producers rather than food gatherers

fun culture the rituals, shared understandings, and relationships formed in the context of the search for fun times and novel excitement

functional interdependence the integration that comes from individuals' performing different but interconnected tasks, all of which are necessary for the society to achieve its goals

fundamentalism a religious doctrine that emphasizes the importance of tradition, faith, and spirituality, while disavowing worldly temptations

Gemeinschaft **society** a society based on primary relationships and feelings of unity, cohesion, and commitment

Gesellschaft **society** a society based on rational calculation of rewards and costs and on self-interest

herding or pastoral society a human group that relies on its knowledge and skills to domesticate and use what herd animals like cows, sheep, or goats have to offer

horticultural society a human group that has sufficient knowledge and technology (simple hand tools like a hoe or digging stick) and environmental conditions to allow it to raise edible crops

hunting and gathering society a human group whose survival depends upon the knowledge and skills to gather and eat edible vegetation and/ or to capture and eat animals

idea diffusion the only thing an inventor has to go on is an idea or suggestion

Industrial Revolution a social revolution that occurs when human and animal power are replaced in large part by the power of machines

industrial society a human group that has the knowledge and technology to use advanced forms of energy to run machines to produce goods and services

iron cage the likelihood that bureaucracies would evolve to a point where they were efficient and widespread but also disenchanting and confining

McDonaldization of society the transformation of a society so that the rules of efficiency, calculability, predictability, and control have pervaded practically all sectors of social life

mechanical solidarity a division of labor that produces unity by virtue of the fact that people perform similar or identical tasks

natural will *(Wesenwille)* a sentiment that predominates in *Gemeinschaft* society that generates a preponderance of primary relationships in which interactions are deep and extensive

nuclear family a family unit that includes a limited number of individuals, usually parents and their children

obligated self characterized by immersion in a web of relationships where a high degree of mutual responsibility and personal sacrifice exist

organic solidarity a division of labor that produces unity by virtue of the fact that specialized tasks are interdependent enough that performance of each one is vital for the preservation of the group

political institution the social institution that organizes human relationships oriented toward the possession and use of legitimate power (and efforts to keep it or to get more of it)

postindustrialism and **postindustrial society** characterized by an advanced economy based more on the provision of services in exchange for financial payment than on manufacturing and production; information processing, the possession of specialized knowledge, and the capacity for creative thought and action are of great value

rational will *(Kürwille)* a sentiment that predominates in *Gesellschaft* society that leads to a profusion of secondary relationships characterized by calculation and control

reform movement a social movement that produces gradual and ongoing changes in a society

religious institution   the social institution that organizes human relationships that are oriented toward spirituality and other sacred matters and supplies answers to questions about death and the possibilities of an afterlife

revolutionary movement   a social movement that produces dramatic and sweeping changes in a society, often intended to overthrow an entire governmental apparatus

slash-and-burn cultivation strategy   burning of standing shrubs, trees, or other vegetation to produce a layer of ash in which to grow crops

social movement   an organized and enduring social initiative that causes sociocultural change

sociocultural change   the alteration over time in systems of shared knowledge, institutional structures, and interpersonal relationships

three-field system   innovation regarding agriculture in which one field of four lies dormant, allowing the soil to be replenished for the next growing season, whereupon it is cultivated and a different field is allowed to rest

References

Baird, Vanessa. 1998. "The World Made Flesh." *New Internationalist* 1:7–10.

Banner, Lois. 1983. *American Beauty.* New York: Alfred A. Knopf.

Bendix, Reinhard. 1962. *Max Weber: An Intellectual Portrait.* Garden City, NY: Anchor.

Blasi, Anthony. 1998. "American Ritual and American Gods." Pp. 109–16 in *The American Ritual Tapestry: Social Rules and Cultural Meanings,* edited by Mary Jo Deegan. Westport, CT: Greenwood.

Blau, Joel. 1999. *Illusions of Prosperity: America's Working Families in an Age of Economic Insecurity.* New York: Oxford University Press.

Brownmiller, Susan. 1984. *Femininity.* New York: Linden Press.

Chirot, Daniel. 1994. *How Societies Change.* Thousand Oaks, CA: Pine Forge.

Crane, Diana. 2000. *Fashion and Its Social Agenda: Class, Gender, and Identity in Clothing.* Chicago, IL: University of Chicago Press.

Crichton, Michael. 1999. *Timeline.* New York: Alred A. Knopf.

Davidson, Alan. 1999. *The Oxford Companion to Food.* New York: Oxford University Press.

Deegan, Mary Jo. 1998a. "Weaving the American Ritual Tapestry." Pp. 3–17 in *The American Ritual Tapestry: Social Rules and Cultural Meanings,* edited by Mary Jo Deegan. Westport, CT: Greenwood.

———. 1998b. "The Americanization of Ritual Culture: The 'Core Codes' in American Culture and the Seductive Character of American 'Fun.'" Pp. 75–83 in *The American Ritual Tapestry: Social Rules and Cultural Meanings,* edited by Mary Jo Deegan. Westport, CT: Greenwood.

Diamond, Jared. 1999. *Guns, Germs, and Steel: The Fates of Human Societies.* New York: W. W. Norton.

Durkheim, Emile. 1933. *The Division of Labor in Society,* translated by George Simpson. New York: Free Press.

Easterbrook, Gregg. 2001. "America the O.K." Pp. 208–14 in *Sociology 01/02,* 30th edition, edited by Kurt Finsterbusch. Guilford, CT: McGraw-Hill/Dushkin.

Elias, Norbert. 2000. *The Civilizing Process: Sociogenetic and Psychogenetic Investigations,* revised edition. Translated by Edmund Jephcott and edited by Eric Dunning, Johan Goudsblom and Stephen Mennell. Malden, MA: Blackwell.

Farb, Peter and George Armelagos. 1980. *Consuming Passions.* Boston: Houghton Mifflin.

Finkelstein, Joanne. 1998. *Fashion: An Introduction.* Washington Square: New York University Press.

Finn, Janet. 1998. *Tracing the Veins: Of Copper, Culture, and Community from Butte to Chuquicamata.* Berkeley: University of California Press.

Frenkel, Stephen, Marek Korczynski, Karen Shire, and May Tam. 1999. *On the Front Line: Organization of Work in the Information Economy.* Ithaca, NY: Cornel University Press.

Giugni, Marco, Doug McAdam, and Charles Tilly, editors. 1999. *How Social Movements Matter.* Minneapolis: University of Minnesota Press.

Hage, Jerald and Charles Powers. 1992. *Post-Industrial Lives: Roles and Relationships in the 21st Century.* Newbury Park, CA: Sage.

Harris, Marvin. 1999. *Theories of Culture in Postmodern Times.* Walnut Creek, CA: Altamira.

Heberle, Rudolfo. 1957. "Preface." Pp. xi–xii in *Community and Society (Gemeinschaft und Gesellschaft),* by Ferdinand Tönnies translated and edited by Charles Loomis. East Lansing: Michigan State University Press.

Hopcroft, Rosemary. 1999. *Regions, Institutions, and Agrarian Change in European History.* Ann Arbor: University of Michigan Press.

Hughes, John, Peter Martin, and W. W. Sharrock. 1995. *Understanding Classical Sociology.* Thousand Oaks, CA: Sage.

Husain, Humaira, editor. 1998. *Decades of Beauty.* New York: Facts on File.

Jackson, Linda. 1992. *Physical Appearance and Gender.* Albany: State University of New York Press.

Lachmann, Richard. 2000. *Capitalists in Spite of Themselves: Elite Conflict and Economic Transitions in Early Modern Europe.* New York: Oxford University Press.

Lenski, Gerhard, Patrick Nolan, and Jean Lenski. 1995. *Human Societies: An Introduction to Macrosociology,* 7th edition. New York: McGraw-Hill.

Lieberson, Stanley. 2000. *A Matter of Taste: How Names, Fashion, and Culture Change.* New Haven, CT: Yale University Press.

Loomis, Charles and John McKinney. 1957. "Introduction." Pp. 1–29 in *Community and Society (Gemeinschaft und Gesellschaft),* by Ferdinand Tönnies, translated and edited by Charles Loomis. East Lansing: Michigan State University Press.

Lupton, Deborah. 1998. *The Emotional Self: A Sociocultural Exploration.* London: Sage.

Margolis, Diane Rothbard. 1998. *The Fabric of Self: A Theory of Ethics and Emotions.* New Haven, CT: Yale University Press.

McCall, Leslie. 2001. "Sources of Racial Wage Inequality in Metropolitan Labor Markets: Racial, Ethnic, and Gender Differences." *American Sociological Review* 66:520–41.

McLaughlin, Janice, Paul Rosen, David Skinner, and Andrew Webster. 1999. *Valuing Technology: Organisations, Culture, and Change.* London: Routledge.

Mellor, Philip and Chris Shilling. 1997. *Reforming the Body: Religion, Community and Modernity.* Thousand Oaks, CA: Sage.

Midlarsky, Manus. 1999. *The Evolution of Inequality: War, State Survival, and Democracy in Comparative Perspective.* Stanford, CA: Stanford University Press.

Miller, Eleanor and Carrie Yang Costello. 2001. "The Limits of Biological Determinism." *American Sociological Review* 66:592–8.

Nietschmann, Bernard. 1995. "When the Turtle Collapses, the World Ends." Pp. 229–35 in *Peoples of the Past and Present: Readings in Anthropology,* edited by Jean-Luc Chodkiewicz. Toronto: Harcourt Brace.

O'Connor, James. 1973. *Fiscal Crisis of the State.* New York: St. Martin's.

Ogburn, William. 1932. *Social Change.* New York: Viking Press.

———. 1964. *On Culture and Social Change.* Chicago, IL: University of Chicago Press.

Patrick, L. 1982. *The World Encyclopedia of Food.* New York: Facts on File.

Perry, John and Erna Perry. 1993. *The Social Web: An Introduction to Sociology,* 6th edition. New York: HarperCollins.

Pescosolido, Bernice and Beth Rubin. 2000. "The Web of Group Affiliations

Revisited: Social Life, Postmodernism, and Sociology." *American Sociological Review* 65:52–76.

Ritzer, George. 1999. *Enchanting a Disenchanted World: Revolutionizing the Means of Consumption.* Thousand Oaks, CA: Pine Forge.

———. 2000. *The McDonaldization of Society,* New Century edition. Thousand Oaks, CA: Pine Forge Press.

Rubin, Beth. 1996. *Shifts in the Social Contract: Understanding Change in American Society.* Thousand Oaks, CA: Pine Forge.

Snow, David and Pamela Oliver. 1995. "Social Movements and Collective Behavior: Social Psychological Dimensions and Considerations." Pp. 571–99 in in *Sociological Perspectives on Social Psychology,* edited by Karen Cook, Gary Alan Fine, and James House. Boston: Allyn and Bacon.

Solberg, Carl. 1976. *Oil Power: The Rise and Imminent Fall of an American Empire.* New York: New American Library

Stephens, Debra, Ronald Hill, and Cynthia Hanson. 1994. "The Beauty Myth and Female Consumers: The Controversial Role of Advertising." *The Journal of Consumer Affairs* 28:137–153.

Sullivan, Deborah. 2001. *Cosmetic Surgery: The Cutting Edge of Commercial Medicine in America.* New Brunswick, NJ: Rutgers University Press.

Tönnies, Ferdinand. 1957. *Community and Society (Gemeinschaft und Gesellschaft),* translated and edited by Charles Loomis. East Lansing: Michigan State University Press.

Walter, Dave. 1992. *Today Then: America's Best Minds Look 100 Years into the Future on the Occasion of the 1893 World's Columbian Exposition.* Helena, MT: American and World Geographic Publishing.

Weiss, Jessica. 2000. *To Have and to Hold: Marriage, the Baby Boom, and Social Change.* Chicago, IL: University of Chicago Press.

Yang, Fenggang and Helen Rose Ebaugh. 2001. "Transformations in New Immigrant Religions and Their Global Implications." *American Sociological Review* 66:269–88.

Zelizer, Viviana. 1994. *Pricing the Priceless Child: The Changing Social Value of Children.* Princeton, New Jersey: Princeton University Press.

Author Index

Subject Index